NATURE AND LANDSCAPES

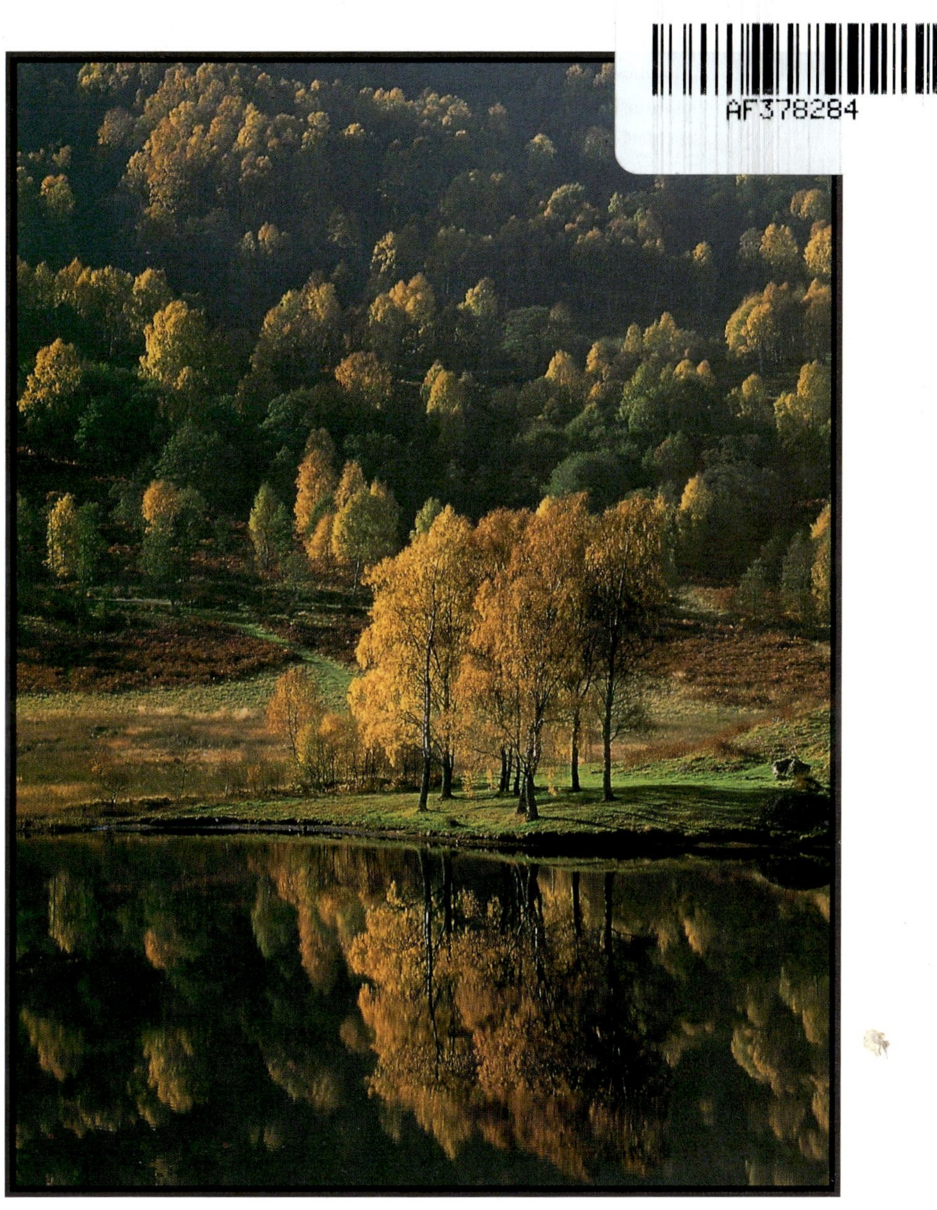

Creating a sense of place

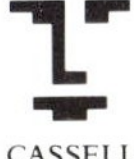

CASSELL

ACKNOWLEDGEMENTS

Front cover; (main) Zefa, (left inset, centre inset) Michael Busselle/Eaglemoss, (right inset) Simon Fraser, 1-4 ICL, 5 ICL/Landscape Only, 6 ICL, 7-10 Michael Busselle/Eaglemoss, 11 TPL, 12-16 Michael Busselle, 17-20 Michael Busselle/Eaglemoss, 21-24 Simon Marsden, 25(t) Jennifer Rigby, 25(b) RHPL, 26(tl) Neil Holmes, 26(b) Alastair Scott, 26-27 Michael Busselle, 27(b) Michael Busselle, 28(tl) Neil Holmes, 28(tr) Michael Busselle, 28(b) Alastair Scott, 29-33, 34(t) Michael Busselle/Eaglemoss, 34(b) TSI, 35 Patrick Eagar, 36 TSI, 37(t) Michael Busselle, 37(b) Zefa, 38(t) NHPA, 38(cl) Zefa, 38(cr) Jeffrey Beazley, 38(b), 39(t) Michael Busselle, 39(cl,b) Zefa, 40-44 Michael Busselle, 45-48 Clive Boursnell, 49 GPL/Bob Estall, 49(b), 50, 51(tr) S&O Mathews, 51(tl) Jerry Harpur, 51(b) TPL, 52(t) GPL/Vaughan Fleming, 52(l) Neil Holmes, 52(b) S&O Mathews, 53(tl,tr) Michael Busselle, 53(b), 54(tl) Jennifer Rigby, 54(b) RHPL, 54-55 TSI, 55(b), 56(tl) Michael Busselle, 56(tr) Jennifer Rigby, 56(b) Zefa, 57,58 TSI, 59(t) Michael Busselle, 59(b)Chris Kapolka, 60(t) RHPL, 60-61 E.A.Janes, 61(t) Mike Peters, 61(b) Roger Howard, 62(t) ICL, 62(bl) Zefa, 62(br) John Heseltine, 63-74 Michael Busselle, 75(t) TSI, 75(bl,br) Zefa, 76(bl) Simon Fraser, 76-77 ICL, 77(t) Michael Busselle, 77(b) Ardea/Ake Lindau, 78(t) Biofotos/Heather Angel, 78(b) TIB, 79 TSI, 80(t) RHPL/Adam Woolfitt, 80(b) RHPL, 81(t) TIB, 81(b) TSI, 82(t) TIB, 82(b) Zefa, 83(t) Ed Buziak, 83(b) ICL, 84-85 ICL, 85(cr) Roger Howard, 85(br) Zefa, 86(tr) RHPL, 86(bl) TIB, 87(t) John Heseltine, 87(b) Zefa, 88(t) TIB, 88(b) Van Greaves, 89(t) Zefa, 89(b) Tim Woodcock, 90(t) John Heseltine, 90(b) Zefa, 91-94 Michael Busselle/Eaglemoss, 95(t) TSI, 95(b) TIB, 96(t) TPL, 96(b) TSI, Back cover Zefa.

Key: GPL - Garden Picture Library; ICL - Images Colour Library;
       NHPA - Natural History Photographic Agency;
       RHPL - Robert Harding Picture Library; TIB - The Image Bank;
       TPL - The Photographers Library; TSI - Tony Stone Images

Consultant editor: Roger Hicks

First published 1993 by Cassell
Villiers House, 41/47 Strand, London WC2N 5JE

Distributed in Australia
by Capricorn Link (Australia) Pty Ltd
P. O. Box 665, Lane Cove, NSW 2066

British Library Cataloguing-in-Publication Data
A catalogue record for this book is available from the British Library

ISBN 0-304-34352-8

Printed in Spain by Cayfosa Industria Grafica

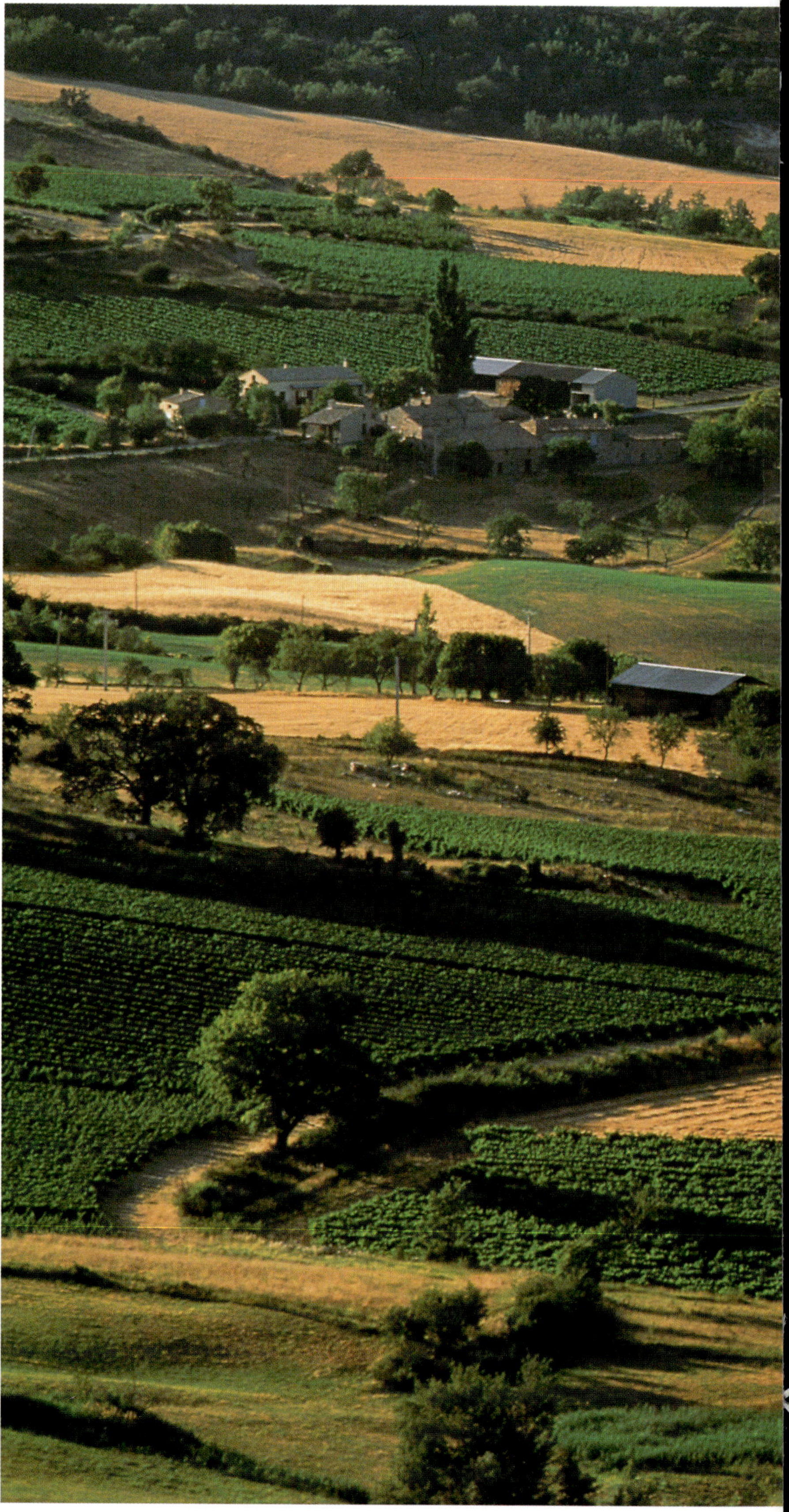

CONTENTS

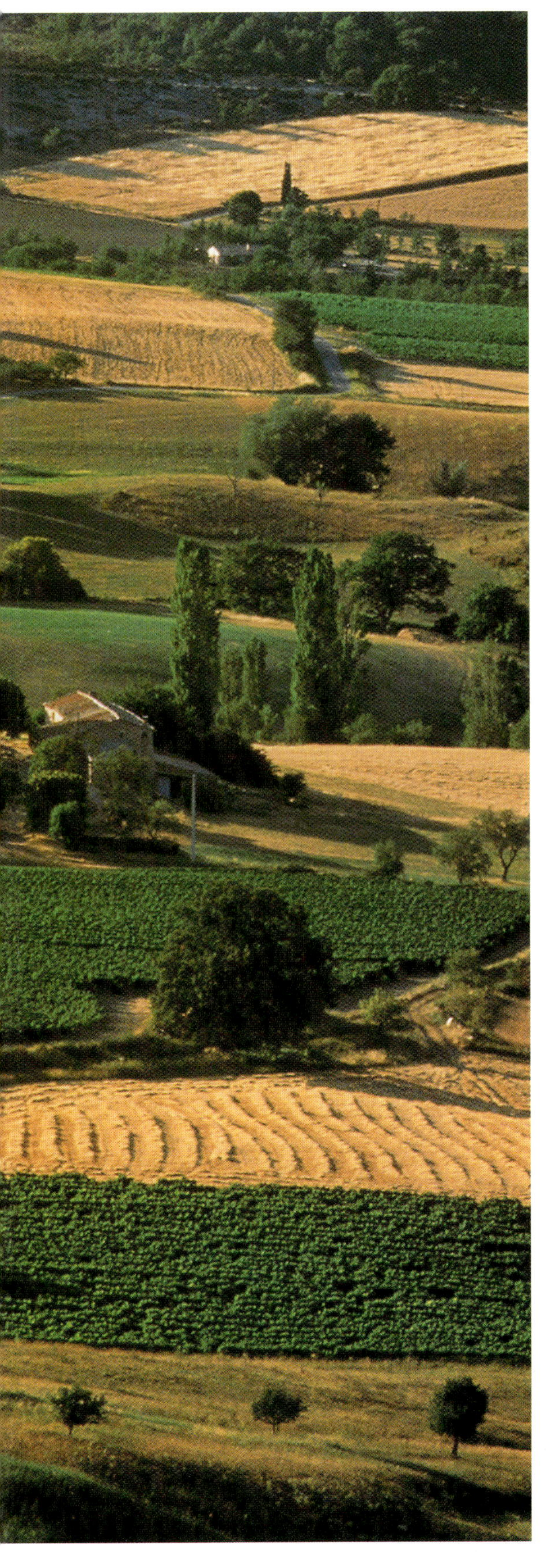

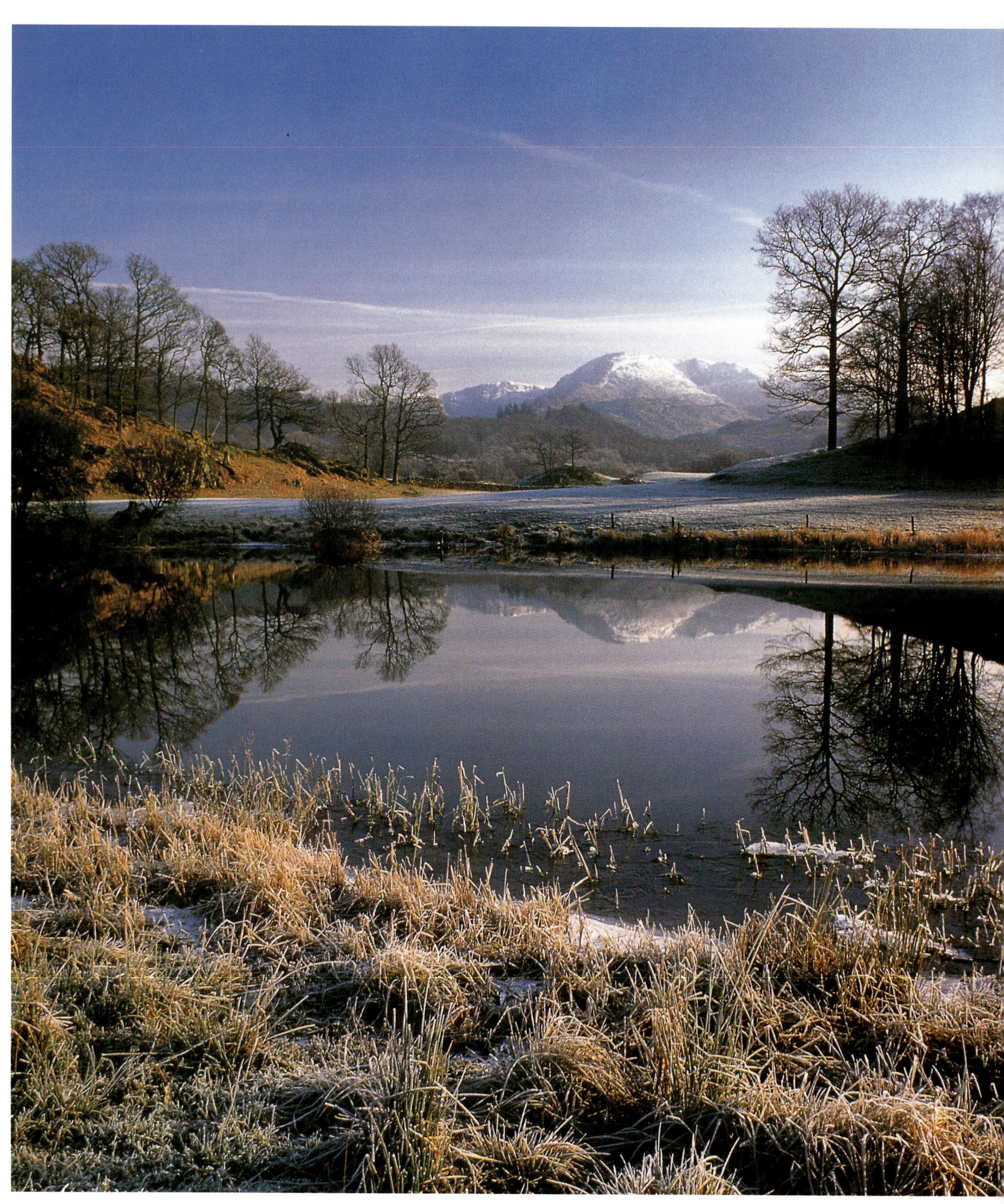

INTRODUCTION

WHETHER we live in beautiful, unspoiled countryside, or in the heart of a busy city, we all share certain haunting images of beauty. The subdued colours of a misty morning; the sea, tranquil on a summer's day or crashing in a winter's storm; the majesty of a mountain range; the magic of a single leaf. There is something timeless and peaceful about the natural world around us which appeals to everyone, and perhaps this is why landscapes and nature are such popular photographic subjects.

There are many types of good landscape pictures, and one way to use this book is to flick through it until you find images that specifically appeal to you, or images you wish you were able to achieve but somehow don't quite manage to do. Try not to allow preconceptions to blinker your vision, though. Mike Buselle's cloudscapes (on pages 29-32) are beautiful pictures of an inherently unpromising subject - clouds on a rainy day. And there are many pictures where viewpoint is everything, and the same subject could easily have been made to look dull or boring: the spring flowers on pages 49-52, for example.

Once you find your inspiration, study the text carefully to learn exactly how the photographer did it. For instance, Clive Boursnell gets up very early in the morning to achieve the beautiful, soft renditions of country

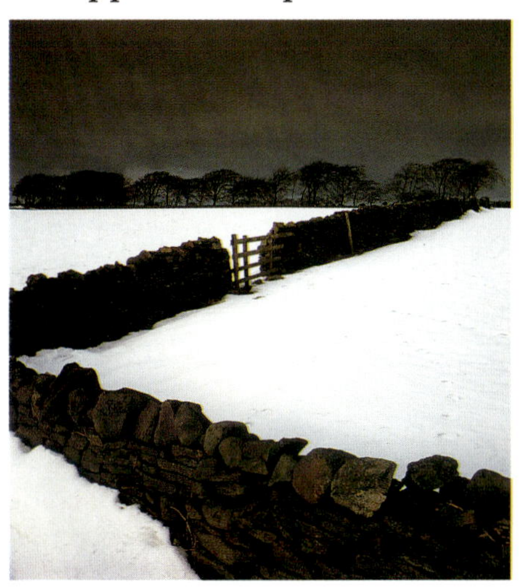

gardens on pages 45-48, but the range of lenses he uses on his Hasselblad is very modest: the equivalent of no more than a single "standard zoom" (28-105mm) on a 35mm camera.

The next step is to find the right place to take the kind of pictures you want. There are no substitutes here for time and patience. You need time to scout out the locations in the first place, and then both time and patience to wait until all the elements that go to make a great landscape picture - the angle of the light, the sun, the clouds, the people, the reflections - are just right.

Curiously, few photographers take landscapes for a living – it takes too long, and the rewards are too uncertain. On the other hand, almost all photographers - even top professionals working in advertising or fashion photography - take landscapes for pleasure. It is an area in which some of the very best landscape photographers are amateurs in the strictest sense: those who take their pictures for love, not money.

In the end, landscape photography brings double rewards. In the first place, there is the perennial satisfaction of achieving really good pictures. In the second place, there is the magic of seeing beautiful places – watching mist dissolve in the early morning sun, the sudden sight of a heron, the beauty of a frost-rimmed leaf.

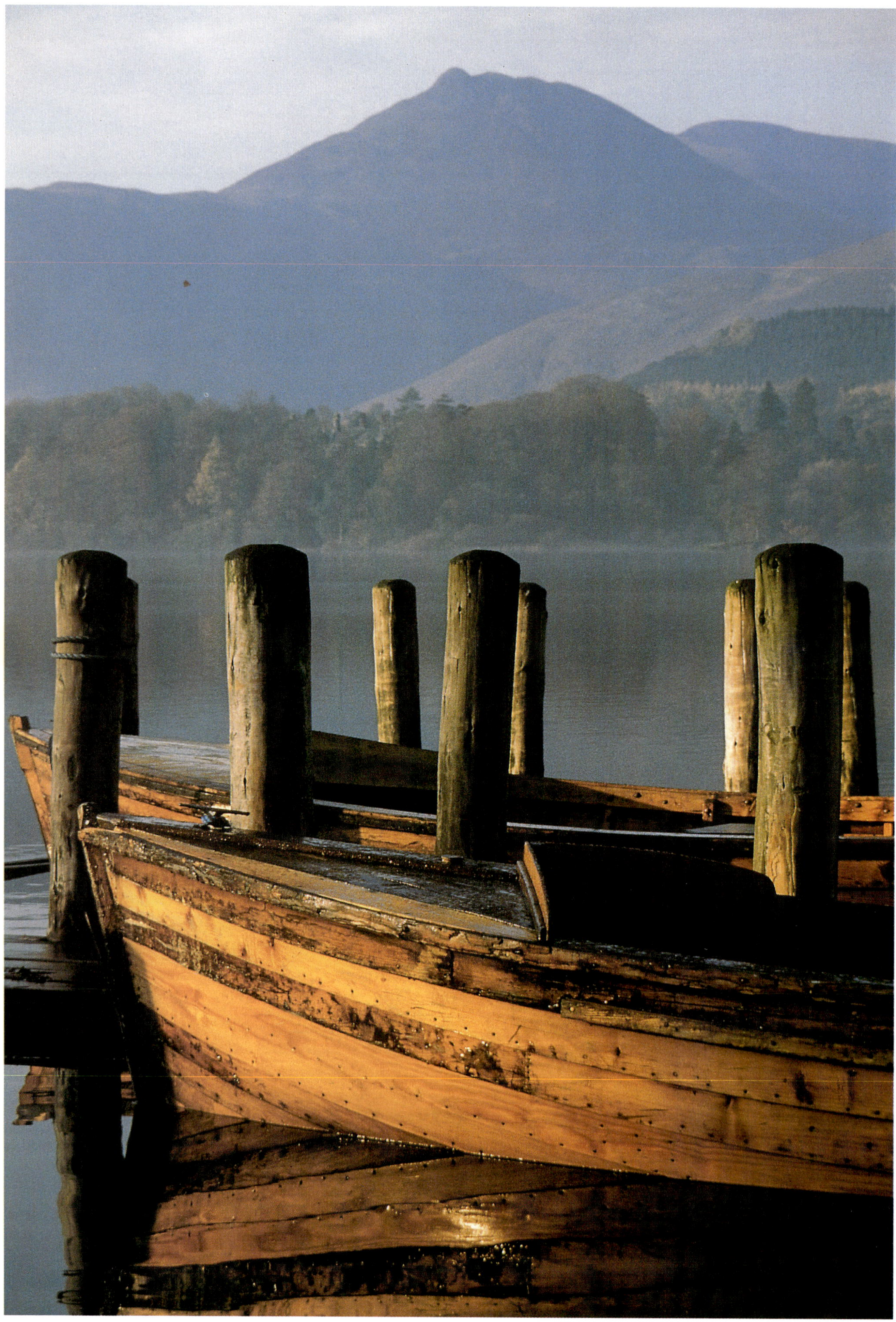

Landscape photography

To take a top class landscape you need a well trained eye, the right accessories and lots of patience.
Mike Busselle shows David Jones how it's done.

Mike and I spent a good hour driving around looking for locations before we finally settled on this one – 'a view with definite possibilities,' he decided. 'We're lucky' he added, 'because midsummer is easily the worst time for taking landscapes.

'Most crops have already been planted so plough lines are scarce, and everything's covered in dense green foliage which leaves you only a limited palette to work with.'

Mike chose this spot because of the colourful variety of trees in the foreground and the distinctive plough lines in the rolling hills behind. Once we'd set up the shot, the long wait for the sun began. But when the clouds eventually parted

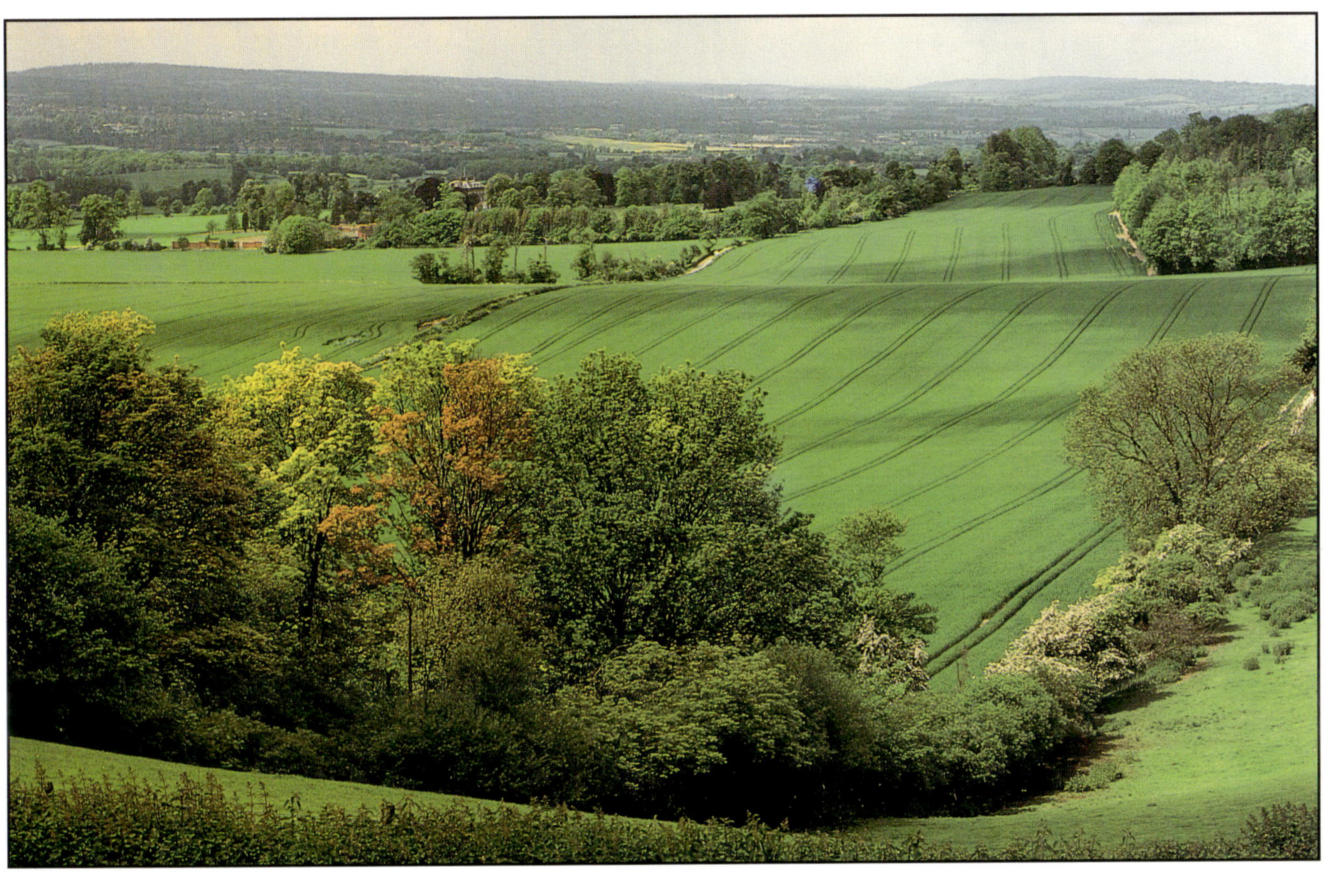

▲ *This is the shot that Mike waited for so patiently. There's enough sunlight to highlight the trees in the foreground, but not so much that the scene looks too evenly lit. Together, Velvia film and the polarizing filter produce rich, saturated colours.*

The set up

Mike and David were photographing the rolling landscape from a roadside just above it. The sun was directly above their heads, and as Mike was using filters there was a strong risk of flare (reflections of sunlight falling on the filter). To prevent this, he shielded the top of the lens with his left hand. Both photographers used a tripod, and made sure it was steady before they went to work.

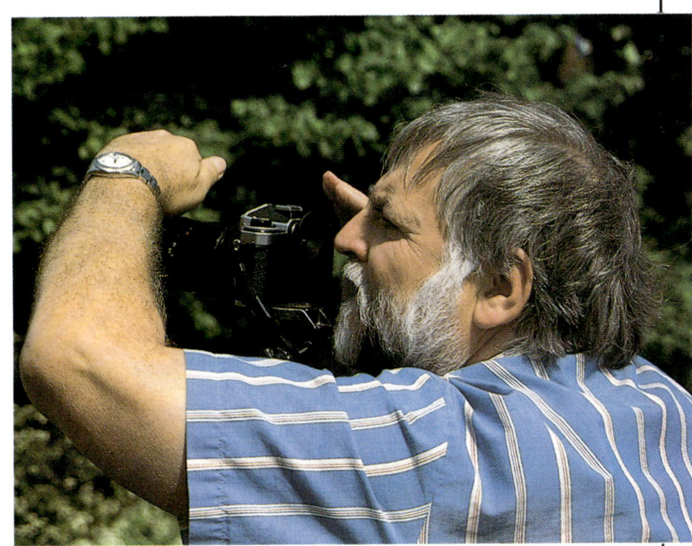

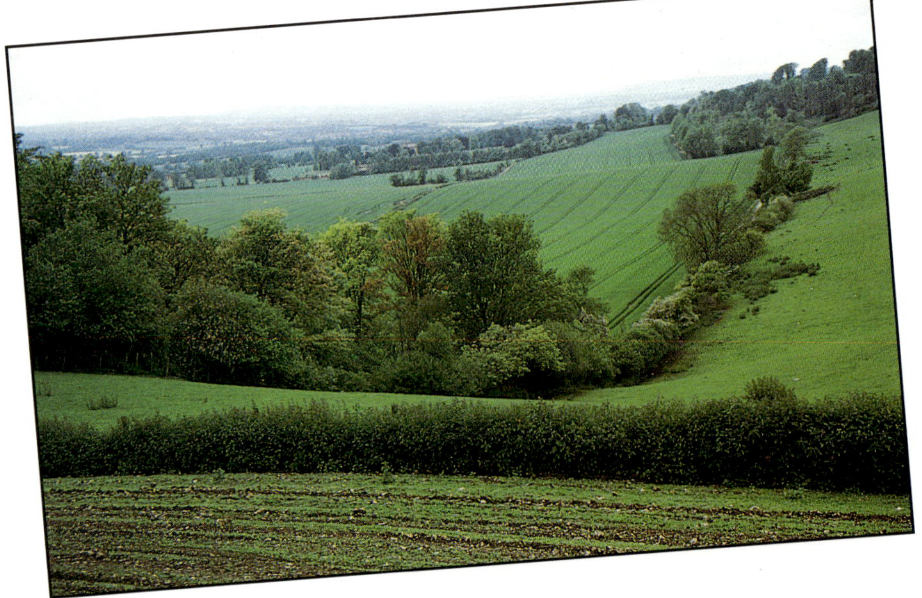

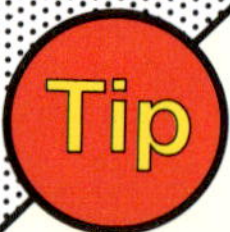

Composing landscapes

'An element of contrast is vital to a good landscape photograph' says Mike Busselle. 'Whether it's clashing colours or opposing areas of light and shade, contrast gives a landscape the dramatic quality it needs.'

◀ *It's hard to believe that this is the same view. Without sunlight, David has ended up with a flat picture that does the landscape no justice. He tried to add interest by including some ploughed foreground, but nothing can compensate for the dull light.*

A CALMER APPROACH

1 WAITING FOR THE SUN

While the sky was overcast, Mike carefully set up his shot using a polarizing filter for rich colour, a neutral density graduated filter to darken the sky, a straw coloured Kodak Wratten 81EF filter for warmth and a tripod. In this initial shot there's actually too much sunshine and not enough contrast and shadow.

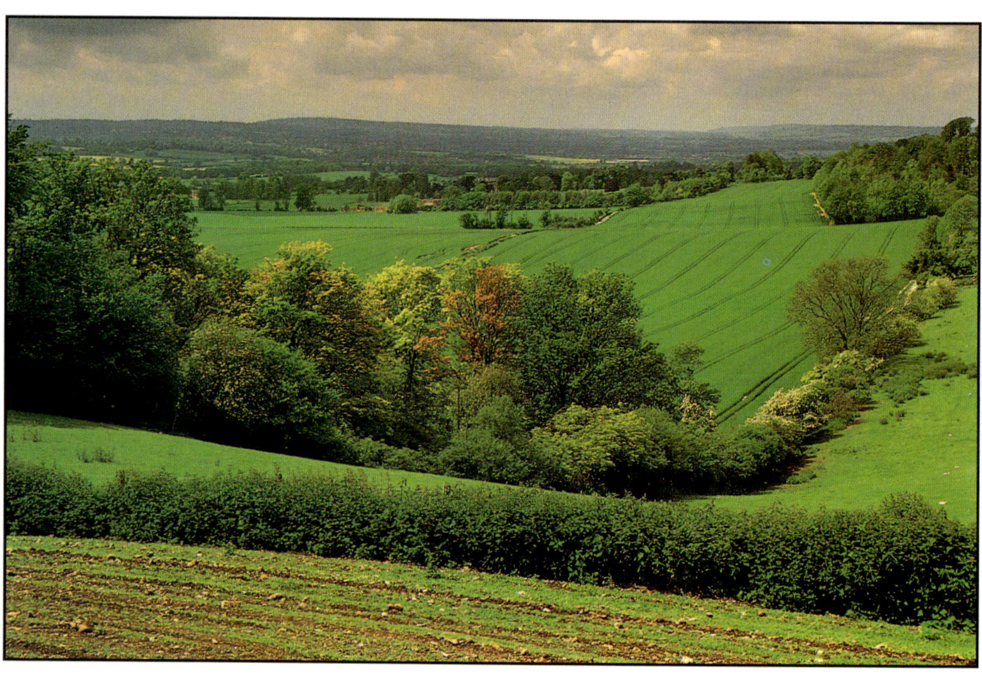

and Mike started shooting I began to realize how satisfying taking landscapes can be.

A lack of sunshine

It was my turn first. I chose an SLR because its lenses are interchangeable and it can be used with all types of filters, so armed with Mike's Nikon FE2, a 35 to 70mm lens and some Fuji ISO 50 slide film (slow film is excellent for landscapes), I found a vantage point on the roadside overlooking the copse and began setting up my shot.

When we first spotted this view the trees and field were bathed in warm sunlight. But by the time I was ready to shoot the sun had disappeared behind heavy cloud cover leaving the landscape looking far less attractive.

I was determined not to start until the sun returned, but after 15 minutes I gave up hope and began shooting. I pulled back a little to include some ploughed land and made sure I didn't include too much of the dull sky, but what the shot really needed was sunshine. I should have waited a bit longer.

A richer picture

Mike, meanwhile, was taking his time. He knew there was no point in trying to photograph the scene without the sun, so he spent his time setting up the shot and making sure he'd be ready if and when the light returned.

He used an FE2 as well, with the same lens but different film. He chose the richer colours of Velvia slide film – still at the same slow speed of ISO 50.

Filters are very useful for landscapes – Mike used a polarizing filter to increase colour saturation and bring out cloud detail, a neutral density graduated filter to reduce the brightness of the sky, and an 81 EF filter to warm the shot.

Using slow film and filters forces you to shoot on a slow shutter speed, so a tripod is essential if you

2 ZOOMING IN

Zooming in a little closer to the copse, Mike tried removing the ploughed foreground to create a different composition. There's plenty of cloud shadow now – the only trouble is it's all falling on the trees, muting the leaf colours and killing the shot.

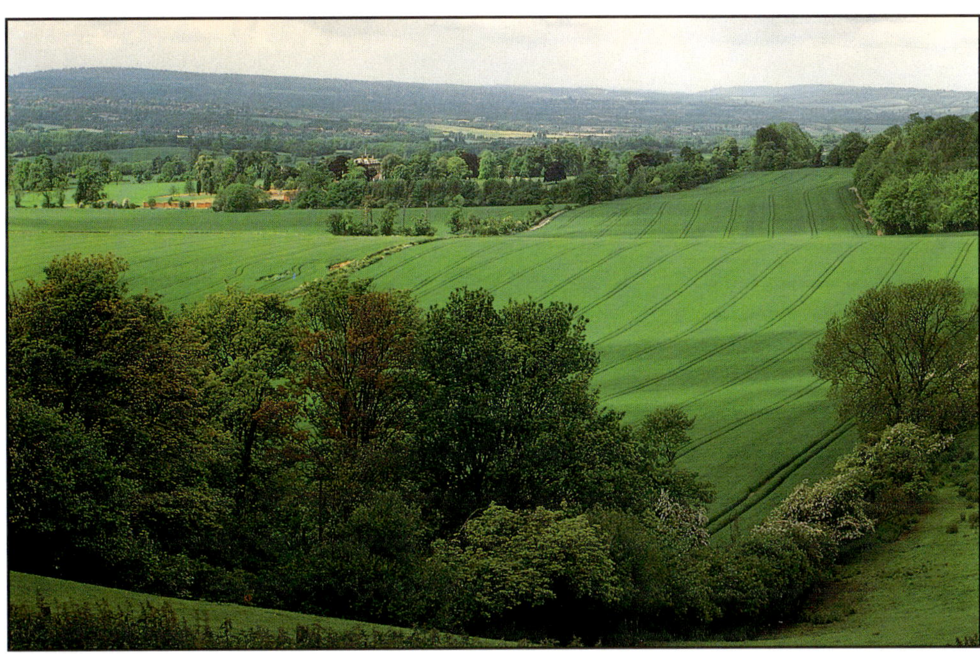

3 TRYING ANOTHER ANGLE

For this shot, Mike moved about 20 metres along to his left, so that he's almost directly behind the trees. The lighting problem is reversed – the foreground is now bathed in sunshine, but the background is dark. It's a better picture, but Mike still thinks he can improve on it.

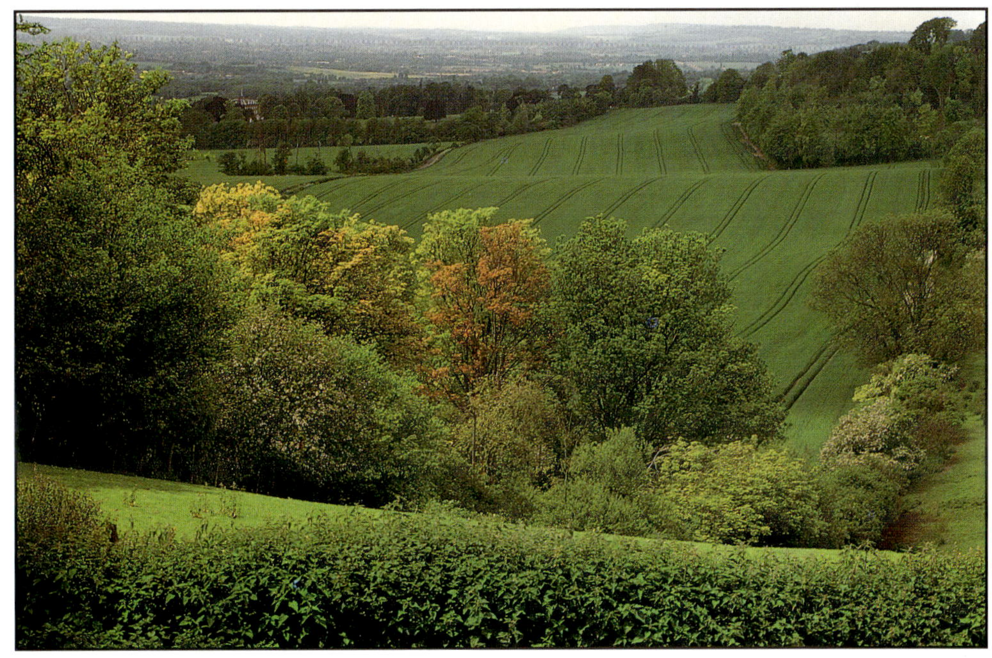

want to avoid shake. A tripod also lets you set up a shot and hold it until the light is right – which is exactly what Mike did.

The return of the sun completely transformed the view. At first there was too much of it, but Mike soon had the balance of shade and sunlight he felt would produce the best results. His initial shots included the ploughed foreground as I had, but he decided it was an unnecessary distraction and zoomed in closer to the trees.

Finally, with the sun lighting up the most colourful trees in the middle of the copse, and the clouds casting rolling shadows across the field, Mike found the shot he'd been waiting for.

Using a polarizer

Polarizing filters are very useful for outdoor photography. They have three functions:
❑ darkening blue sky and bringing out cloud detail
❑ reducing reflections
❑ dramatically increasing colour saturation.
Mike Busselle uses polarizers for about 80% of his landscapes shots. 'They're invaluable for bringing the natural colours out', he says. 'The only problem is although they're supposed to be neutral they can make an image a bit cold. So I generally use a warming filter – such as an 81EF – as well. It's essential with very green landscapes: they can look drab without artificial help.'
To use the polarizer with two other filters – the neutral grey graduated and the 81EF – Mike uses a 'system' filter holder. This has two slots for sliding filters and one for rotating filters such as the polarizer.

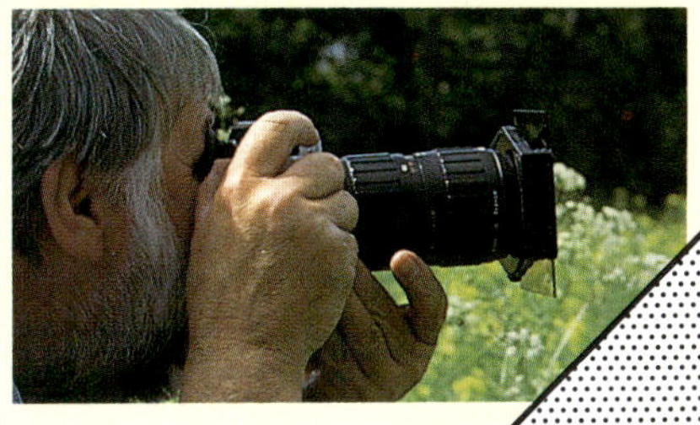

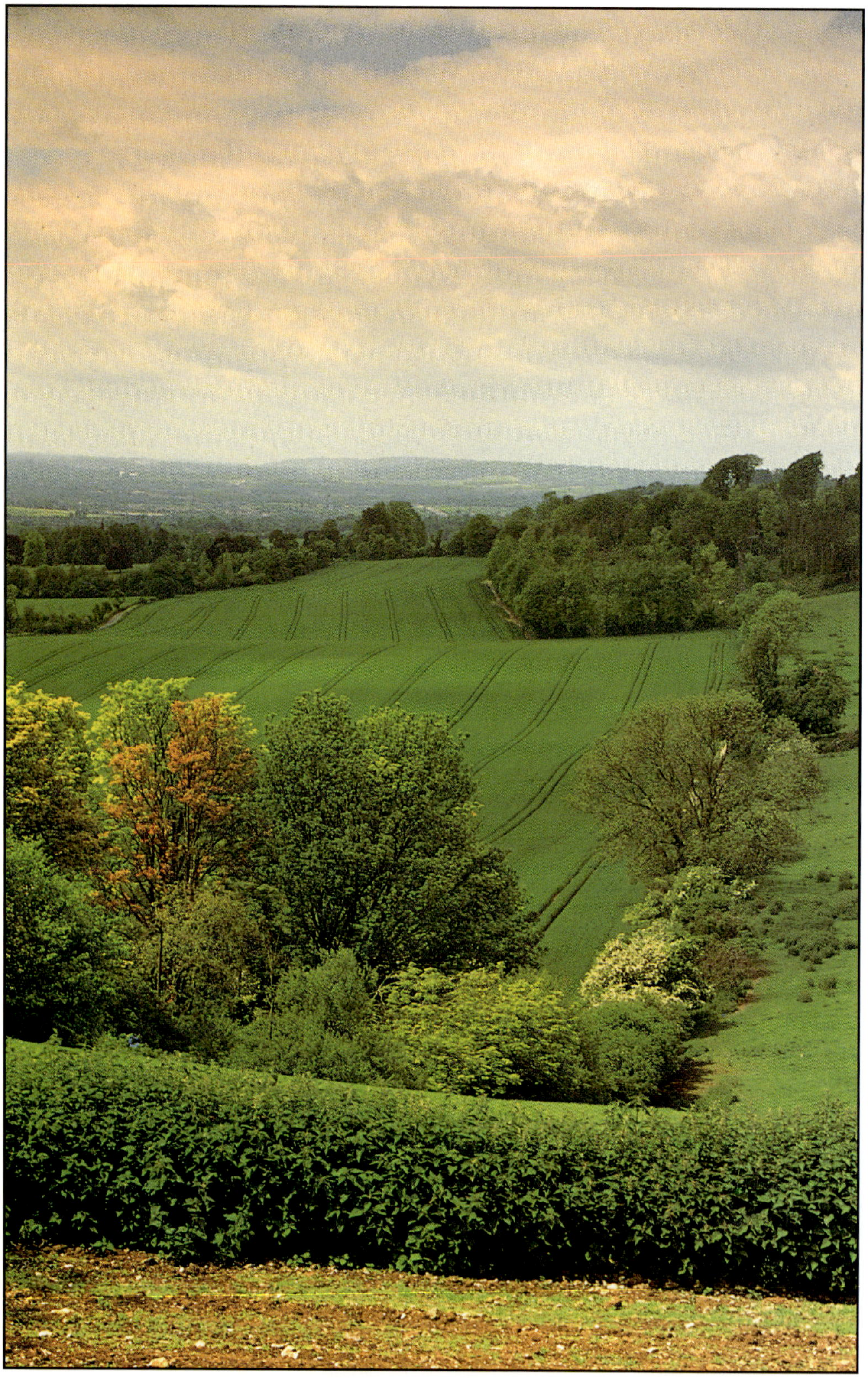

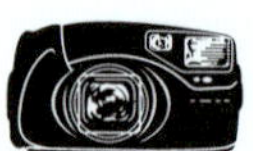

Compact tips

❑ **Filters** Good landscape photography is possible with zoom compacts and hybrids. A range of filters is available for compacts, but you may find the fixed lens a bit limiting.

❑ **Tripods** Remember that a tripod is always helpful, whatever the camera type.

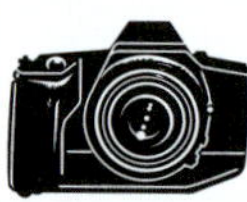

SLR tips

❑ **Cable release** When you're using slow film at a very slow shutter speed, even the act of pressing the shutter release can be enough to cause camera shake. So if you're serious about your landscape photography, a cable release is a sound investment. It reduces the risk of shake, and allows you to take photographs at some distance from the viewfinder.

❑ **Shutter delay** When an SLR's shutter release is pressed, the mirror which lets you see through the lens flips up out of the way of the shutter, so you can take a photograph.

At slow speeds this can cause shake, so some cameras – including Mike's FE2 – have solved the problem with a special self-timer. When the shutter release button is pressed the mirror flips up, but the picture isn't taken until several seconds later, when all the shaking has stopped.

4 THE RIGHT BALANCE
Finally, Mike moved back along the road. He switched to a vertical format and reincluded the ploughed foreground, which looks far better bathed in sunlight.

The shot has just the right balance of light and shade, with plenty of interesting contrast in the background, and the polarizer has brought out some beautiful cloud detail.

Rural idyll

It is often easier than you think to capture the breathtaking views found in the countryside.

1 Mood

The bonus with rural landscapes is that often, if you're prepared to get up really early, you can take advantage of mist to transform the shot's atmosphere.

If it's in the distance, mist can also cloak and lighten confusing background detail, so that the subject is emphasized.

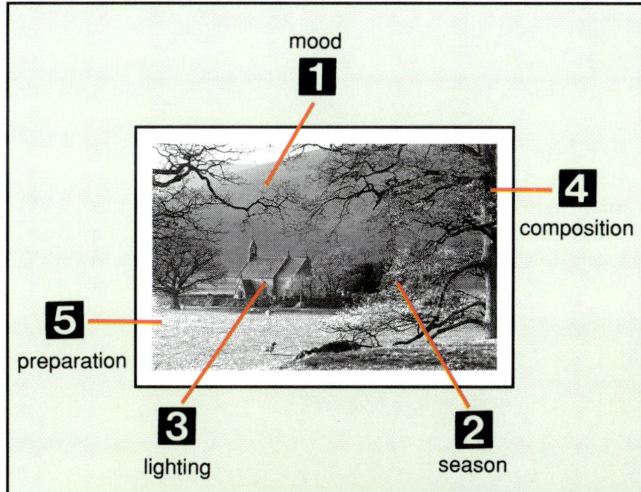

▼ *After exploring, the photographer found a view where tree branches frame the country church.*

2 Season

Each time of year brings different features and colours to the landscape. That's why it's well worth visiting a country scene – even one that looks unpromising from a photographic point of view – at different times of the year, to see how it changes.

You may find it's most photogenic in autumn, for example, when the falling leaves display a multitude of reds and browns. Or perhaps the landscape looks more dramatic in winter, when the branches are bare and it turns monochromatic.

▼ *A panoramic camera is perfect for showing off the rich colours of this tree lined lane in Vermont, USA.*

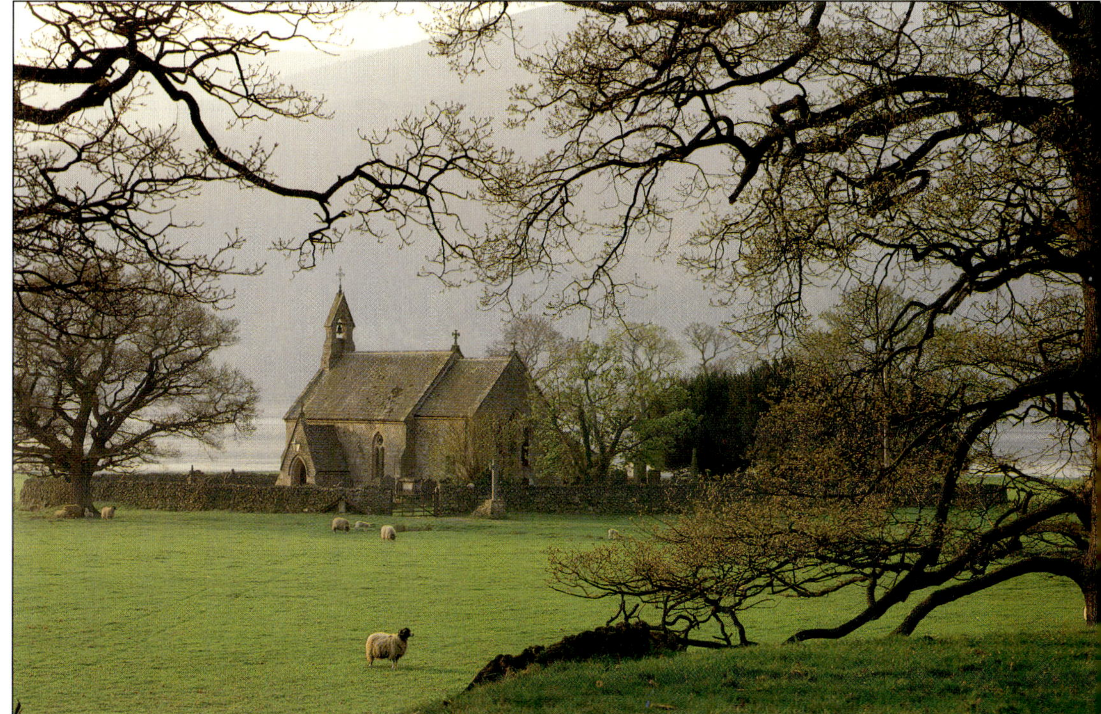

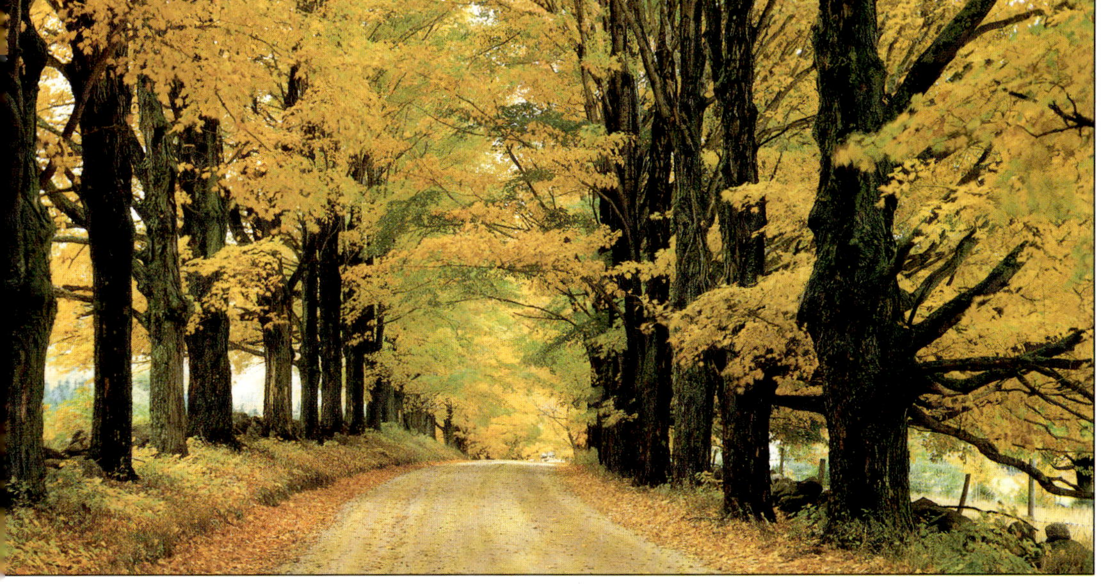

3 Lighting

It's surprising how the right lighting can transform a landscape. Try shooting when the sun is quite low in the sky. It brings a lovely warm, golden light and picks out the texture of tree bark and leaves.

Think of shafts of sunlight breaking through a wood, or a gap in the clouds causing a patch of sun to highlight a solitary building.

Equally, you can turn a sunless day to your advantage if you want to convey a cold or bleak landscape.

4 Composition

It's very easy to be overwhelmed by a breathtaking view and simply start shooting at once, resulting in disappointing photographs.

A mistake is to include a huge expanse of featureless sky in the shot which doesn't improve the picture at all. Remember that a successful shot doesn't have to include any sky. A panoramic camera helps you avoid the problem and still capture the full beauty of a scene.

A tripod is also a very good idea. In landscape photography, it has two main uses.

Firstly, it lets you use slower shutter speeds, which means you can set a narrower aperture for greater depth of field. This lets you keep the foreground sharp without losing detail in the background.

Secondly, a tripod slows down the whole business of picture taking. If you're forced to set up the tripod each time you want to take a picture, you'll soon stop shooting at every opportunity, and save your film for really worthwhile views. Try it and see on your next expedition.

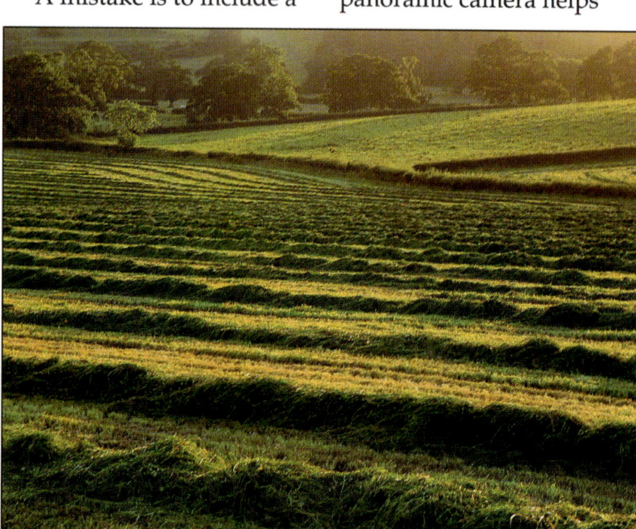

▲ *A touch of flare in the top right hand corner adds to this photograph by emphasizing how low the sun is in the sky.*

▶ *Here the photographer rose early to be sure of finding mist. The resulting image captures the chilly feel of an autumn morning.*

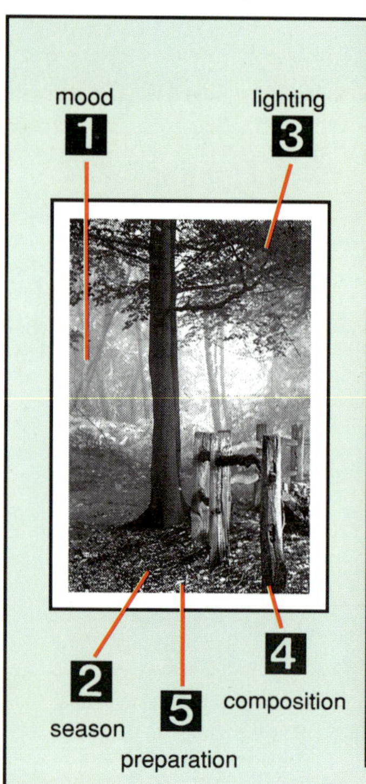

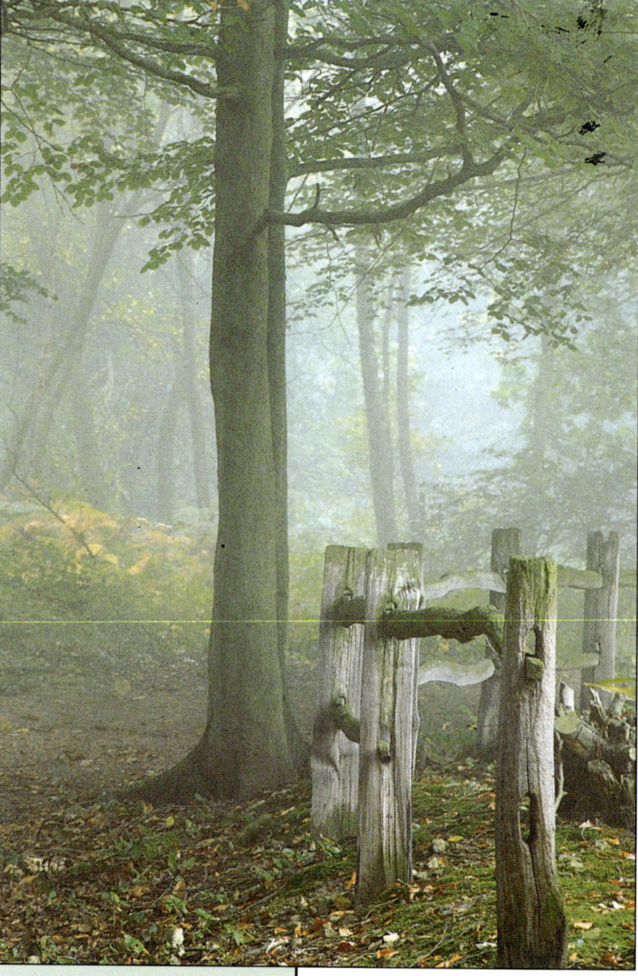

Camera: panoramic or SLR.

Lens: normally a wide angle is best – anything from 17-35mm.

Film: take both slow (ISO 25, 50 or 64) and medium (ISO 100) slide film in case the light changes.

Camera support: tripod strongly recommended.

Filters: UV or skylight. A polarizer can darken blue sky; with black and white film, a yellow, orange or red filter will darken the sky for more dramatic pictures.

Lens hood: recommended.

Lighting: early morning or late afternoon sun is recommended; but experiment in other weather conditions.

Time of day/year: depends on the mood and scenery you want. It's well worth returning to a scene at different times.

Other equipment: camera bag to hold film, filters and perhaps a second camera body loaded with different film; map, walking boots.

5 Preparation

Depending on the location, you could find that you have a long walk if you forget a vital filter or run out of film.

So if you're going on an expedition by foot, make sure you have everything you need – photographic or otherwise – before you set off. A camera bag which straps on to your back like a rucksack is most comfortable for long walks.

Don't forget that the weather in the morning could well be completely different by the afternoon. So it's a good idea to take both slow and medium speed films with you in case the light changes dramatically.

Mike Busselle – Master of landscapes

Leading landscape photographer Mike Busselle regularly travels the roads of Britain, France and Spain in search of that rare combination of beautiful scenery and spectacular light.

'I spend a lot of my time driving around the country-side looking for good locations', says Mike Busselle, 'and luckily for me I enjoy it. There's a great sense of excitement when you see a really special view for the first time and the light's exactly as you want it. You've got to grab those moments, because the weather can change so quickly. There's a nice spontaneous feeling about pulling over and leaping out of

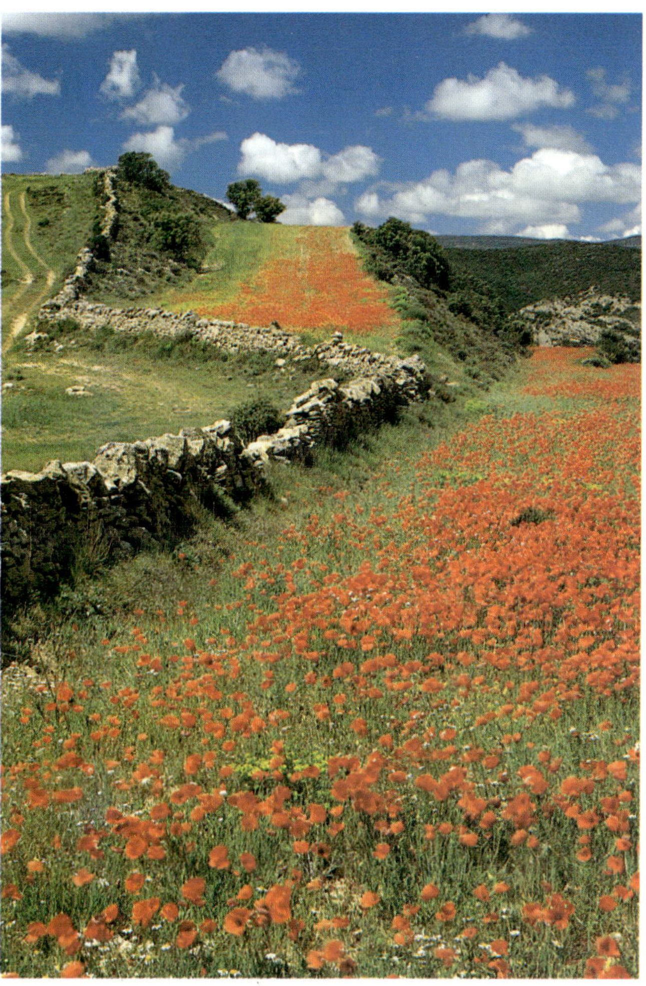

"I was driving through the Auvergne region of France in the late spring when I came across this magnificent view. The weather had been dismal all day, and this patch of sunlight only appeared for a few seconds. I used a neutral graduated filter to keep the mountains and sky dark and a Wratten 81B to warm up the foreground."
Taken on the Nikon FE2 with a 75-150mm lens on Fuji 50 at 1/15th sec and f16.

"I found this field of flowers in an area of southern Spain that's normally very harsh and bleak, but in spring it really comes to life. I tried shooting the scene horizontally first but it worked much better vertically. I used a polarizer to help bring out the blue sky as well as an 81C warm up filter."
Taken on the Nikon FE2 with a 75-150mm zoom lens on Fuji ISO 50 slide film at 1/25th sec and f16.

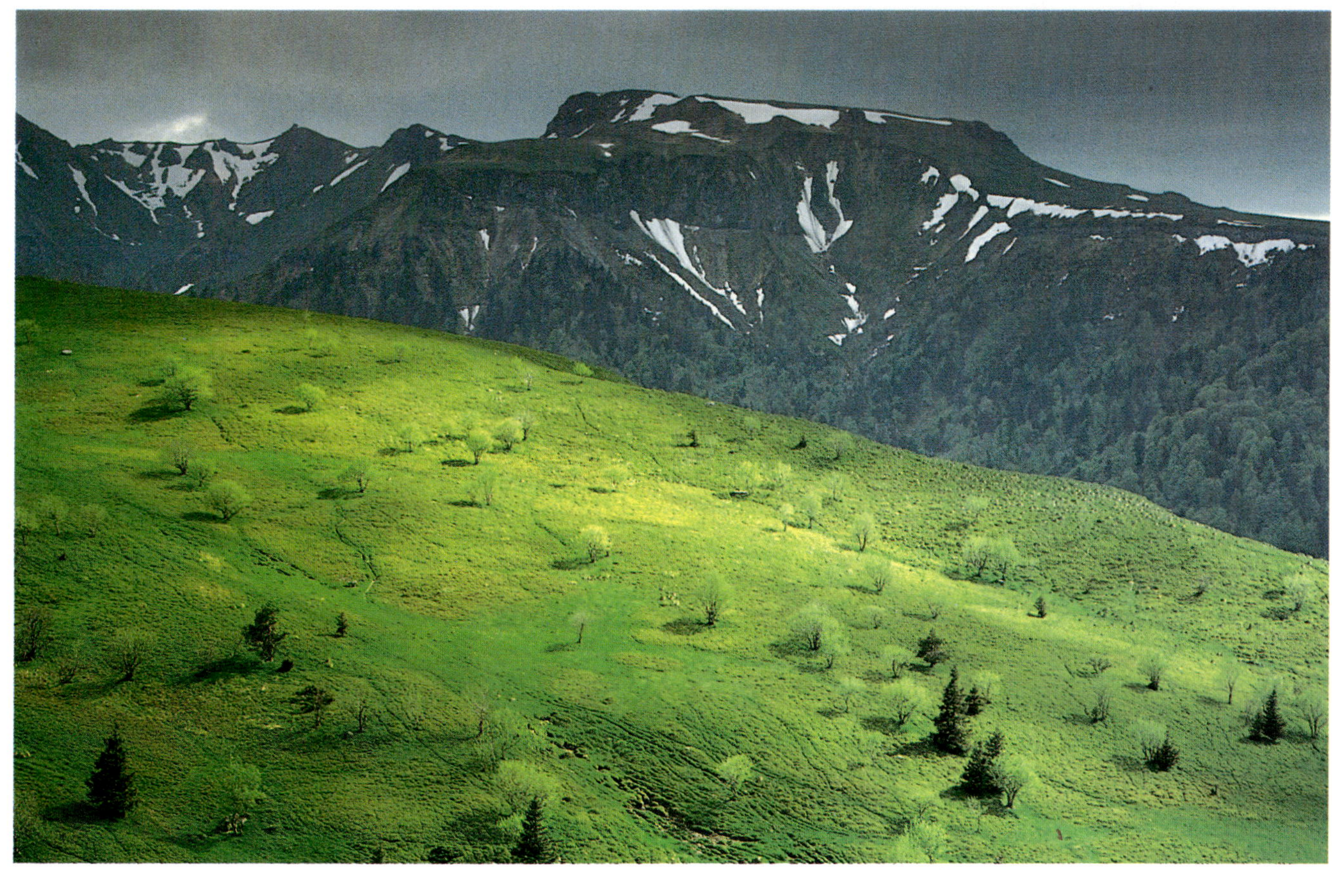

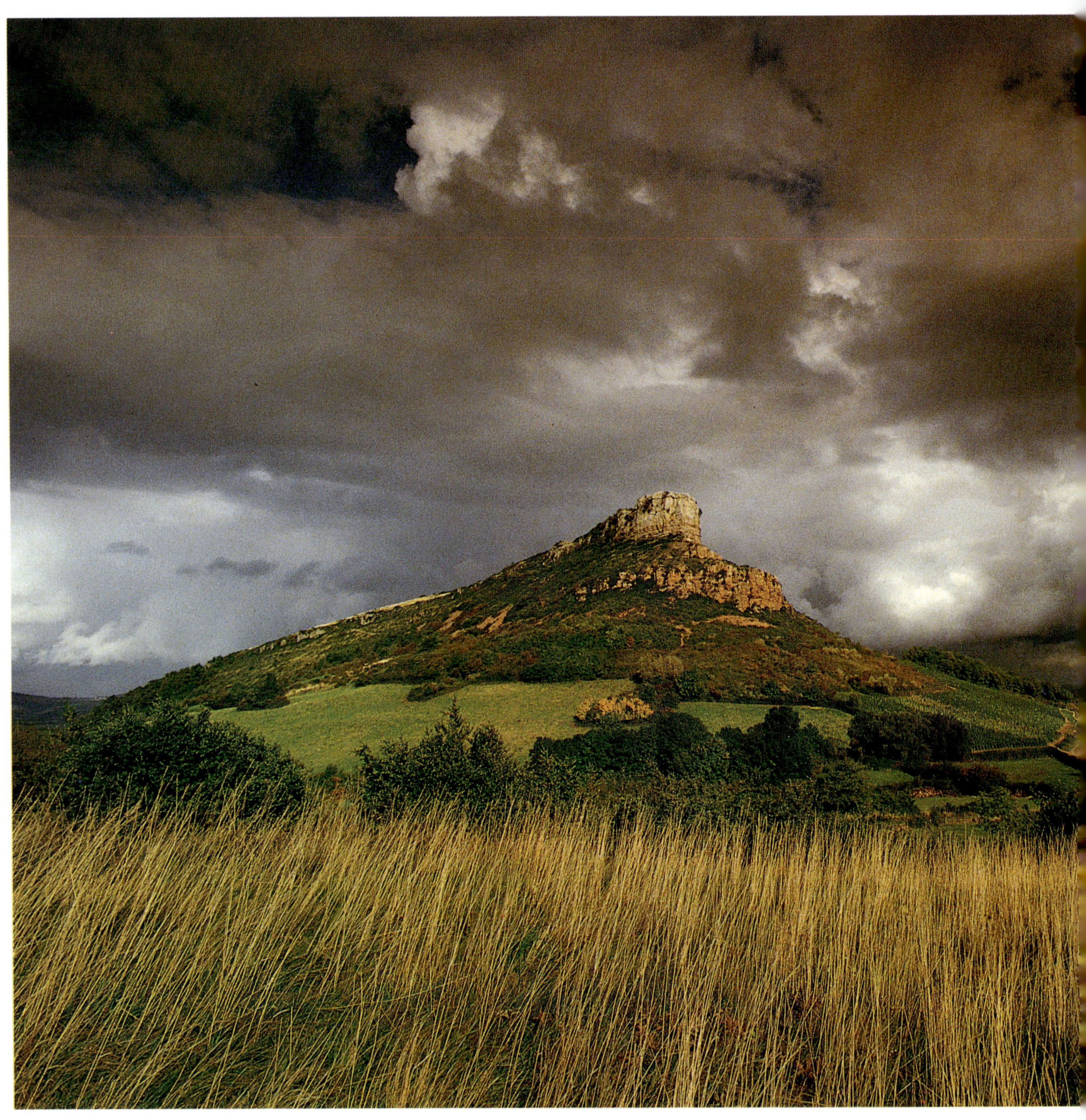

the car to shoot a roll of film before the last rays of sunshine disappear.

'But landscape photography can also be very frustrating', he admits, 'because you're completely dependent on the weather. You can spend hours looking helplessly at a staggering view and end up with no pictures at all because the light's no good. Patience often pays off in the end though – I've taken some of my best shots at the end of rainy, overcast days when the sun decides to make a brief appearance. The combination of dark sky and sunny foreground you sometimes get in those circumstances can look very effective.'

A studio start

Mike began his career as a studio photographer, shooting portraits, products and still lifes. He then became involved in writing and supplying the pictures for books on photographic technique. It was when he decided to build up his own library of images that he began photographing landscapes seriously. 'For the first time in ages I found myself going out every day to take pictures that I liked and enjoyed, and most of them were landscapes. I then got involved in doing travel books on Britain, France and Spain, so I've been shooting landscapes non-stop ever since.'

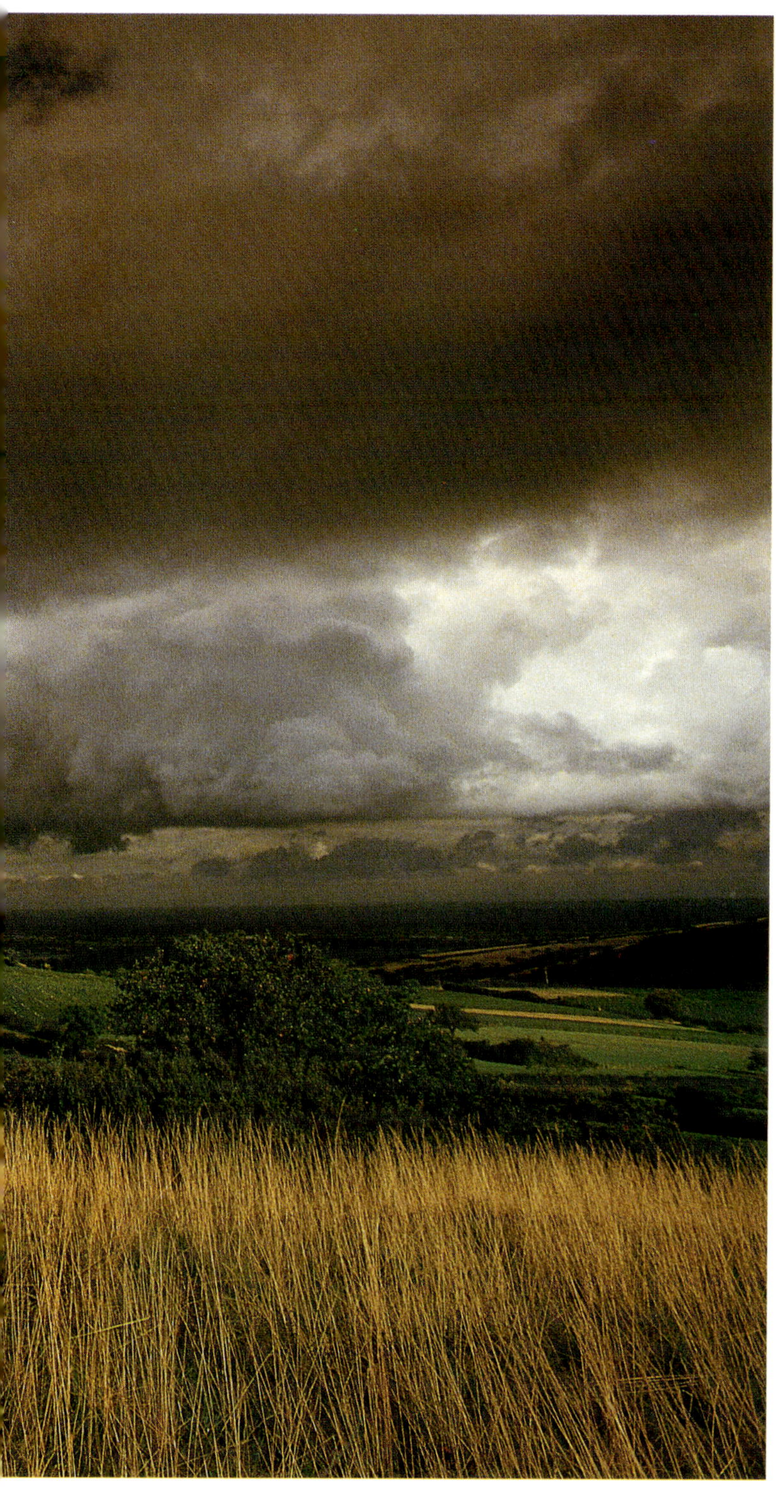

Switching to medium format

At first Mike used 35mm for all his travel and landscape work, but he recently decided that he needed a larger image size for some of his shots. He already had a Rolliflex 6 x 6cm camera but felt that the square format was totally unsuitable for landscapes. Then he came across the Mamiya 645. 'It's the perfect camera for my needs – much more portable than any of the big 6 x 7cm cameras but capable of producing images of similar size and quality. It has a cheap and comparatively small shift lens, which I tend to use a lot, and the 645 format is perfect for presentation. I now alternate between the Mamiya and my Nikons.'

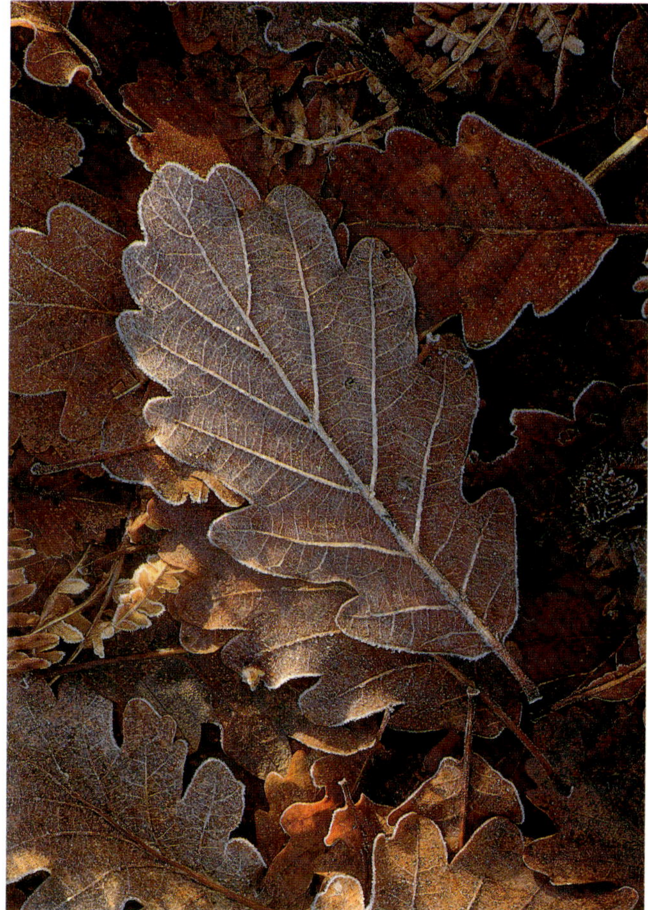

You can do it

'If you want your landscapes to look natural', says Mike, 'it's best to keep most manmade objects out of them. Although roads and ploughed land often add to a landscape, electric pylons, signposts and litter, for example, can ruin an otherwise perfect picture. I'm a bit obsessive about it, but it's surprising the things you don't notice when you're shooting that can spoil a certain kind of landscape. You've got to be vigilant.'

This is a place called Saloutre in the Mâcon wine region in France. That hill is a very special place – a lot of early human remains have been found there and the locals sometimes hold ritual bonfires up there. I used a graduated filter to exaggerate that dark, heavy sky and an 81C filter to warm up the foreground."
Taken on the Nikon FE2 with a 28mm lens on Fuji ISO 50 slide film at 1/25th sec and f16.

"I shot this detail for a book I was doing in a wood near my home on a frosty winter's morning. I used an extension tube on the lens which let me shoot within a metre of the leaves. I didn't use a warm up filter because it would have reduced the subtle colour differences in the image." Taken on the Mamiya 645 with a 150mm lens and extension tube on Fuji Velvia ISO 50 slide film at 1/25th sec and f22.

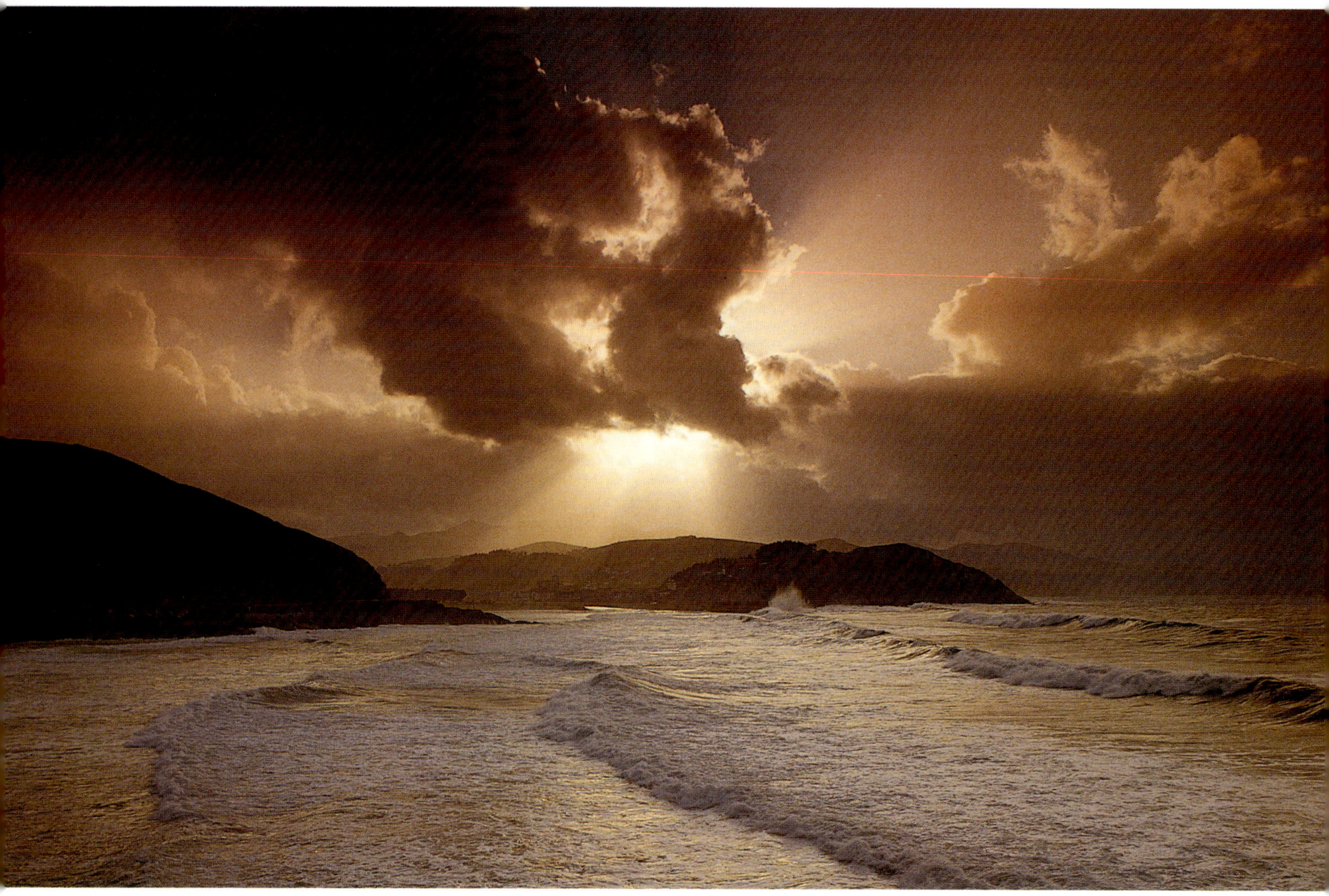

Technical details

'The dark sky in this shot was a bit of a dilemma for me', explains Mike. 'The problem was that the clouds looked dark enough without a graduated filter, but the intense blast of sunlight might have burnt out on film without one. So I either had to settle for lighter sky with the risk of burn out or darker sky and a perfectly exposed sun. I tried shooting it both ways, but I think this shot with the graduated filter worked best.'

"This seascape was taken near San Sebastian in northern Spain. It was another situation when the clouds broke for a second to light up a beautiful view. I was supposed to be photographing castles that day but this scene looked so dramatic that I just had to stop the car and take it."
Taken on the Nikon FE2 with a 28mm lens on Fuji 50 at 1/15th sec and f11.

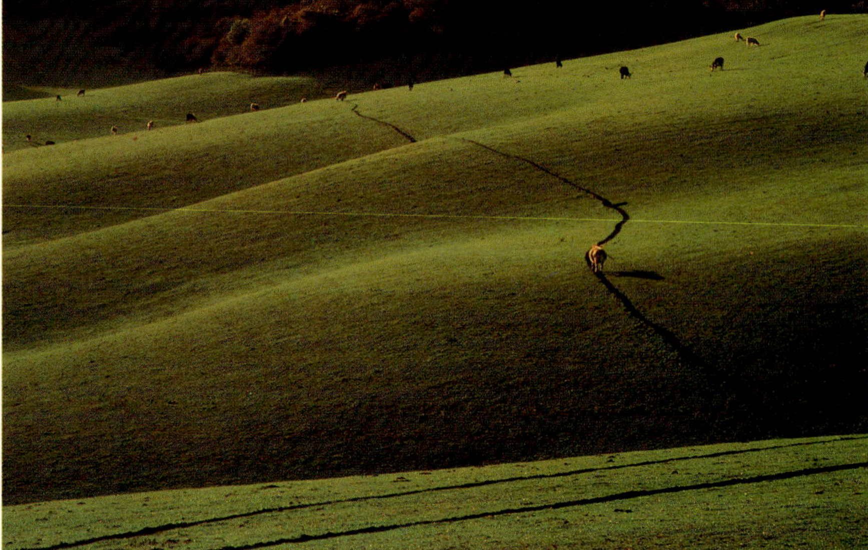

A landscape in black and white

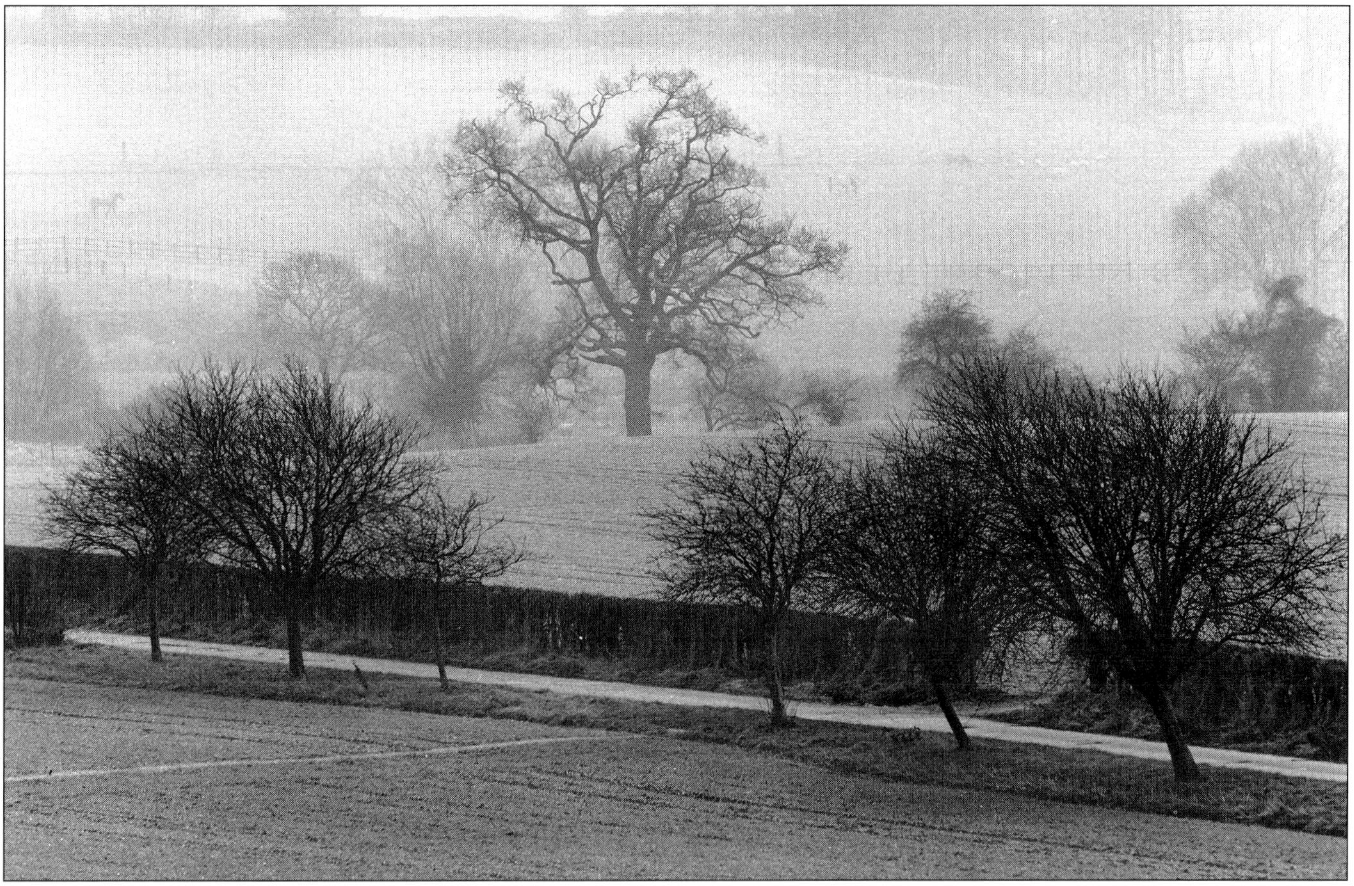

To shoot a strong black and white landscape you need good tonal range and plenty of contrast. So lighting conditions are very important, as Mike Busselle shows David Jones.

A photographer looks at things differently when working in black and white. A landscape that takes your breath away in colour may not look as good in monochrome, and alternatively a scene with strong lines and good contrast often looks more striking in black and white.

While sunshine and blue skies are generally good news for colour photography, they're not always helpful if you're looking for an atmospheric shot in mono. Brilliant sunlight casts harsh shadows, which can dominate and complicate a simple rural scene. For subtler pictures a bright but cloudy day is ideal.

Those weren't quite the prevailing conditions on the morning Mike Busselle and I set out. It was a cold and misty day so visibility was limited, and the sky was overcast but completely blank, which made the light exceptionally flat. The mist cut brightness down to the minimum and made the countryside look rather dull.

It had been brighter early in the morning, so we went to work hoping and praying that the weather would improve as the day went on. After a short search we came across a stretch of rolling pasture with a bare tree in the foreground that really caught Mike's eye.

▲ *Mike took this rolling landscape early in the day. It's an interesting composition, with plenty of texture in the ploughed fields, a strong diagonal running through the foreground and bold silhouettes created by the trees. But because of the dull, flat light and poor visibility the foreground's a little too dark and the background's far too soft.*

▼ *David's first shots included a wooden fence and an overgrown patch of land in the foreground. But he decided that these were too distracting.*

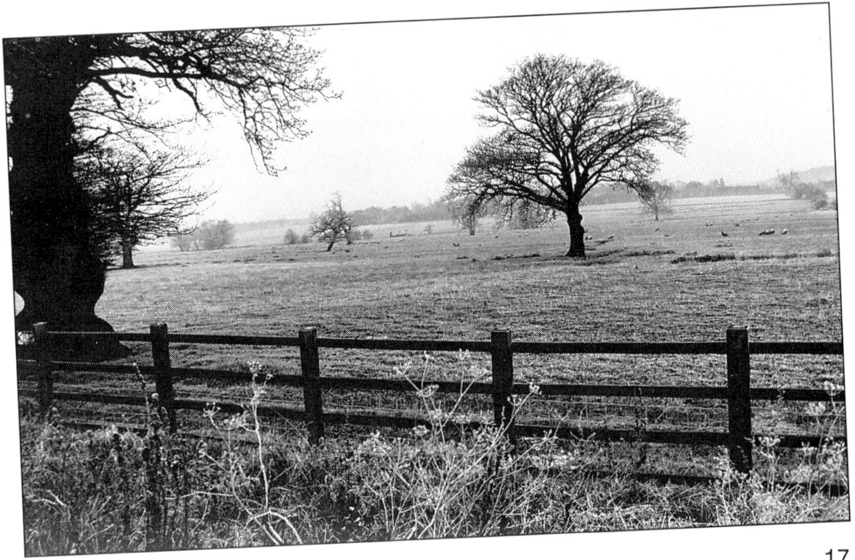

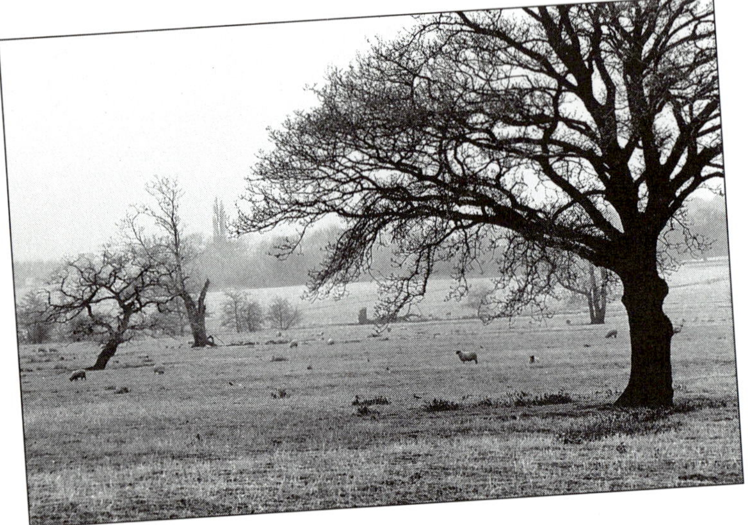

Tip — Improving with printing

'When you're shooting in black and white on a day as dull as this one', says Mike, 'you need all the help you can get from developing and printing. You can bump up contrast on ordinary mono film by increasing developing time. But that's not possible with XP2, because it's developed in the same way as colour film. So it was only possible for me to improve the contrast in the printing.

'By printing on hard paper – Grade 4 or 5 – I was able to increase contrast dramatically. The tree and soil in my final shot came up much darker and the chinks of light in the sky became more distinct. Even on a bad day, you can do a lot to improve a shot after you've taken it.'

The set up

Mike and David were shooting in an area of gently rolling wooded farmland on a cold day at the beginning of winter. It was misty and overcast, and the light was very flat.

Mike tried several different locations before deciding to concentrate on a particular tree. Both photographers used Nikon FE2s on tripods and Ilford XP2 film.

A PERFECT SILHOUETTE

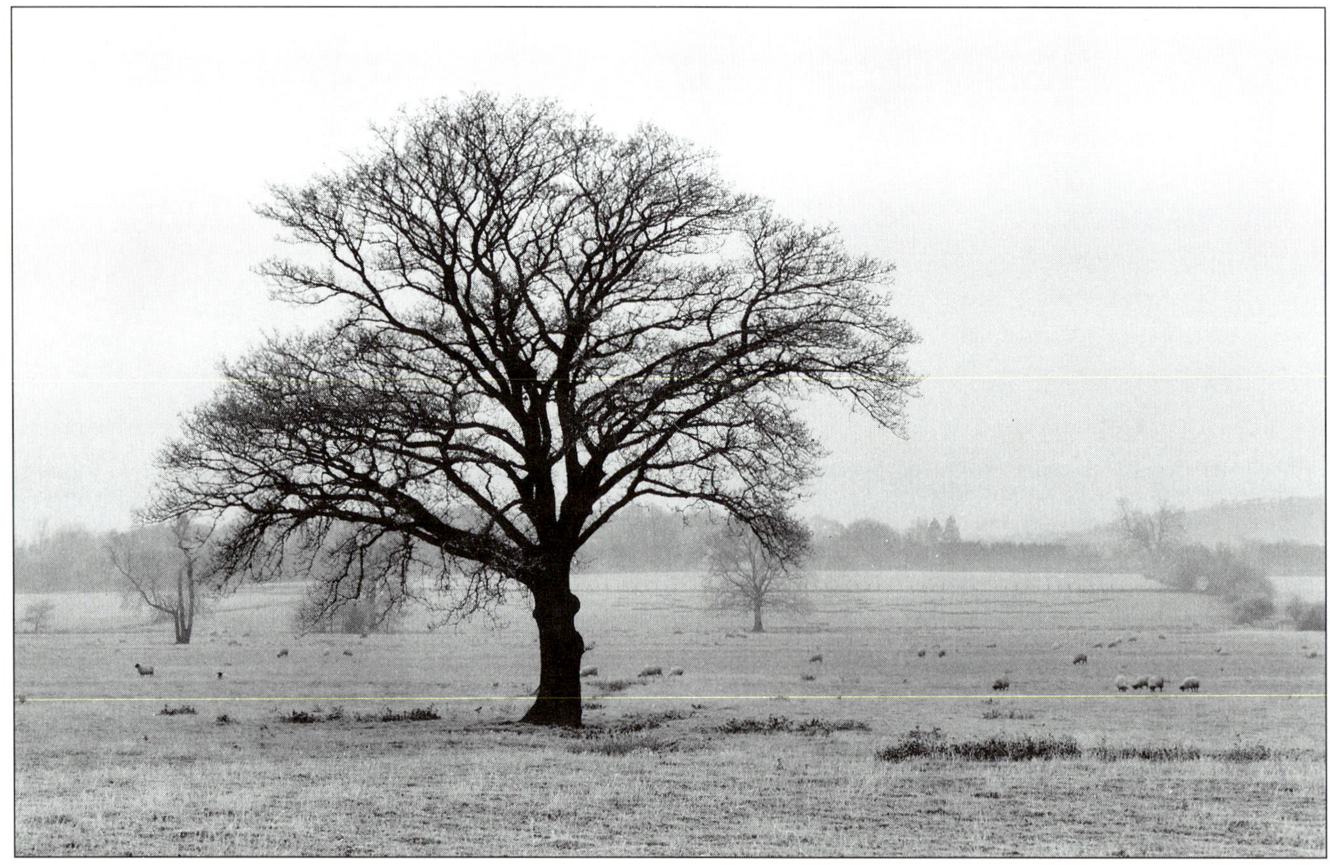

1 STRONGER COMPOSITION

Mike Busselle began by shooting exactly the same scene as David had. He used a 75-150mm zoom lens to close right in so that the shape of the tree really dominated the frame. It's an interesting photograph, but unfortunately a lot of the background has been almost totally washed out by the mist and the sky above it looks blank and boring.

David's shots

I set up by the roadside, using a Nikon FE2 on a tripod with a 35mm lens. I was shooting on Ilford XP2 black and white film for convenience – it can be developed through the ordinary one hour colour process, and you get a set of enprints back instead of a contact sheet.

My first pictures were of a large field sparsely populated with trees and grazing sheep. I tried including a fence in the foreground at first, then used a longer lens to zoom in on a leafless tree. But whatever I tried I didn't get enough contrast to make them interesting. We moved to other locations after this, but these were my best shots.

Looking for contrast

Mike approached the same scene in rather a different way. He was also using a Nikon FE2, XP2 and a tripod, but a 75-150mm zoom lens allowed him to get closer still to the tree. By using the tree as a silhouette he made the scene more interesting. But the background and sky were still too flat, so we moved on.

We tried shooting a number of hilly woodland scenes, but the mist and poor light made them all look dull. Conditions were getting worse instead of better, so Mike decided that his only chance of getting a decent shot was to forget about the sweeping landscapes and concentrate instead on a particular tree.

It was late in the day when he found the tree he wanted in a ploughed field, looking very stark against the pale sky. As he was setting up, Mike spotted a hint of light in the clouds behind – just enough to make the sky interesting.

▼ *When Mike got his XP2 negatives back from the lab, he made up contact sheets to help him choose the best shots.*

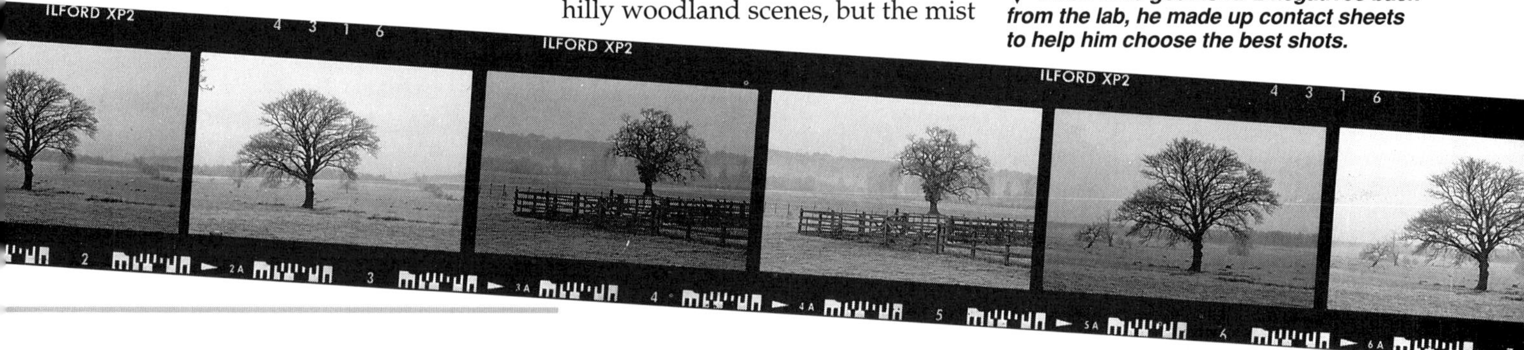

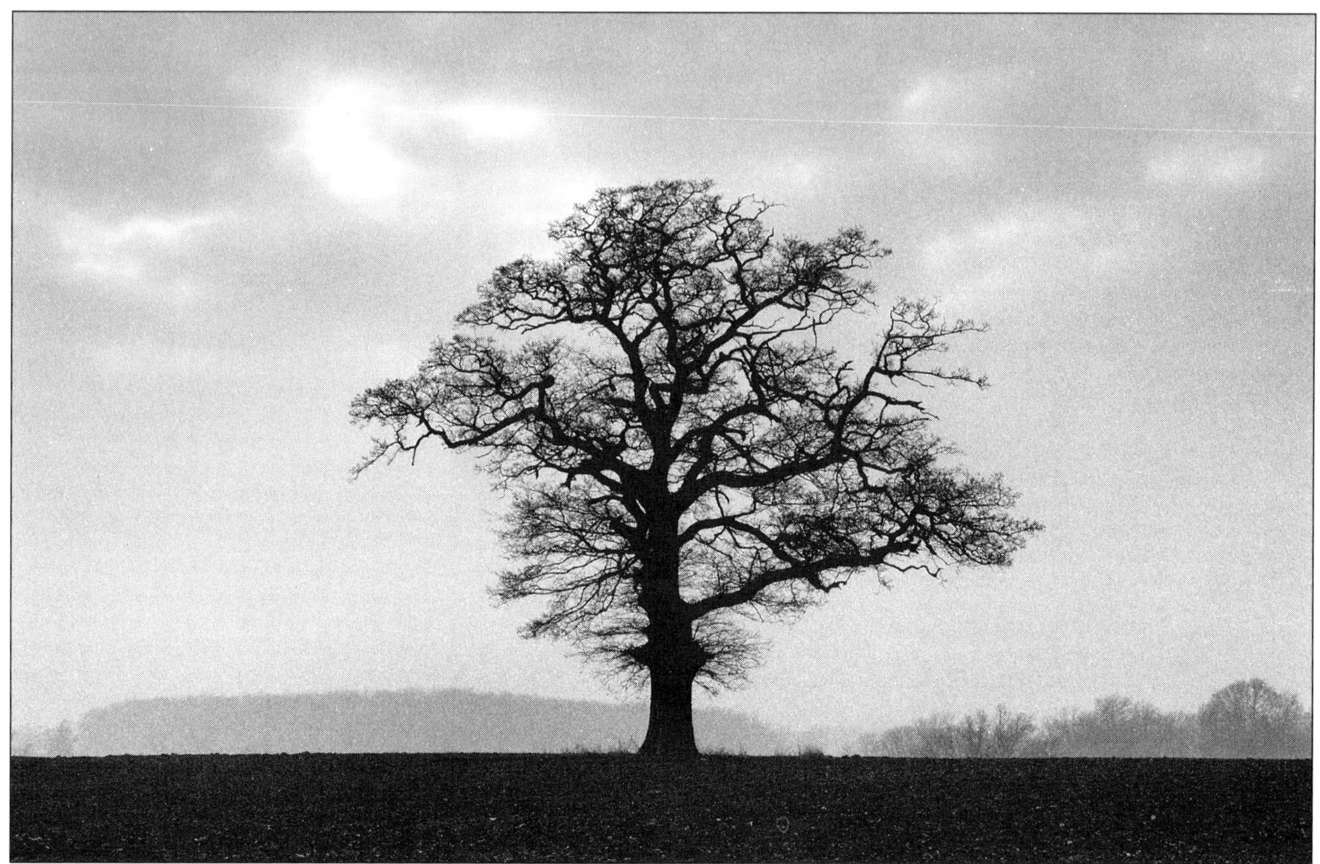

2 **MAXIMUM CONTRAST**
As the evening light was beginning to fade, Mike found the shot he wanted. He tramped through a muddy ploughed field to shoot this gnarled old tree. It stood out very well in silhouette against the sky, which was now broken here and there by little glimmers of light. Printing the photograph on Grade 5 paper has further increased the contrast.

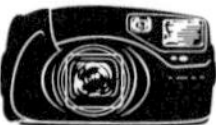

Compact tip

The enprints you get back with XP2 are usually purple, blue or sepia. You should specify which tint you want when you leave your film. Ironically, pure black and white prints are more difficult. To get a true monochrome print, ask for your prints on conventional paper. You'll probably get the best print from a professional lab.

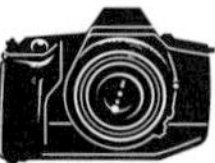

SLR tip

Fine detail such as twigs tests the abilities of a lens to the full. To make sure every stick is sharp, use a moderate setting such as f8 or f11 – no lens performs best at its widest or smallest aperture. Exposure is critical as well. Overexposure spreads the picture's highlights, hiding the fine lines that make a winter tree look so graphic.

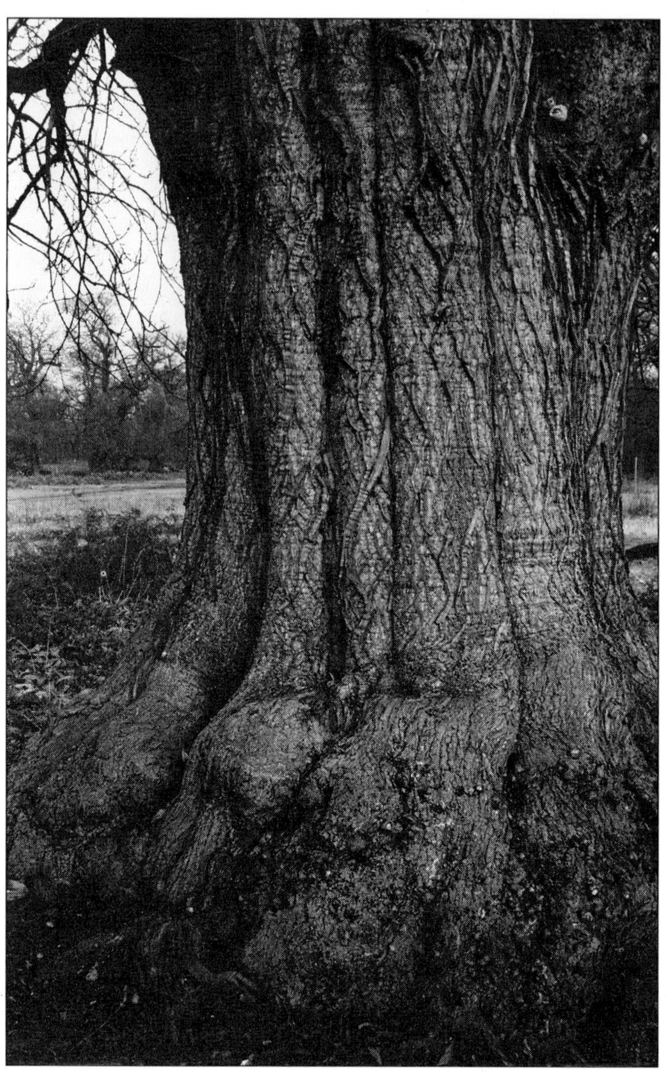

▼ *This is the best sweeping landscape Mike took all day, but it would have looked better if he had shot it on ordinary black and white film. 'It's too soft', he says, 'and I could have solved that by prolonging the developing a little. But you can't do that with XP2.'*

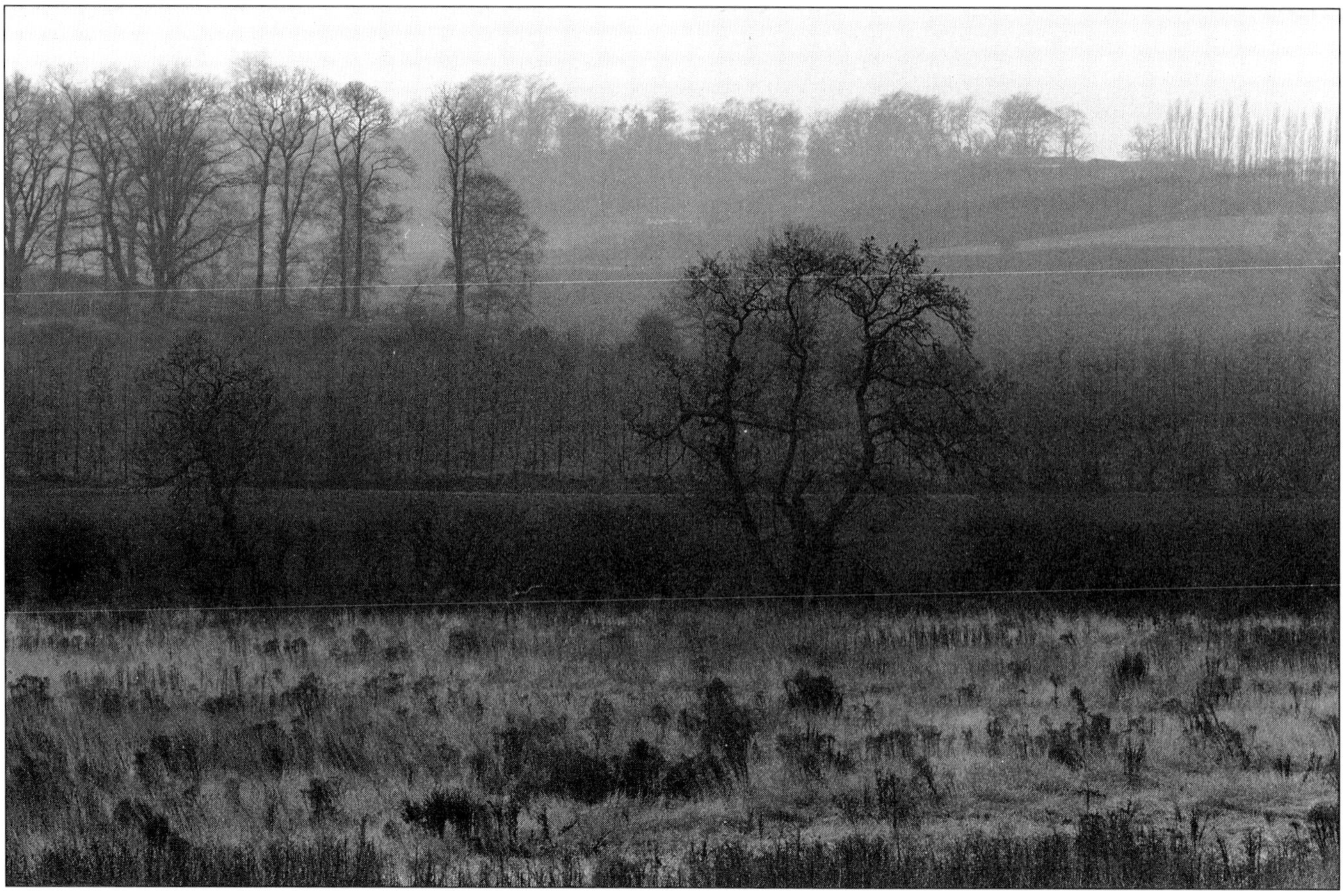

▶ *Another option on dull days is to concentrate on close-up detail. Mike switched to a 50mm lens to reveal the lined bark of this tree trunk. There's plenty of texture in the shot, and the contrast has again been exaggerated in the printing.*

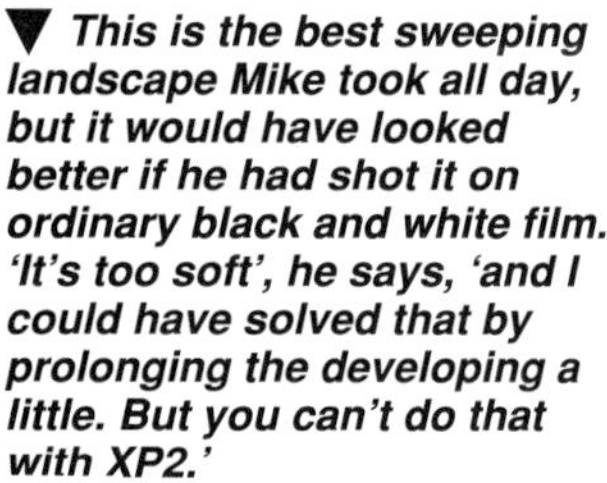

Simon Marsden – Infra-red landscapes

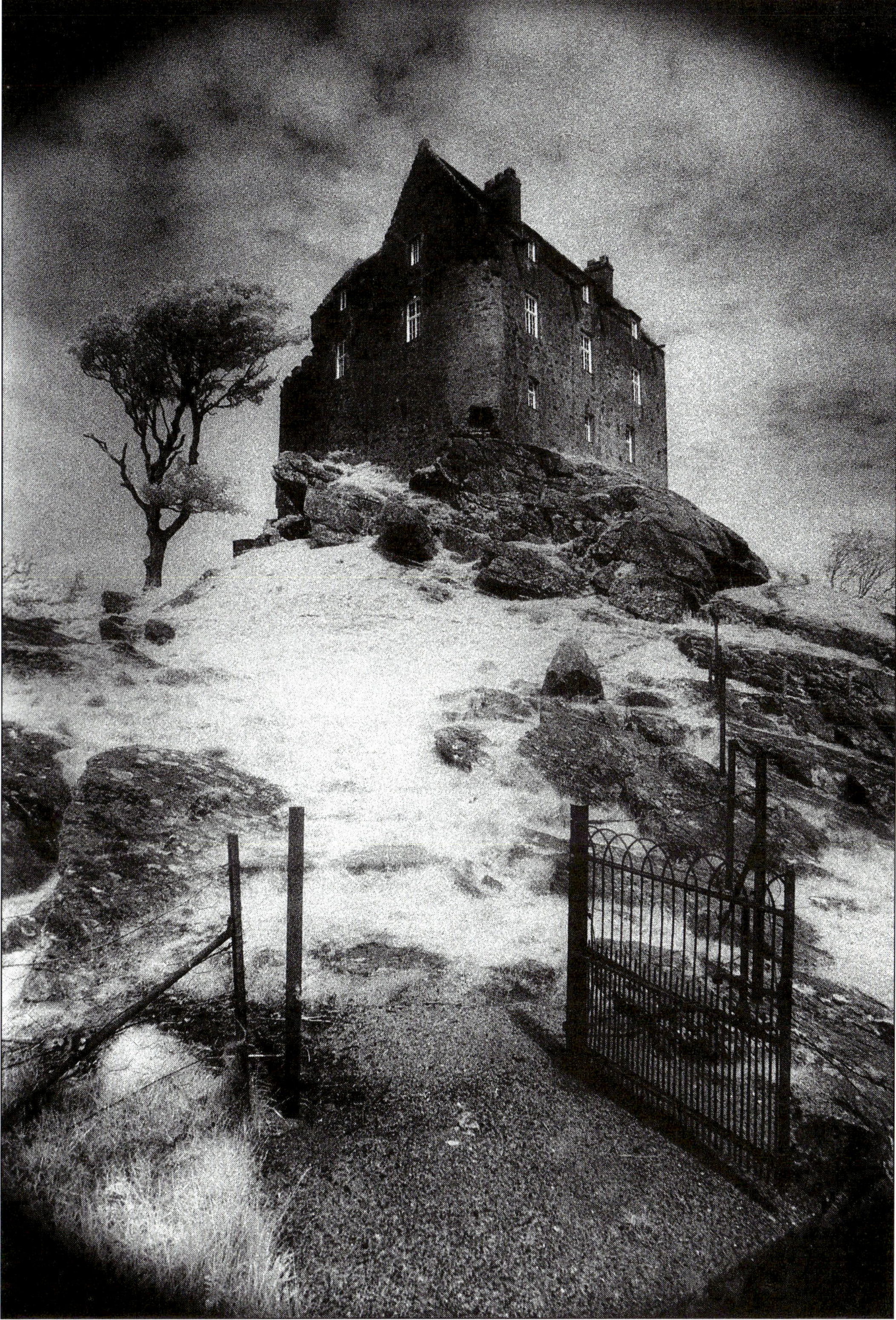

Black and white landscape and architecture photographer Simon Marsden specializes in taking atmospheric infra-red pictures of old and ruined buildings that aptly illustrate his celebrated series of books on haunted houses.

Simon Marsden is something of an expert on the paranormal. He's spent the last ten years travelling around Britain and Ireland in search of haunted homes to include in his series of books on the subject. Finding houses and castles with a ghostly history was comparatively easy. The most difficult task was taking pictures of them that were atmospheric and eerie enough to match the spooky stories.

Simon's answer was to shoot the old buildings on

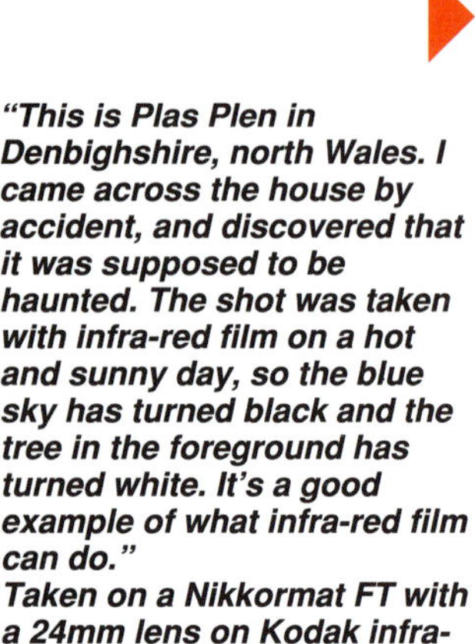

You can do it

'You need sunshine and heat to get the best results from infra-red film', says Simon. On a really hot day a clear blue sky will turn totally black, and anything pale will turn white, giving high contrast and a dramatic overall effect. Infra-red pictures are possible on a cloudy day, but I normally end up doing a lot of work in the darkroom afterwards to enhance the subtler effect.'

It's worth remembering that infra-red film is very unpredictable – you'll only find out how it responds to different conditions by trial and error.

infra-red film. Used with a red filter, infra-red film turns blue sky black and pale colours white, increasing contrast and giving landscapes a surreal feel. This disturbing effect is perfect for the lonely and often ruined buildings that Simon photographs, and he adds to the overall eeriness by shooting almost constantly on a 24mm lens, often from a low or unusual angle. This combination of techniques gives his pictures an unmistakable visual style that compliments the blood curdling stories they often illustrate.

Darkroom skills

His interest in photography began when his father presented him with a Leica on his 21st birthday. 'I went out and shot a roll of film in the garden', he explains, 'and I've been hooked on photography ever since. I

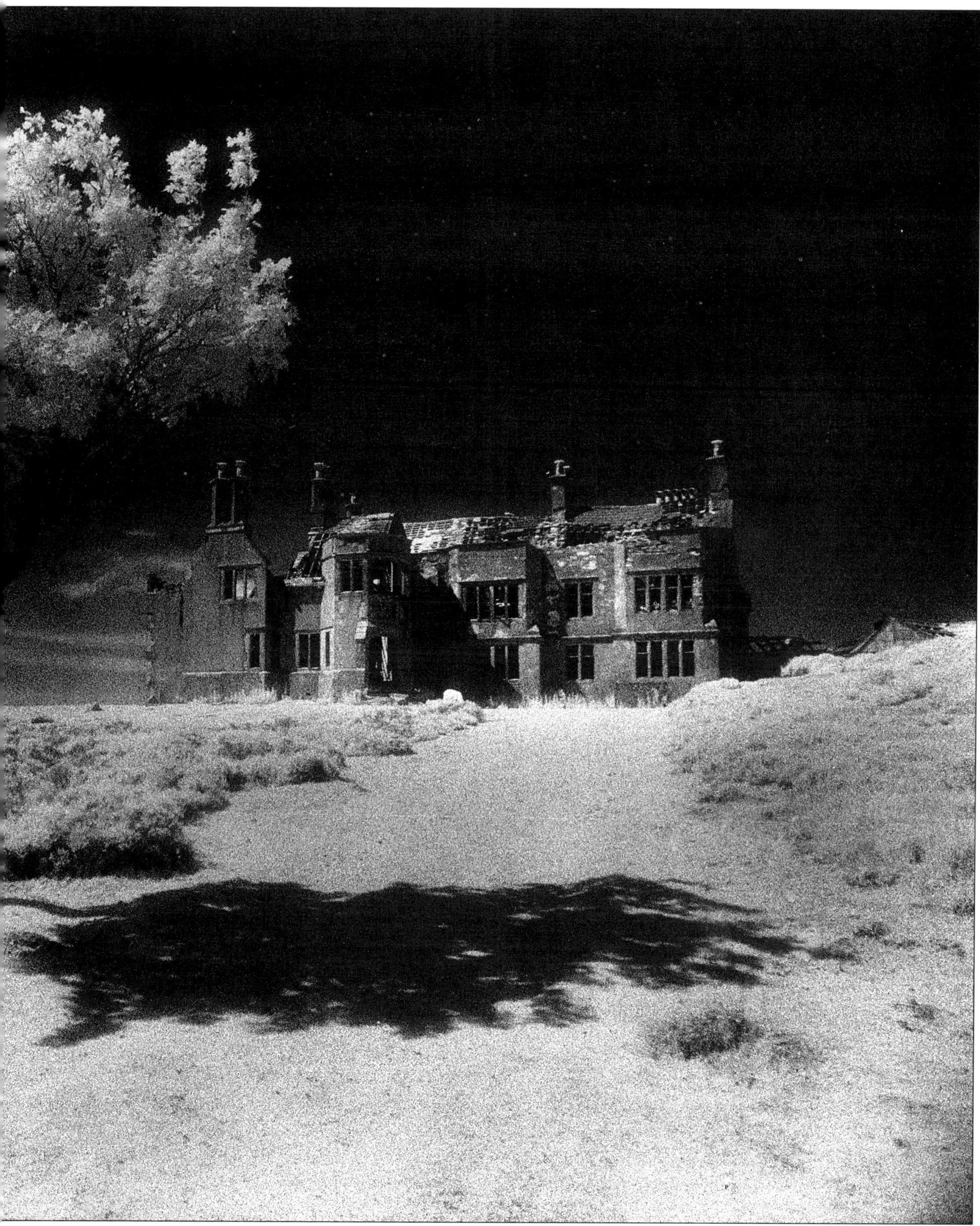

learnt my trade assisting a studio photographer who was technically brilliant. His meticulous approach was very helpful to me, and by a lucky chance his wife was an expert printer. Her kind advice was equally valuable.'

Simon does all his own printing, and spends long hours in the darkroom getting his infra-red prints exactly right. 'I think I spend about 70% of my photo-graphic time in the darkroom as opposed to about 30% actually taking pictures. But printing is a major part of infra-red photography – it can take a long time to get a print exactly right.' He shoots a wide variety of land-scape and architectural subjects, but never works in colour. 'I have absolutely no interest in it', he admits. 'To me, black and white photography is far more of a challenge.'

"This is Glamls Castle in Angus, Scotland, and it's a very strange place. The Queen Mother was born here, and there's a story connected with this place about a family monster, a deformed son who spent his whole life locked up in the top of the house and never saw the light of day. I'd tried some shots of the house on its own but it didn't look atmospheric enough, so I moved back to include this monument in the foreground."
Taken on a Nikkormat FT with a 24mm lens on Kodak infra-red film at 1/250th sec and f4 with a red filter and a polarizer.

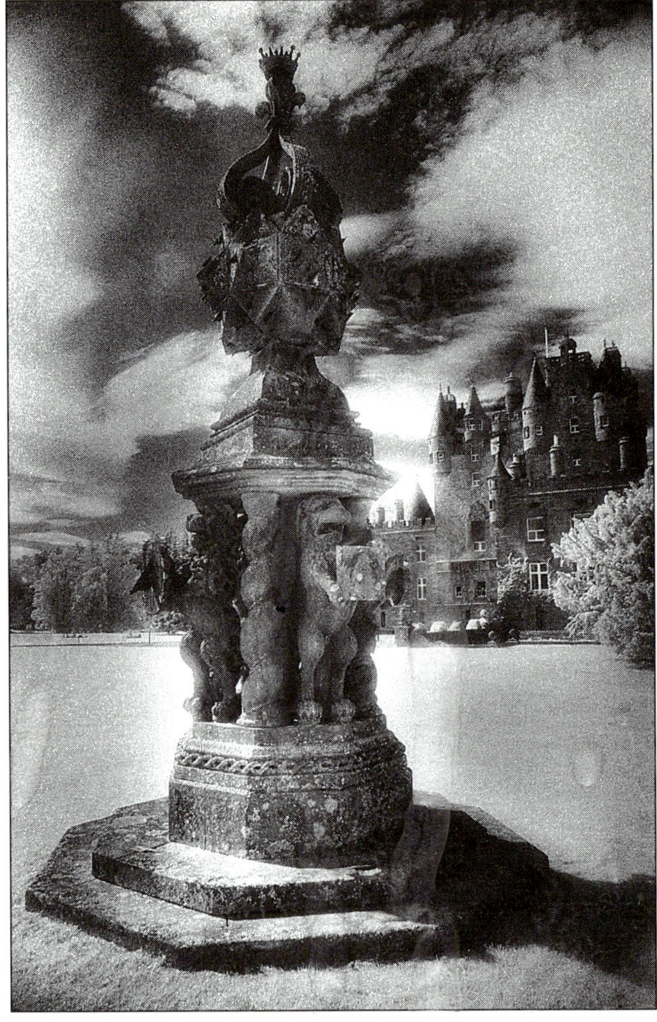

Technical details

When you're shooting on infra-red film, you need to use a red filter – without one, you won't get the effect. The one that's normally used is the Kodak Wratten 88A infra-red filter, but Simon prefers a Kodak 25 red filter. 'The 88A is such a dark red', he explains, 'that you can't see through the viewfinder, so you have to use a tripod, and I find the effect it gives is heavy and exaggerated. A normal red filter is easier to use and gives a subtler effect.'

"This is Gight Castle in Scotland, which was once the home of 'Mad Jack' Byron, an ancestor of the poet. He drank and gambled away the family fortune, and he and his equally demented wife are reputed to haunt the place. It's not a big house, so I moved in very close to make it look bigger."
Taken on a Nikkormat FT with a 24mm wide angle lens on Kodak infra-red film at 1/125th sec and f5.6 with a red filter.

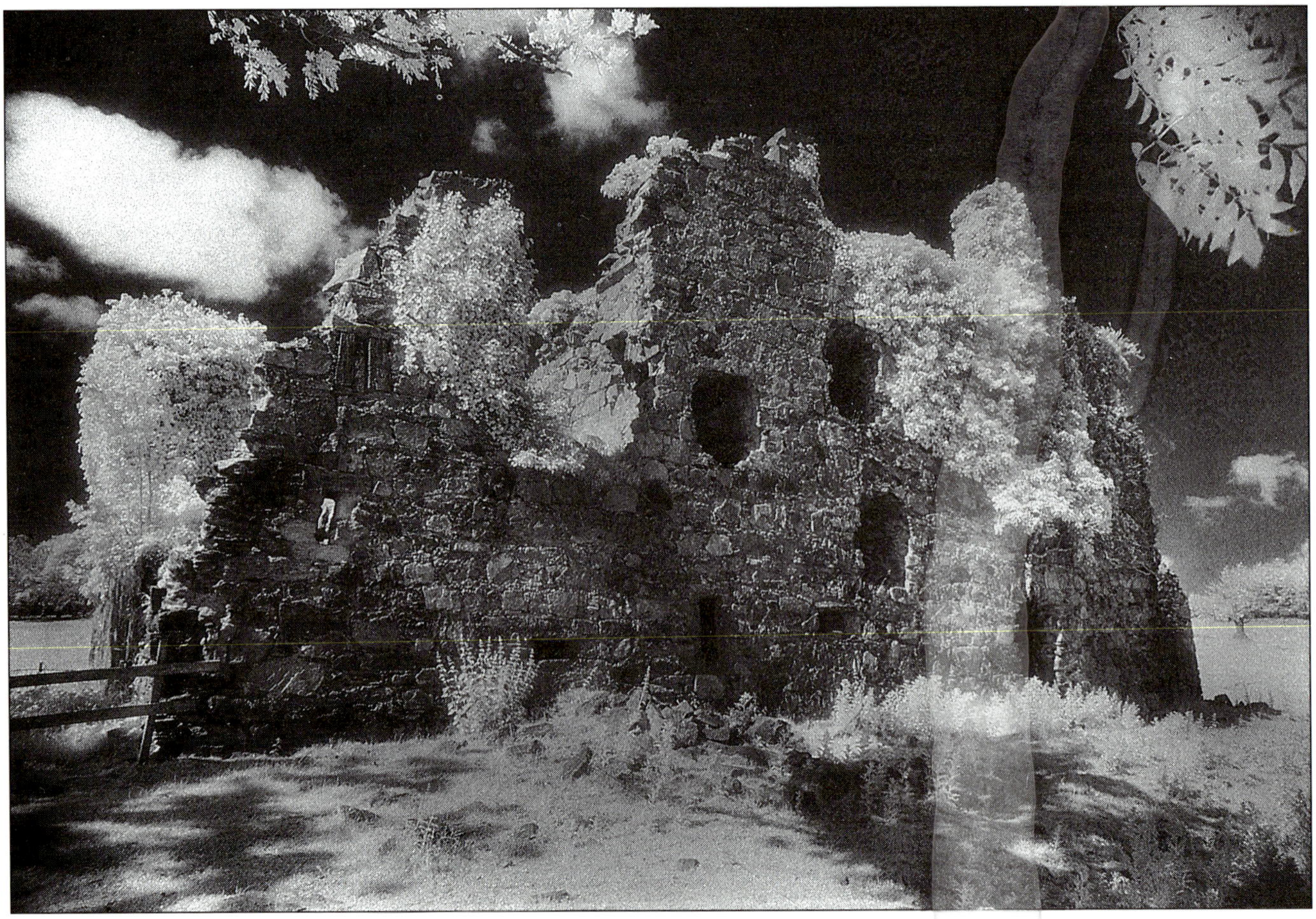

Shooting sunsets

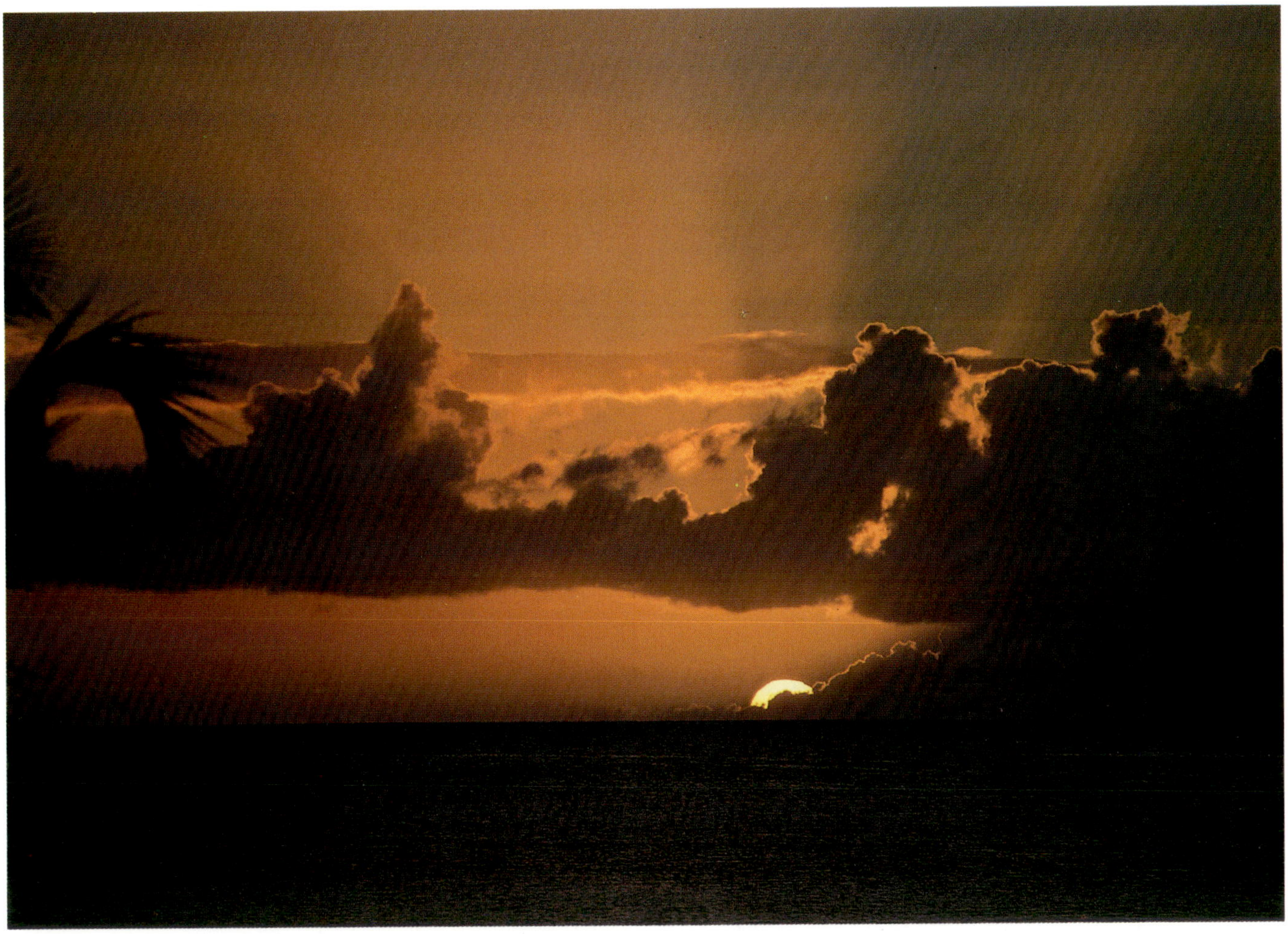

For breathtaking drama and inspiration, nothing beats a good sunset. The secret of success is to backlight carefully chosen features, such as trees and clouds, or to throw them into silhouette.

It's easy to be overwhelmed by a magnificent sunset, but if you take your time composing each shot, you'll be well rewarded.

You may not have time to change film or swap lenses, so have all your equipment ready and waiting. Sunsets are constantly changing, so take plenty of film so you can record as much as possible the variety of colour in the sky.

Instant sunshine

Don't wait for the 'perfect moment' to shoot – you may have waited too long and the sky might already be past its best. If you see a lovely sunset unexpectedly, capture it if you can – be prepared to respond to the beauty of an instant!

▶ **HUMAN INTEREST**
A solitary figure silhouetted against a dramatic sky and sea invites curiosity. Here, an elderly man creates an interesting shape. The photo was taken just as a wave saturated the beach, providing the reflection.

▲ **EVENING SPLENDOUR**
This classic sunset photograph concentrates on the beauty of the sky, with the sinking sun as its focal point. Timing is crucial: the sun moves through its own diameter in two minutes. So when it's setting, you may have only seconds to get the picture right.

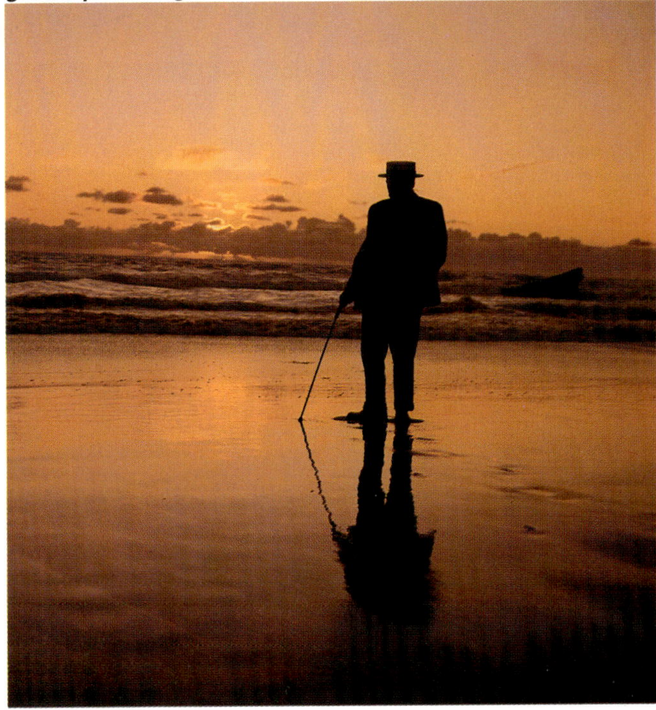

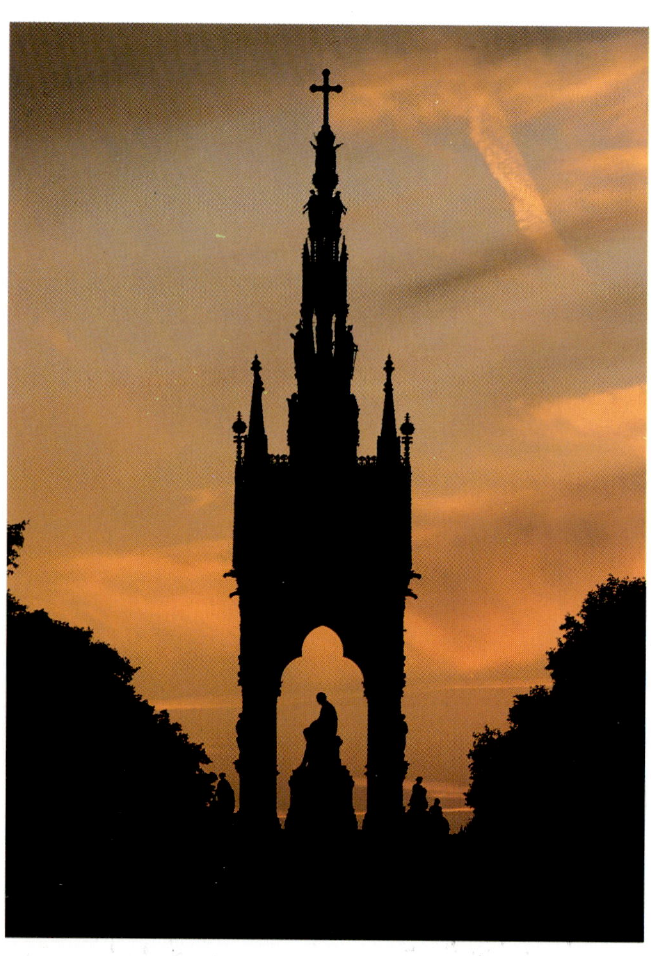

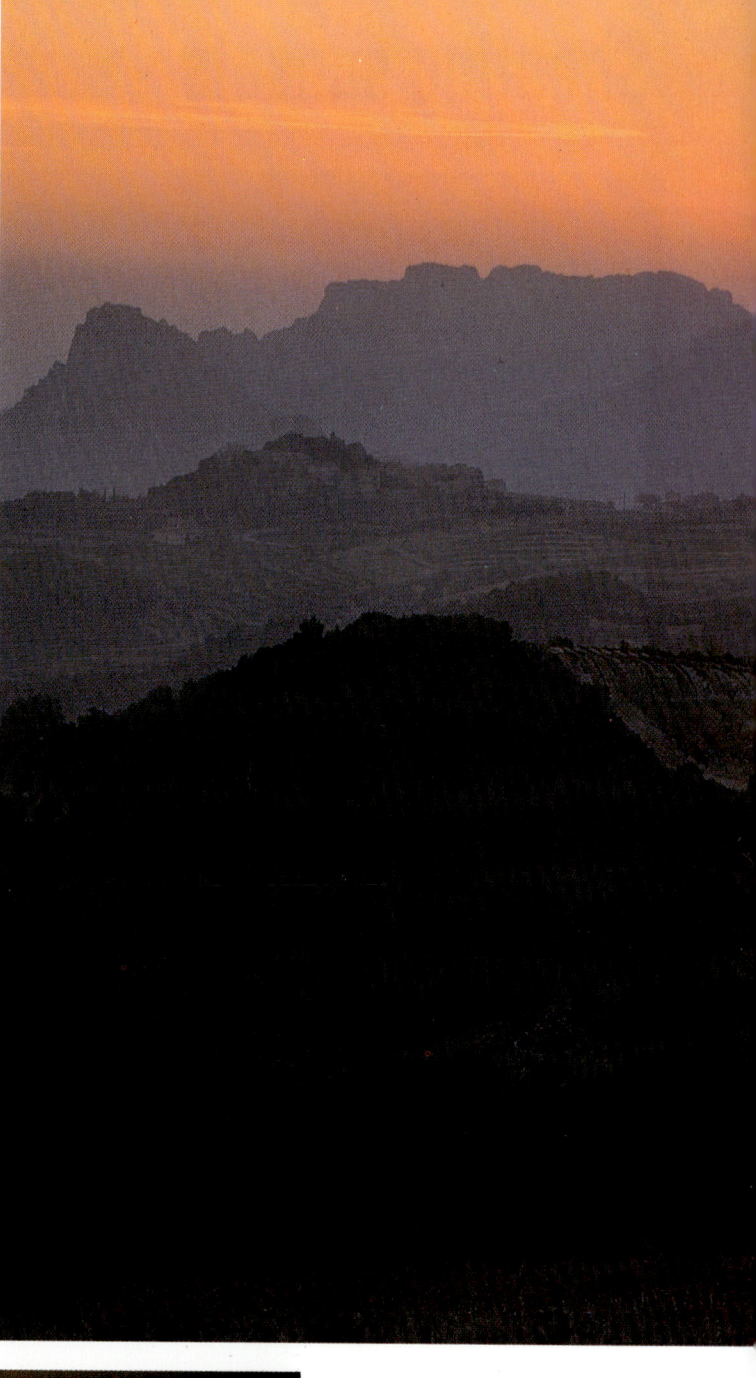

▲ CENTRAL STRENGTH

In silhouette, the Albert Memorial in London displays its intricate outline. The photographer moved round the memorial until the trees on either side balanced each other, making the picture more symmetrical.

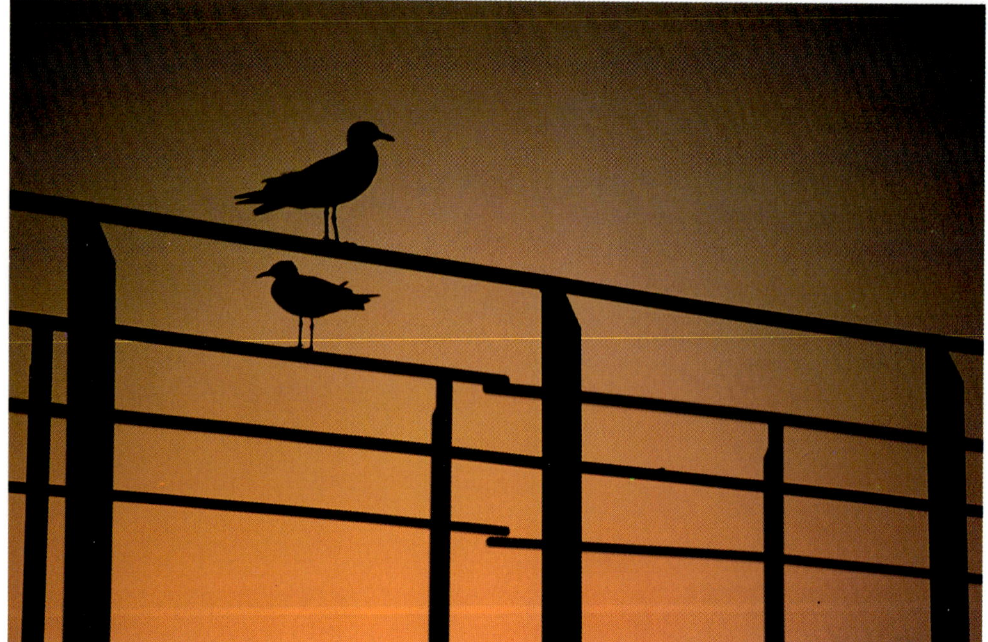

◀ SUPPORTING ROLE

Here the sunset plays a supporting role, silhouetting a foreground pair of sea birds and the railings on which they perch.

Several elements add to the strength of the composition. Look at the low angle of the shot, the mirror-like reversed image of the birds, the slight kink in the railings and their angle in relation to the picture frame. How much weaker it would be, for example, if the railings were parallel to the frame or if both birds faced the same direction.

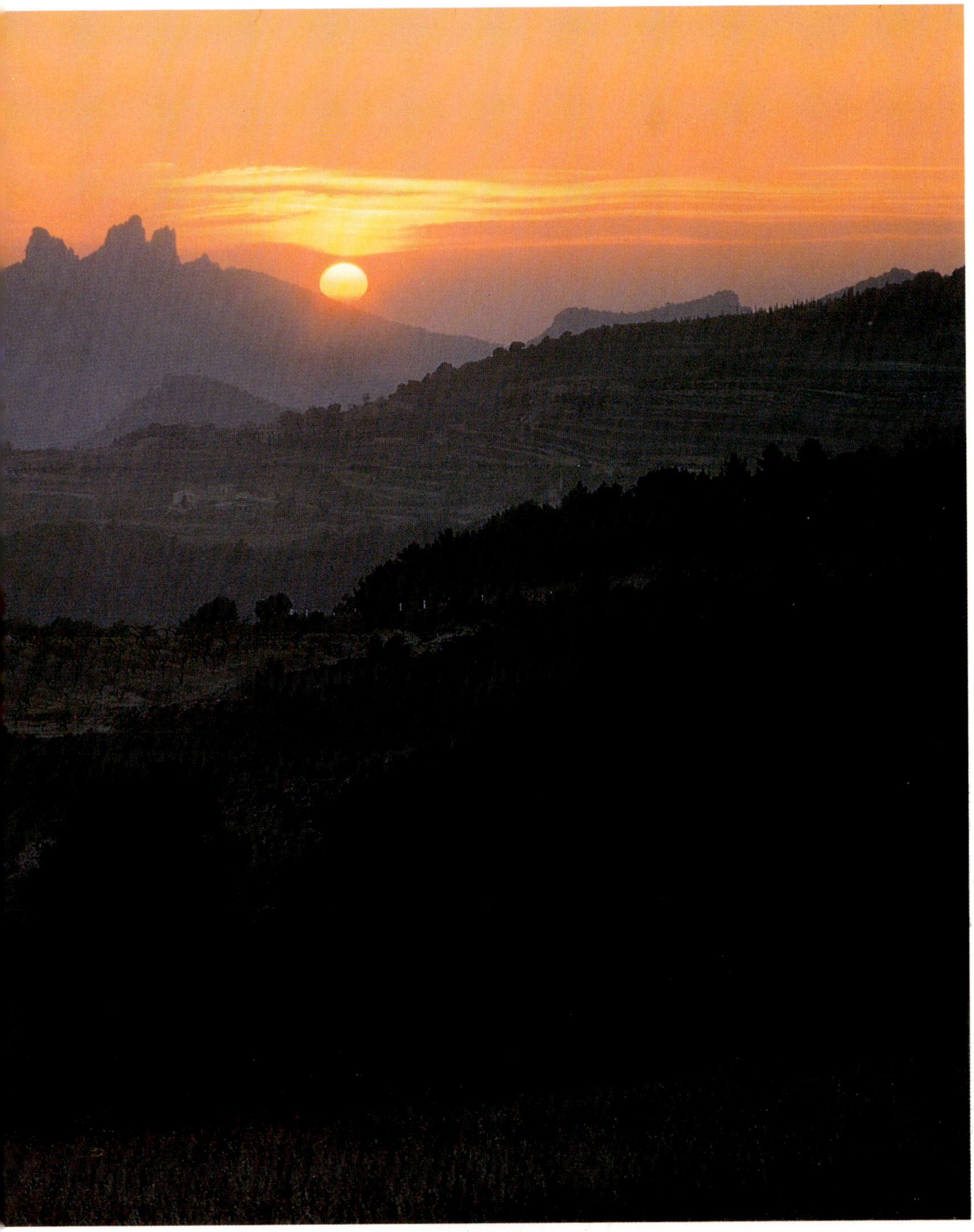

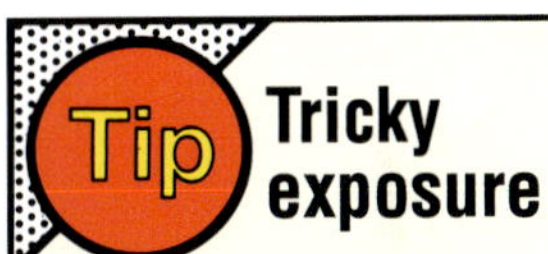

◀ MOUNTAIN MAJESTY
At any time of day, and at any season, mountains are potentially powerful subjects.

In a mountainous area, you can capture the sunset twice: from the foot of the mountain and again from the top.

In this photo, the hints of grassy detail in the foreground meadow and hedgerow trees give a sense of scale and make it possible to relate to the otherwise overwhelming scenery.

Tricky exposure

It's easy to get the exposure wrong when you're taking sunsets, and end up with an underexposed picture which doesn't do justice to the original scene.

If the colour of the sky is your main subject, take a meter reading from the sky where it is at average brightness, away from the sun itself.

It's advisable to bracket exposures if you have enough time.

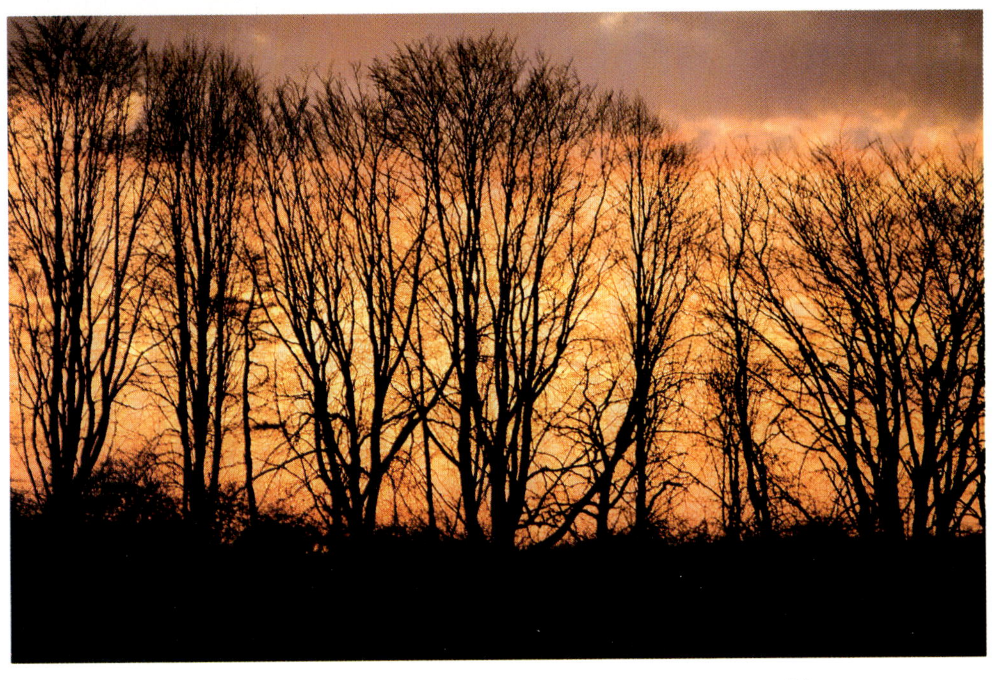

▶ RICH PATTERNS
The horizontal banding of sky and clouds, with the vertical threads of branches woven across them form patterns, emphasized in the evening light, when it is too dark to pick out detail.

If you look closely, you can find signs of thoughtful composition. The slight hummock of ground and the overlap of upper branches on to the purple sky divide the scene into unequal thirds – and add interest.

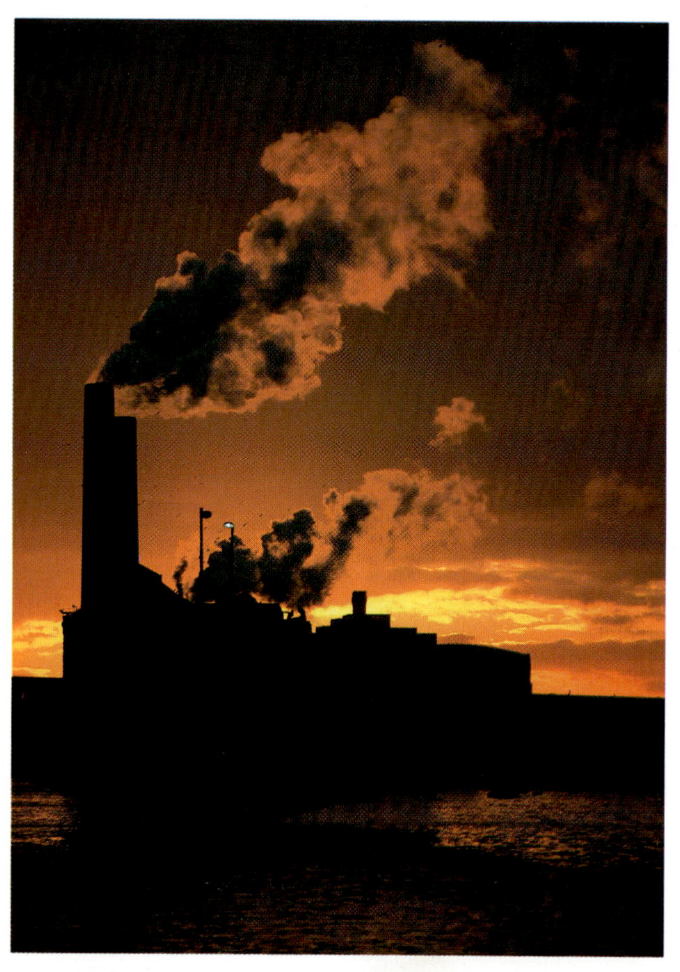

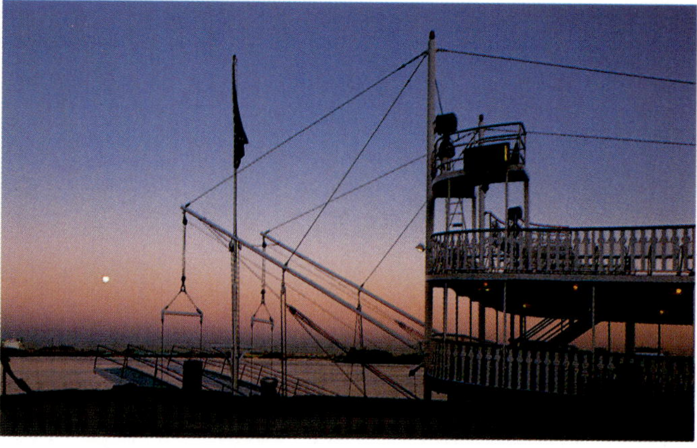

◀ INDUSTRIAL STRENGTH
A potentially ugly subject makes a dramatic image when shot in late evening, when the main dome of the sky is dark. Note how the tiny pinprick of electric light captures the eye, in contrast to the vast but fading evening sky.

▲ DOUBLE BLUFF
This 'sunset' features the moon, a tiny spot of bright light dominating the outline of a New Orleans riverboat. Nautical lights repeat the luminous theme. The image benefits from the solid foreground presence of the quay and upper decks, with their fretwork railings.

▼ NEGATIVE SHAPES
Successful images of silhouetted trees depend on the shapes created between the branches. Here the sinuous branches and lacy twigs of the large tree divide the sky into interesting shapes. The small tree provides balance and a sense of depth and perspective.

The stark black mass at the foot of the picture and the unusual greenish tones combine to suggest an eerie landscape.

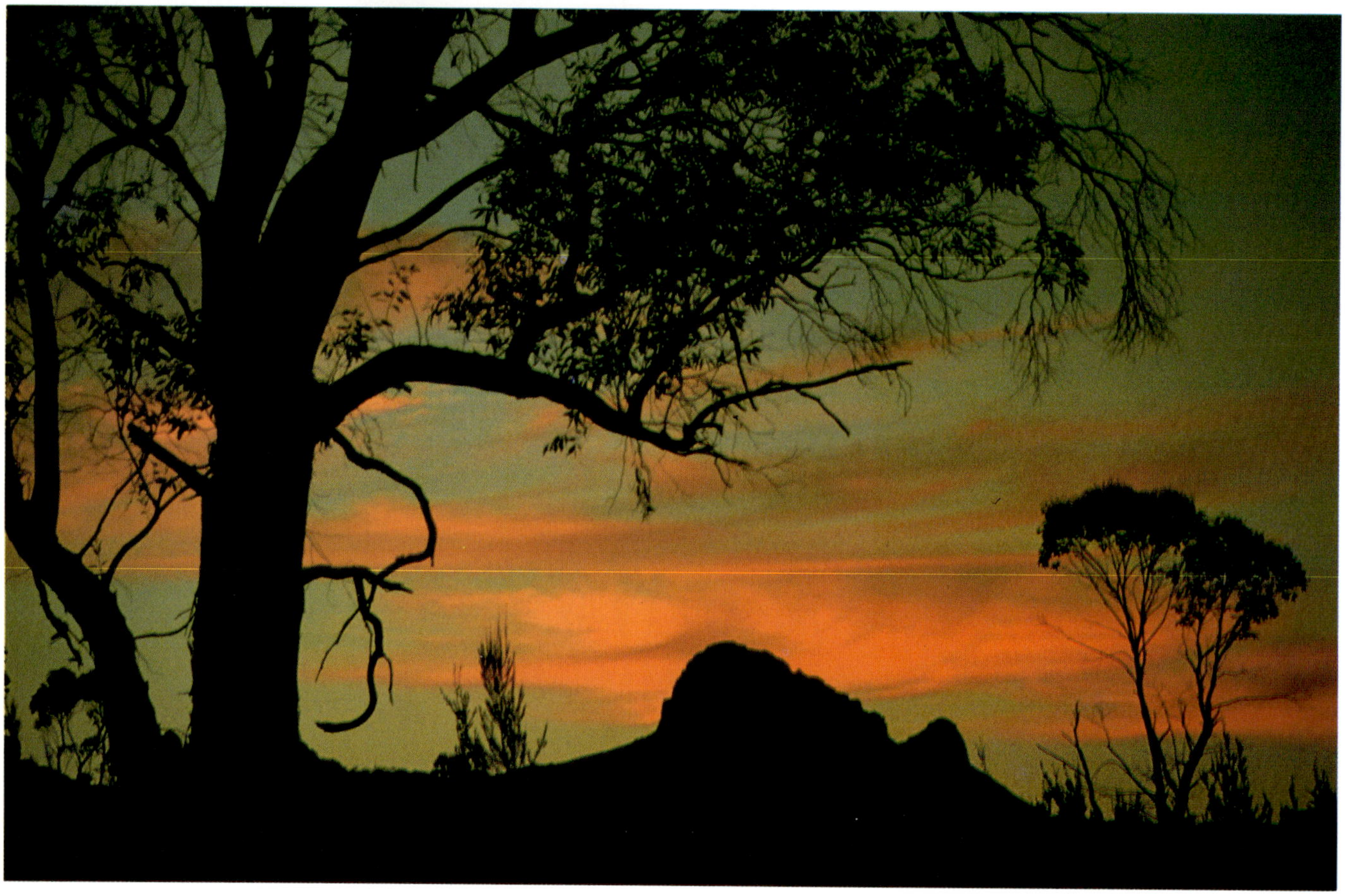

Cloudscapes

Whether it's white clouds scudding across a blue sky or brooding storm clouds looming over the land, cloudscapes can make really atmospheric pictures. Mike Busselle and David Jones photograph the moody skies of central France.

The trouble with setting out to photograph cloudscapes is that you're completely at the mercy of the elements. With most landscape work, you can usually end up with some passable pictures even if the conditions aren't absolutely ideal, but if the sky's not full of cloud and really punchy your cloudscapes just won't work.

We chose the hilly and rainswept Auvergne region in central France for this shoot. All that rain meant a good chance of dramatic storm clouds, and there were plenty of interesting foregrounds to choose from. In a good cloudscape the sky should really dominate the frame, but an interesting foreground is also required to balance up the composition and make the picture strong enough.

A stormy start

When we set out one dull and windy June morning, the sky couldn't have been more promising from our point of view. Dark storm clouds loomed threateningly overhead, making the sky look very dramatic and plunging the ground below into darkness. After driving around for a short while we found a perfect foreground to complement the clouds – a lovely view across woodland and pasture towards a village.

We stopped the car and set up as quickly as we could in order to take advantage of the wonderful sky, because clouds can move away very quickly on a windy day. I was using a Nikon F801s on a tripod with a 35-105mm zoom lens and Fuji ISO 50D slide film, and I

1 ▼ STORM CLOUDS
This is practically the same view as David's (see next page), but Mike composed his picture far more carefully and waited until there was a touch of sun on the land. He used a graduated filter to darken the clouds even further and an 81C warm up filter to brighten up the land.

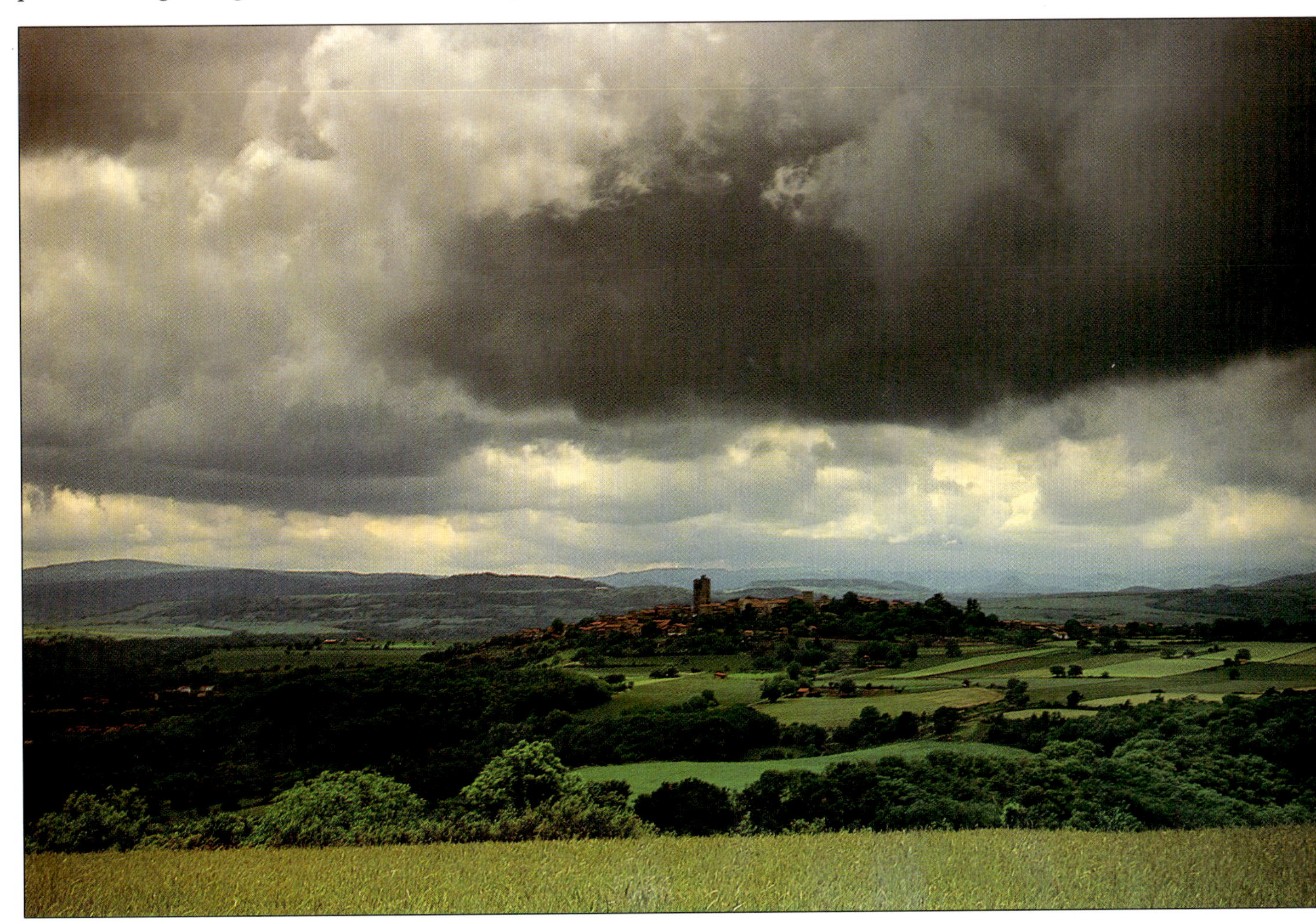

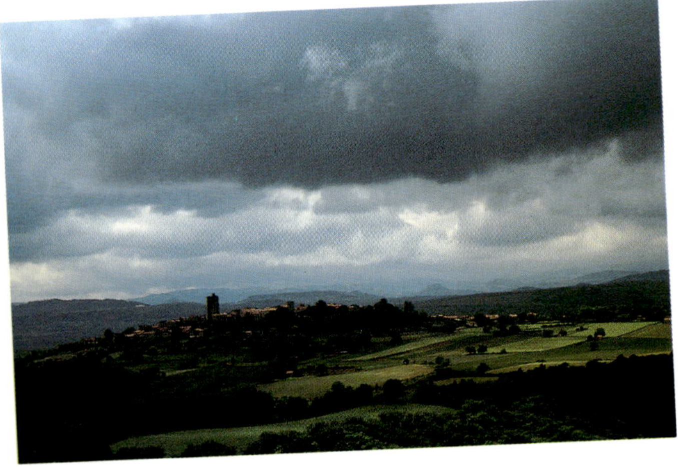

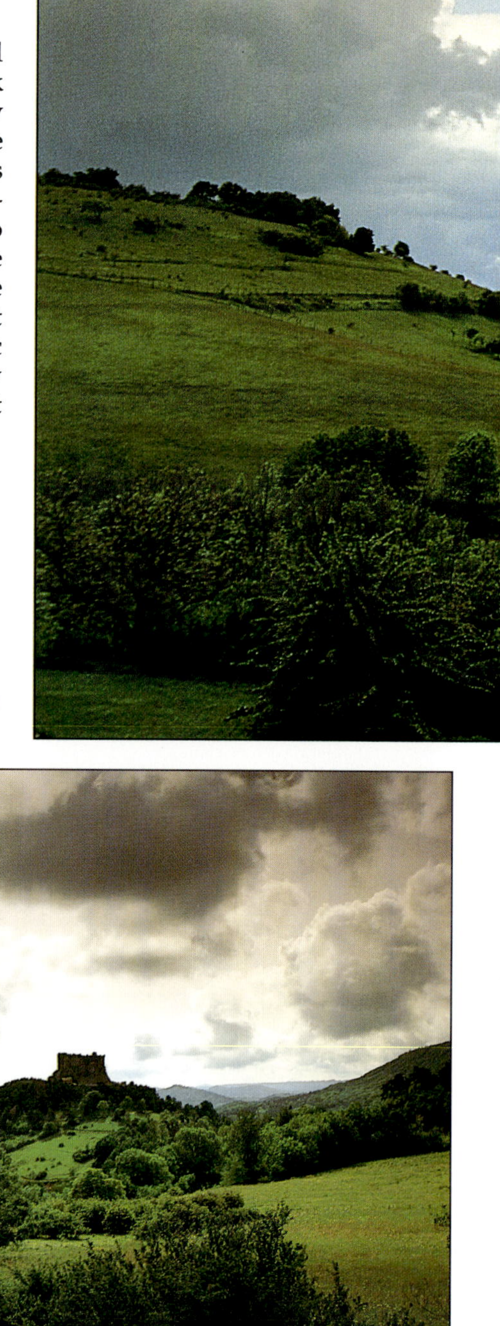

set the lens to about 70mm before taking a series of shots across the fields. I liked the view, and the sky looked very dramatic, but the land was too dark to really stand out and the best of my pictures was just too dull.

Light on the land

Mike concentrated on the same view to begin with, but he realized that the shot would look boring with a dark foreground. He saw a small break in the clouds, and decided to wait and see whether the sun would come out to help him. A few minutes later it did emerge, lighting up the fields and really bringing the foreground to life.

He photographed the scene with a Nikon FE2 on a tripod with a 28-70mm lens and Fuji Velvia ISO 50 slide film. He used a graduated filter to make the sky look even more dramatic, and a warm up filter to brighten up the fields. Then we decided to move on in search of different foregrounds.

Changing skies

By mid morning the wind had really picked up, and by the time we'd found another viewpoint a little further along the road the sky to the east had changed dramatically. There were still a few rain clouds here and there, but most of the sky was brightened up by the sun, which was behind a cloud but just about to appear. A castle on a hill made a very strong focal point in the middle of Mike's shot, but the changing sky was the feature that really dominated the frame.

Half an hour later, the sky had transformed itself again. The dark clouds were gone, replaced by lighter ones backed by clear blue sky. Mike took some shots across trees and farmland towards a distant group of hills, then decided to wait and see how the scene changed. He was hoping for the perfect combination – a strongly lit foreground and a dark, dramatic sky – and after waiting patiently for three quarters of an hour he got what he wanted.

2 ▼ **THE GLOOM LIFTS**
By the time Mike had found another location the sky had brightened considerably. There were still a few dark clouds overhead, but the sky was clearing fast and allowing the sun to shine through. The distant ruined castle makes a good focal point almost in the centre of the frame.

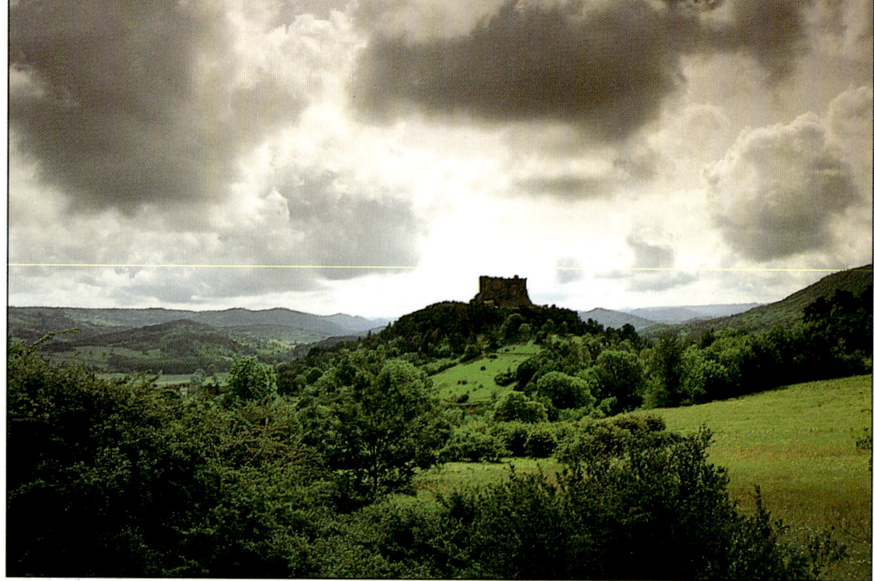

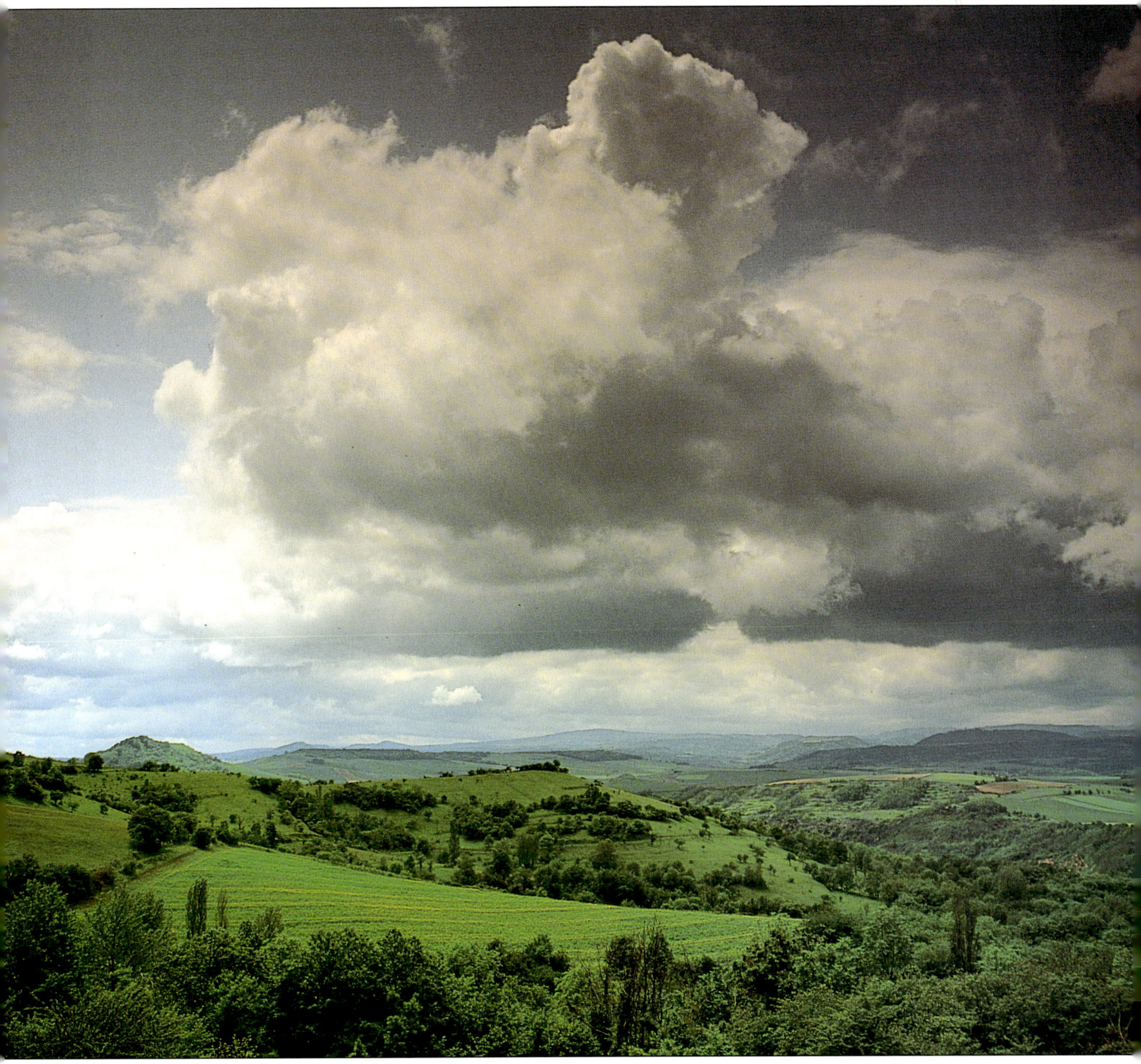

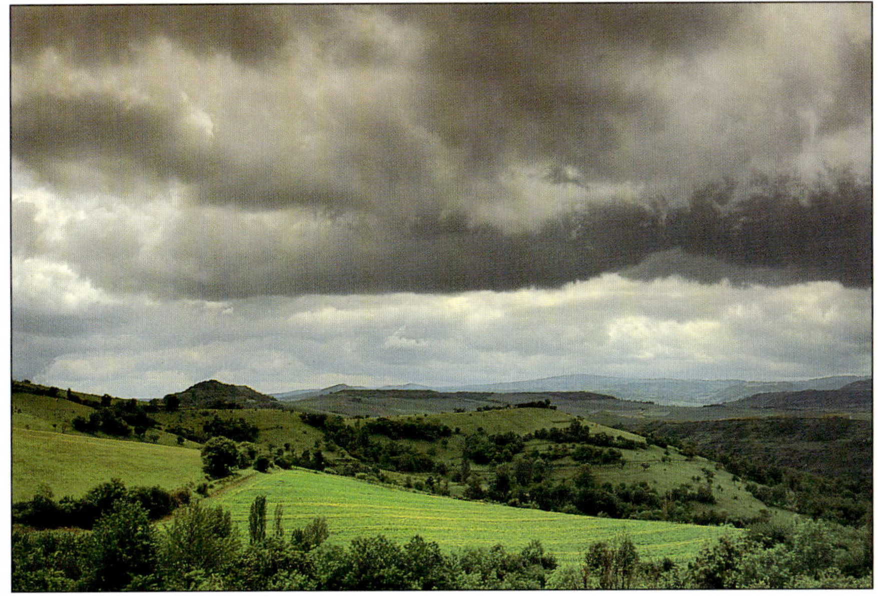

3 ▲ BLUE SKIES
The sky continued to clear as Mike and David drove along, and when they stopped to shoot this view across tree lined farmland patches of blue were clearly visible through the clouds. The extra light was very welcome, but the sky wasn't quite dramatic enough.

4 ▶ THE RAINS RETURN
Mike hung around at the same location for half an hour to see how the sky would change. He was hoping the dark clouds would return without completely killing the sun on the foreground, and that's exactly what happened, but he had to achieve the shot before the rain got too heavy.

The perfect foreground

Mike was pleased with the mix of storm clouds and sun, but he wasn't happy with the foreground so he moved on. A hundred metres down the road we saw a sunlit vineyard. It was an ideal foreground when shot in portrait format to emphasize the moody sky behind it.

5 ▼ STORM AND SUN A few hundred metres down the road Mike came across the perfect foreground. This vineyard really worked well in portrait format, and it was backed by the heaviest storm cloud we had seen all day. He captured this shot just before the sun went in.

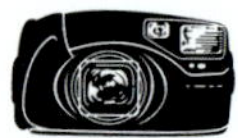

Compact tip

If you're going to use a graduated filter on a compact camera, take special care to make sure that neither the filter holder nor the filter itself obscures any of the windows on the camera. These ports are rarely labelled, but they are all vital to the camera's functions. If the filter or holder obscures any of them, your pictures could end up out of focus, incorrectly exposed, or both.

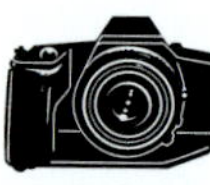

SLR tip

For dramatic skies, use two graduated filters together. This technique generally works well, but take extra care with wide angle lenses. If your camera has depth of field preview, stop down the lens to the working aperture, then look through the viewfinder to check that the dividing line which separates clear and tinted areas of the filter is not too conspicuous. If it's very obvious, stagger the graduated effect by sliding one of the filters up or down a little.

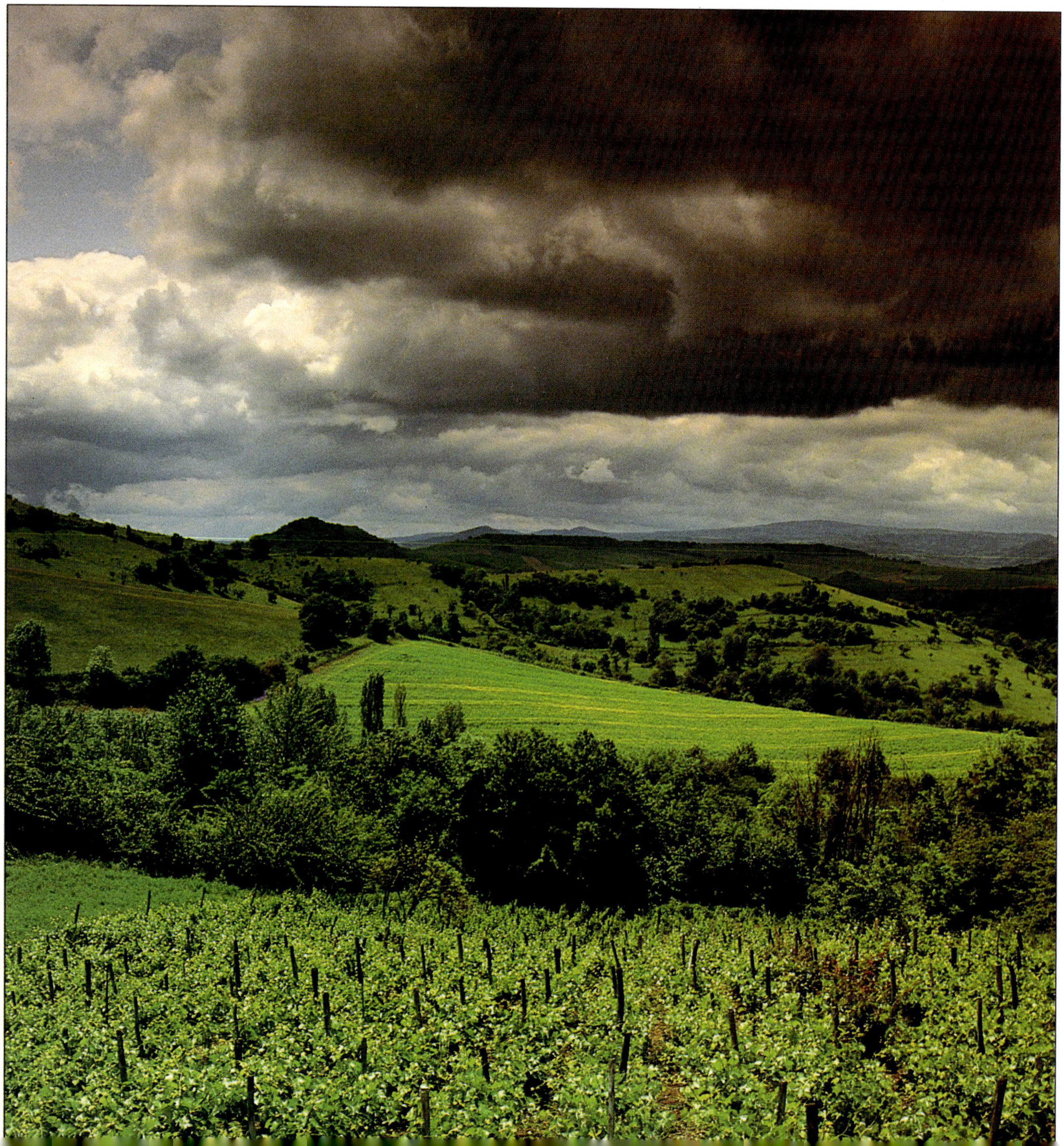

Landscapes plus ...

A landscape can stand alone as a single image, or it can be part of a larger story: a picture story. Like any story, a picture story has a theme, as well as a beginning, a middle and an end.

The first step towards the creation of a good picture story is the selection of a suitable subject. Usually it will be something stimulating and of personal interest, for example an interesting hobby or a family event like a wedding.

A subject which illustrates a process from beginning to end, such as the wine making example we have used here, is ideal; but you can also create a picture story centred around (for example) history, or ecology, or people, relating them all to the landscape – the environment – in which they live and work. Whatever "angle" you choose, you can create a set of pictures which is more than the sum of its parts.

▶ **CHATEAU VINEYARD**
The opening shot should set the scene for the whole essay. The vines lead the eye to the centre of the shot.

▼ **GRAPESHOT**
The next photo was taken some months later when the grapes had ripened. The vine fills the frame.

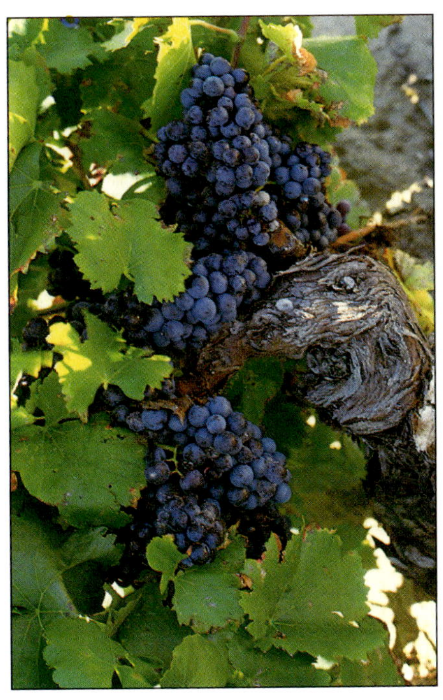

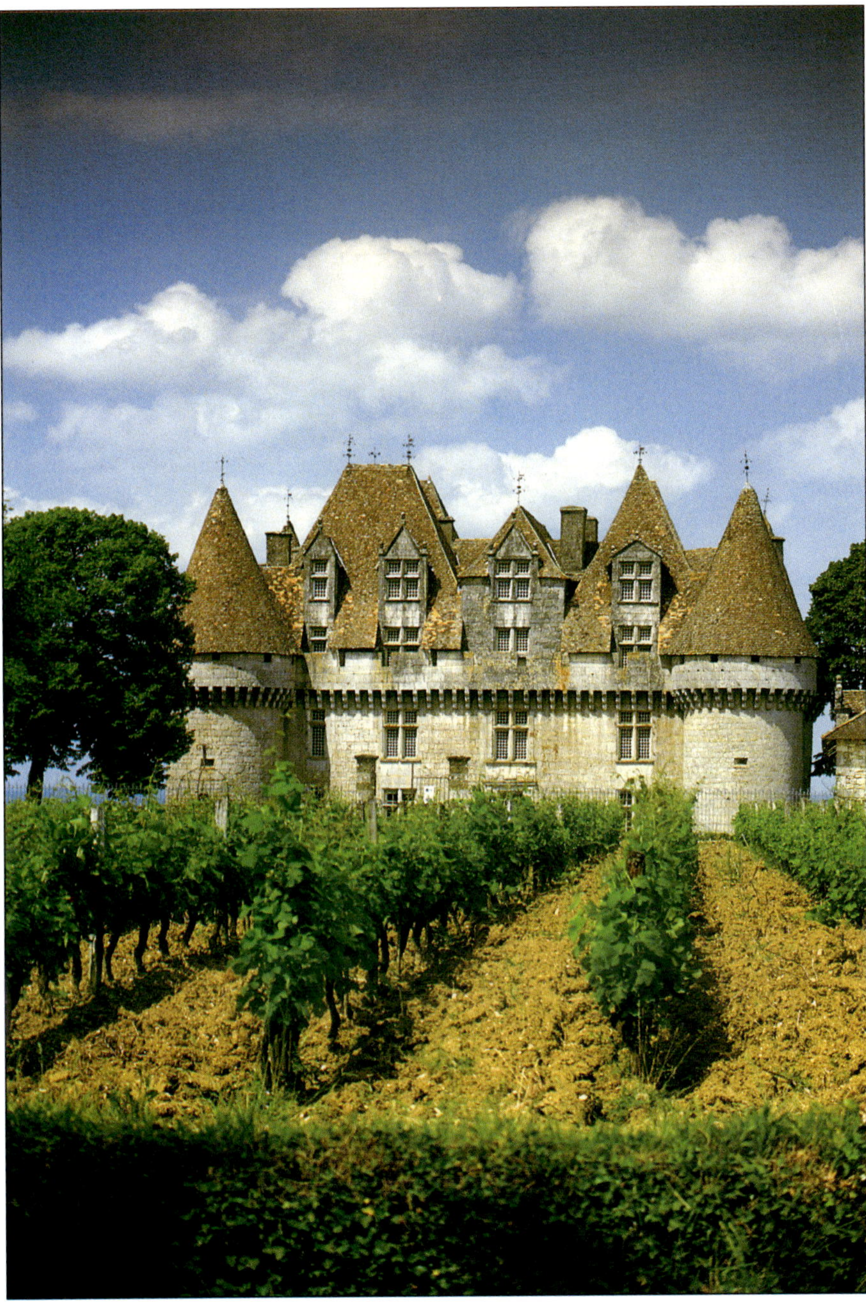

The importance of planning

It's essential that you know what you want to say before you start photographing – or it's very easy to end up with a disjointed series of pictures which have very little impact. Before you start organizing the finer details of the project you should find out as much as possible about your subject.

A good place to start is a visit to the local library. If, for example, your essay is to be on a month in a village, you could find out if there are any legends about the place or when the local festivals are. Talking to local people can also provide important information which you might otherwise miss.

If your essay is on wine making, for example, you would find out, at the very least, when in the year each part of the process takes place, and where the most photogenic vineyards are. You don't have to restrict yourself to the same vineyard. A successful essay can be put together from a variety of different locations.

A little homework will not only give you plenty of ideas for your picture essay – it can also save you a lot of time and wasted film. Armed with the right information you will be able to work out which are the best aspects to photograph.

Structure

Once you've done your initial research, you can make a list of pictures that you believe are essential for the story and tick them off as you shoot.

Remember that for a successful essay you will need a strong structure. It's useful to think how film directors work from a shooting script. First, they set the scene, then they establish the details and characters, and finally there is the climax when everything falls into place.

You can divide your picture essay into three similar sections. You could begin by photographing some establishing shots. A wide angle lens could be used to include lots of detail, such as a château and its vineyard. This might be followed by some close-up shots of a bunch of grapes. These initial pictures are very important as they help provide the framework to build up the rest of the story.

Next, you'll need photos which fill in the story. These should give information about the subject. For an essay on wine making, photos should be taken of every important aspect of the process – the grapes ripening on the vines, the grape picking, the pressing and the storing of the wine.

Finally, you will have to capture the climax of the picture essay – in this case it would be people drinking the finished product.

Remember, don't skimp on film as you will have to do lots of editing when you come to finally putting your picture essay together for display.

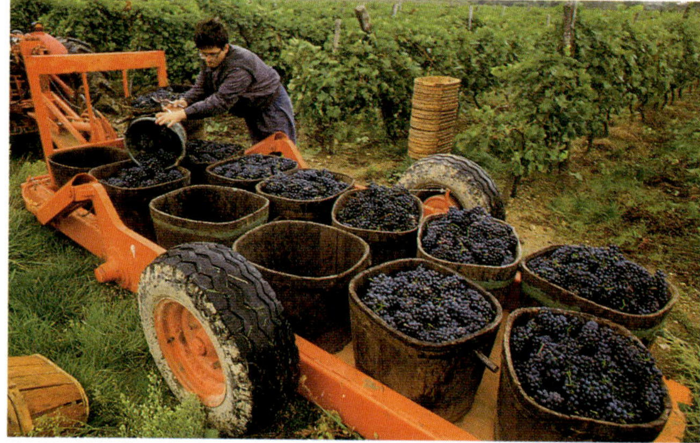

▶ **CARTING THE GRAPES**
The photographer didn't actually have to show the grapes being picked to suggest this stage of the process. The strong contrasting colours and diagonal composition enhance the picture.

▼ **WELLIES AND GRAPES**
A low viewpoint and telephoto lens creates this vivid shot of the grapes underfoot. The blurred figure in the background gives a sense of movement.

▶ **THE WINE CELLAR**
This picture concentrates on the human element in wine making. Daylight film and fill-in flash were used to capture the atmosphere in the cellar.

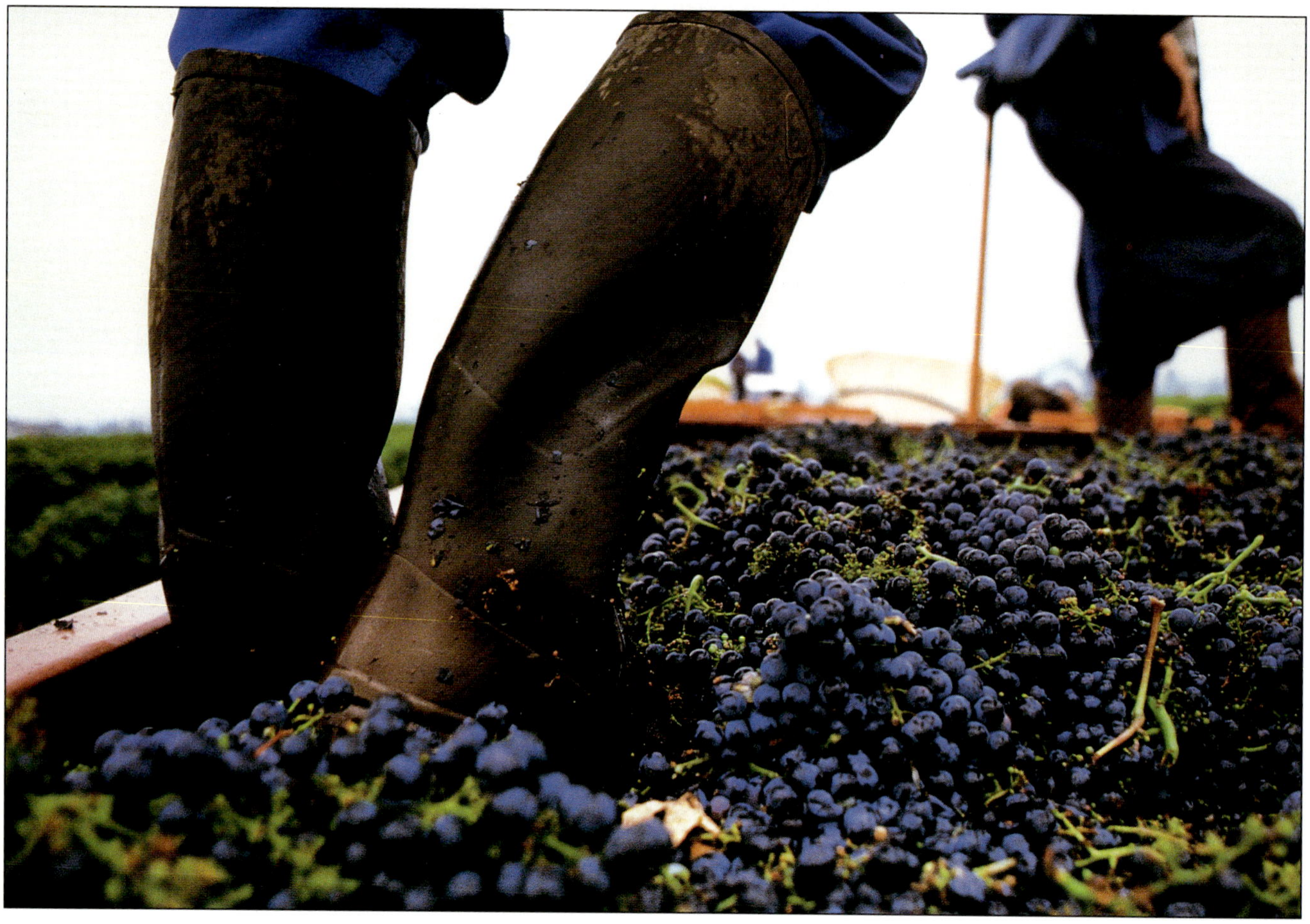

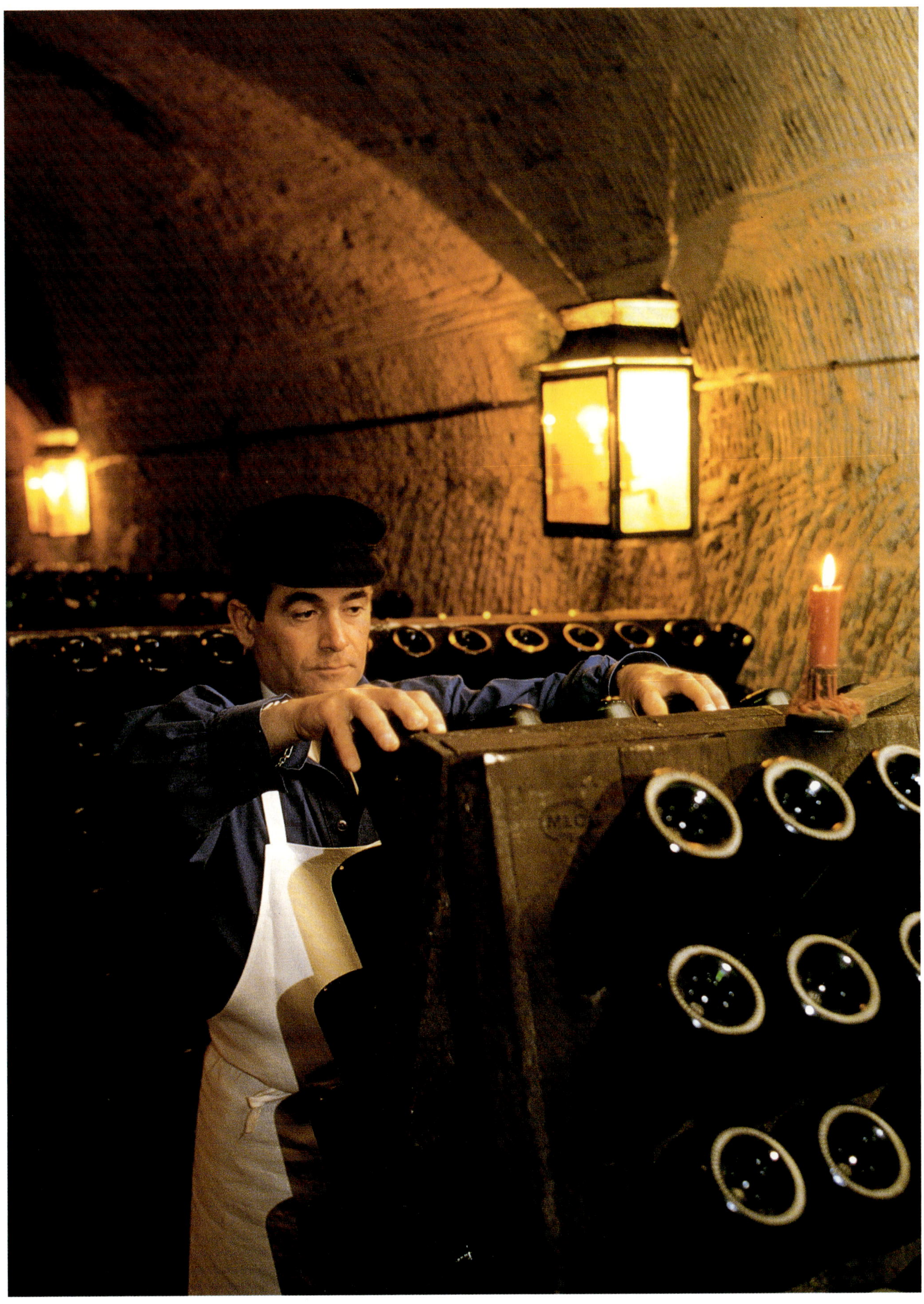

The final stage

The pictures you choose for the final display should illustrate all the important aspects of the subject. They should also have a strong visual appeal so that they help carry the story along.

It's important that each successive photograph should say something different about the subject while at the same time complementing the other pictures. Never include two similar photographs unless they form part of a sequence.

Pictures with a messy background should also be avoided as they will distract from the main subject and you'll risk losing the attention of your viewers.

You don't have to be limited by the size and shape of the prints as they come back from the processing lab. Don't be afraid to crop if it gives the pictures more impact.

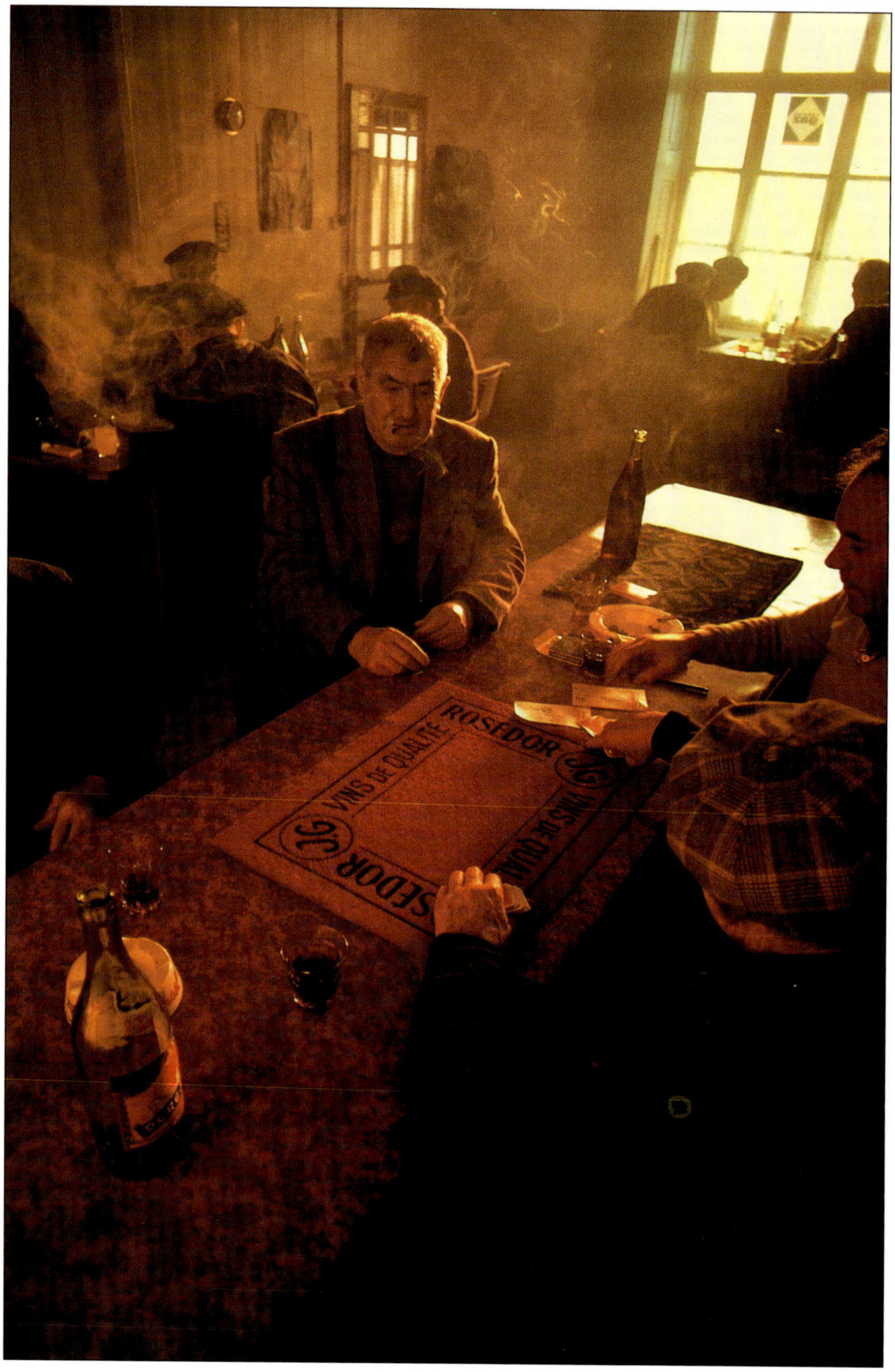

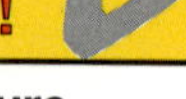

◀ A FINE VINTAGE?
The final picture in an essay should sum up the whole story. For the last shot, the photographer used backlighting to capture the atmosphere of the café where the product was being drunk.

CHECK IT! ✔

To create a picture essay dealing with a process:

❏ research your subject thoroughly before you start taking any photos

❏ shoot a whole variety of photos on each aspect of your subject – don't skimp on film

❏ when displaying your results avoid pictures that are too similar or too messy

❏ don't be afraid to crop your prints

Trees in the landscape

Whether you use trees as a focal point in a larger landscape, or as a subject in their own right, they can be a very rewarding subject. So take advantage of their organic shapes, delicate leaves and varying colours.

Because trees are so much a part of daily life, it's easy to underestimate their photographic potential – but think again.

Even a single tree can present endless opportunities for providing a focal point in a landscape, or for studying the sculptural shapes of its branches, the lacy detail of its twigs and the infinite patterns of its leaves. The seasons multiply your options still further, particularly for colour.

Whether you're photographing the small scale details of a tree in your own neighbourhood, a collage of leaves composed in studio conditions or majestic forests spotted while on holiday, the more you look, the more you'll see – and your photographs will be richer as a result.

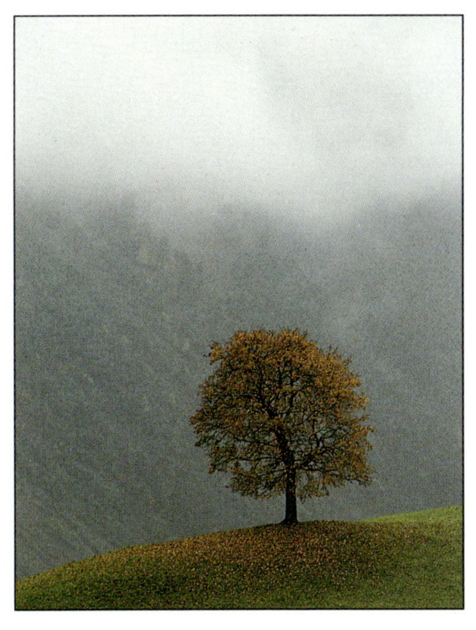

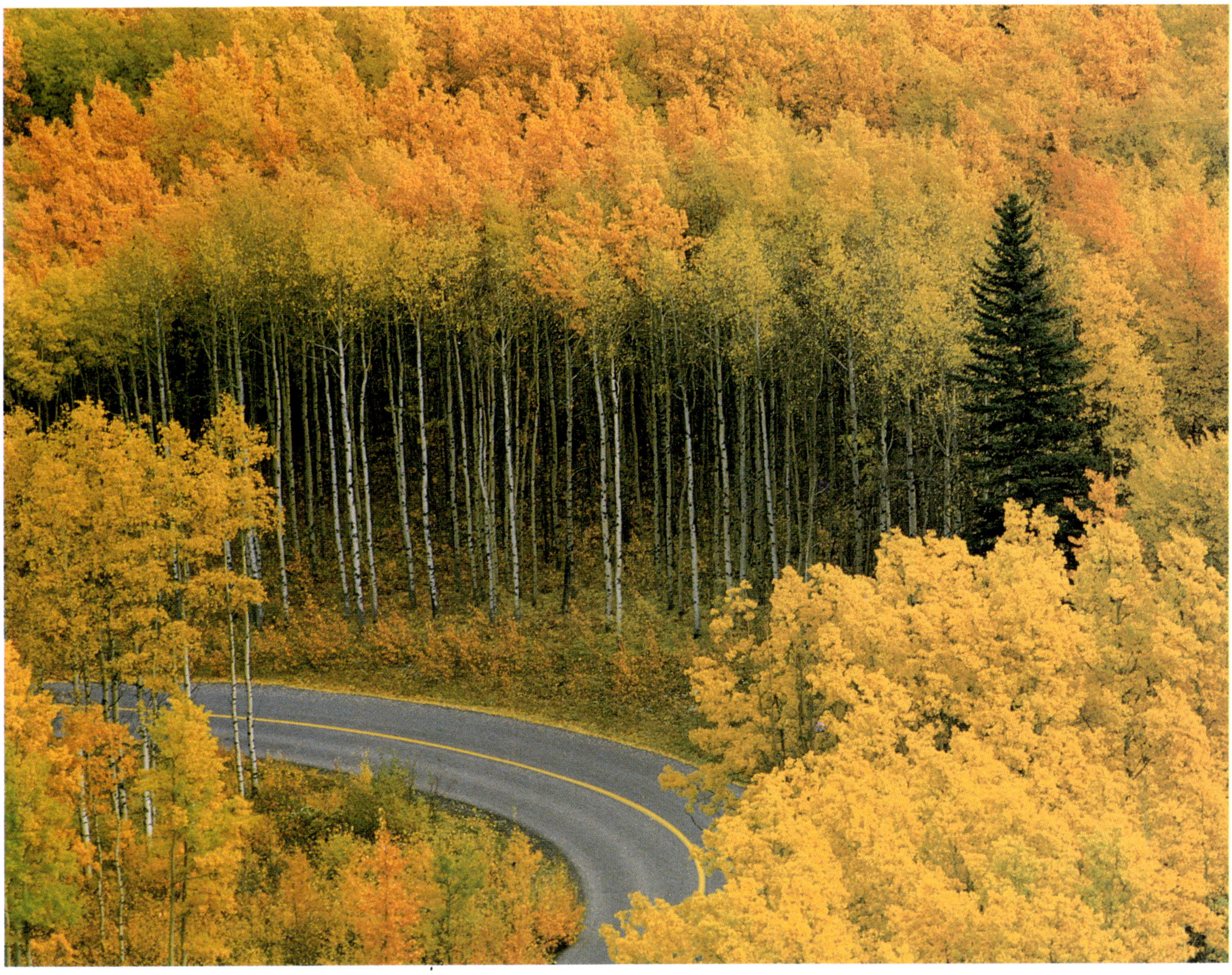

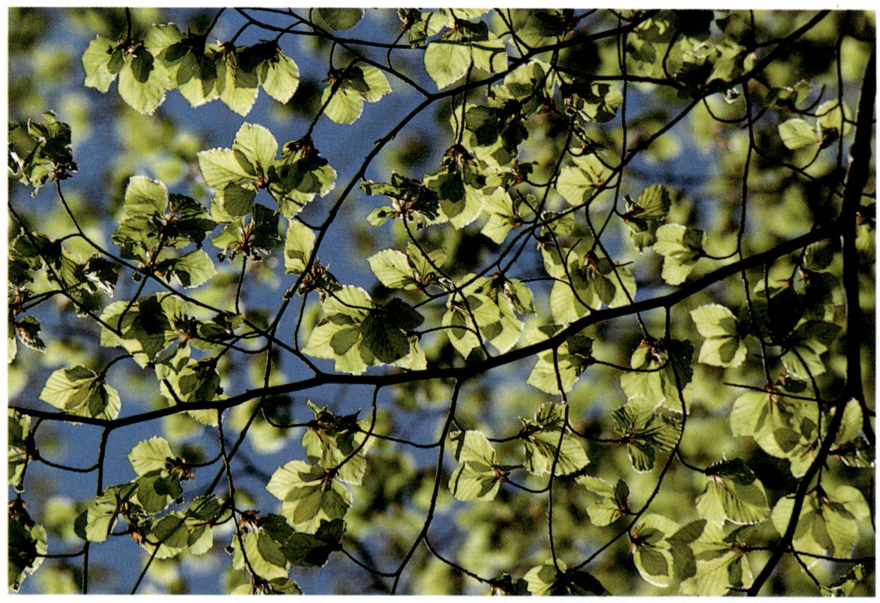

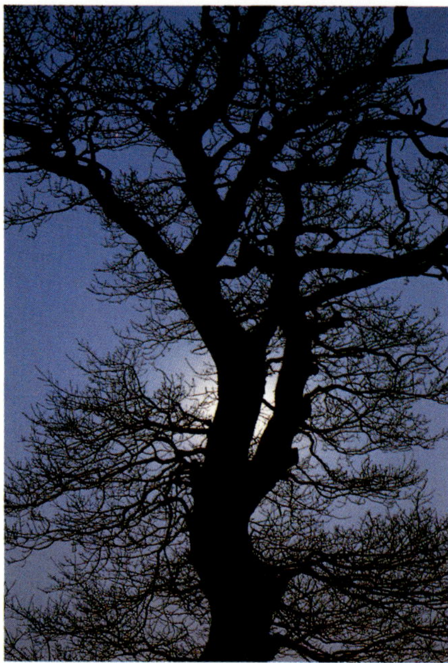

◀ NATURAL DRAMA
*If you find an element that's striking
enough, whether light, atmosphere or
subject matter, it speaks for itself
without stage management. This photo
needs no compositional tricks, which
could detract from the dramatic light.*

▶ CAREFUL COMPOSITION
*By leaving out the top and bottom of this
silhouette, a potentially dull subject – a
bare oak in winter – becomes intriguing.
The glow of the sun, hidden behind the
trunk, creates a sense of depth and a
luminous but not over obtrusive focal
point.*

*The blue sky is an important element
of the picture and adds a sense of wintry
cold.*

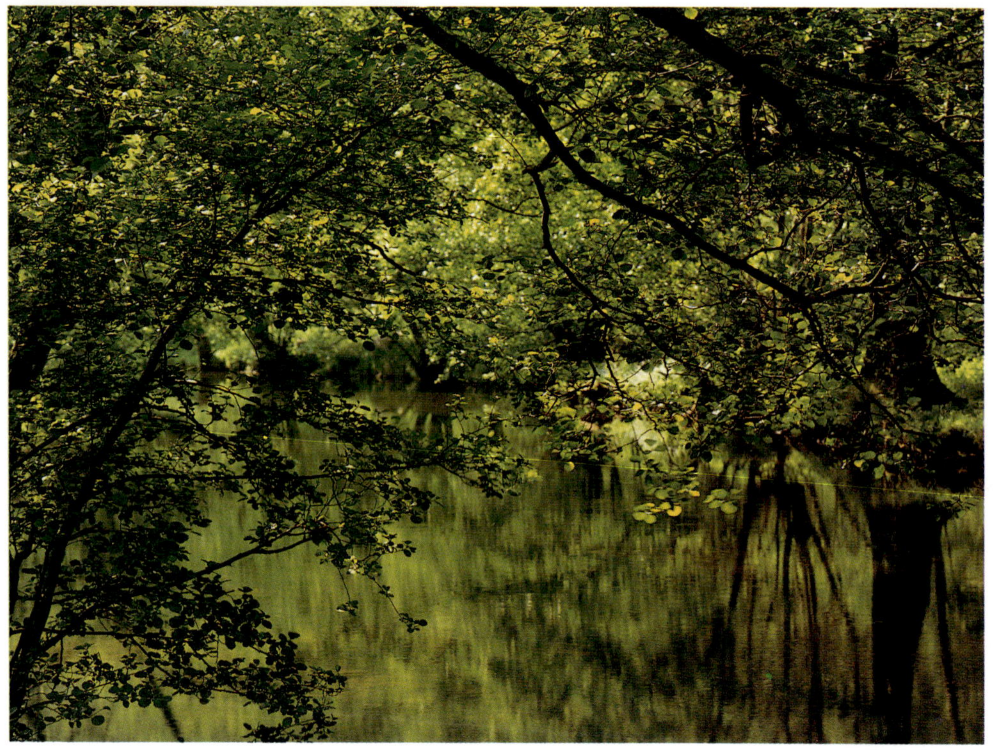

◀ TRANQUIL SCENE
*Spring, when foliage is at its
greenest and freshest, is
often the best time to capture
the play of light on leaves. If
you're prepared to explore,
you can find a scene like this
one, where the quality of light
and its play on water begs a
photograph.*

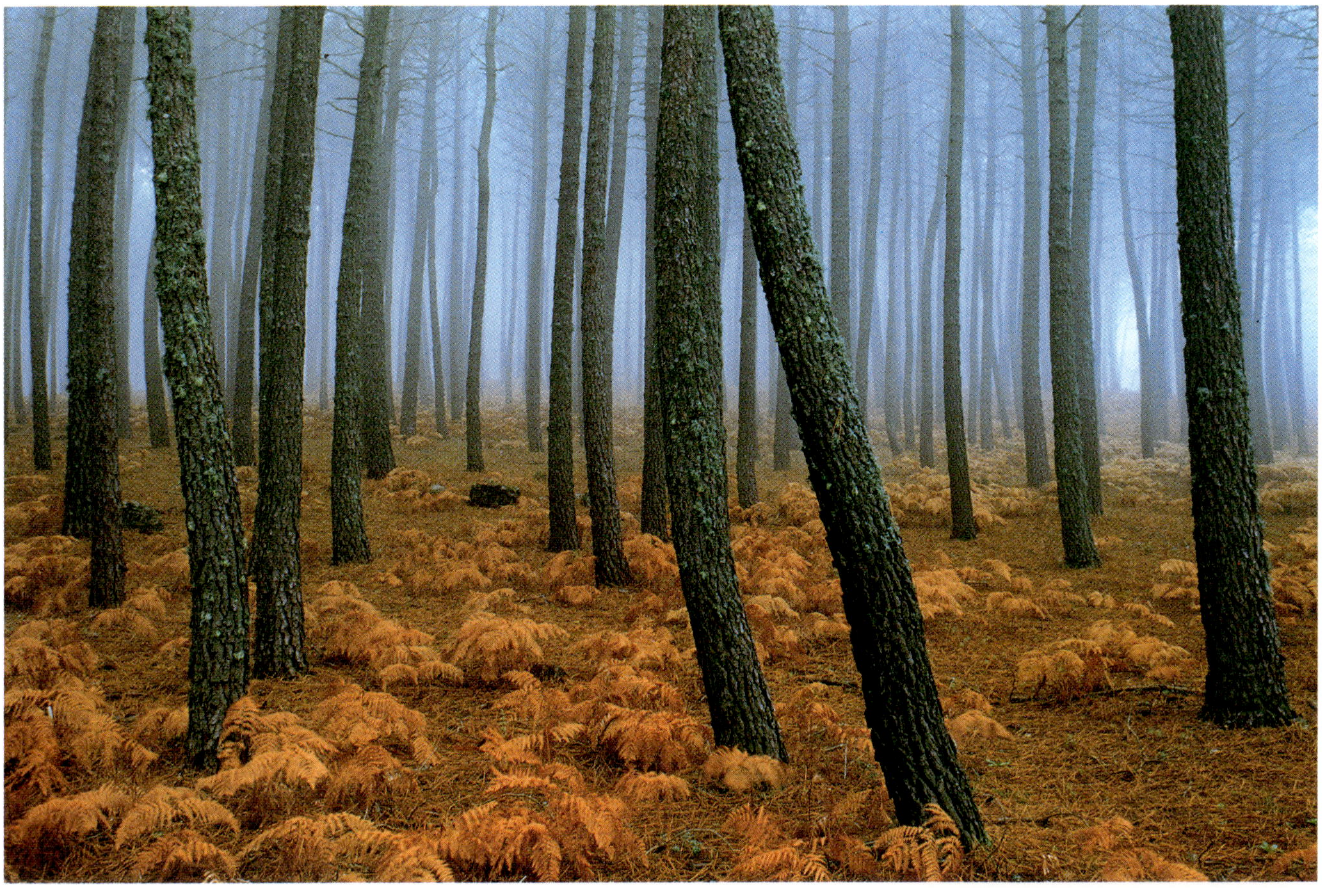

▲ MAJESTIC TREE

A misty atmosphere, especially in winter, can cause subtle changes in depth and density, transforming the most everyday subjects into dreamlike fantasies. The soft tones and diffused light create a painterly quality, in which clarity gives way to mood.

▶ PLEASING PATTERNS

Although this appears to be a random study of fallen cherry tree leaves, they were probably rearranged to improve the composition. The two crossed stalks left of centre form a focus. The serrated leaf edges and veins picked out in frost emphasize the delicacy of the subject and form abstract patterns.

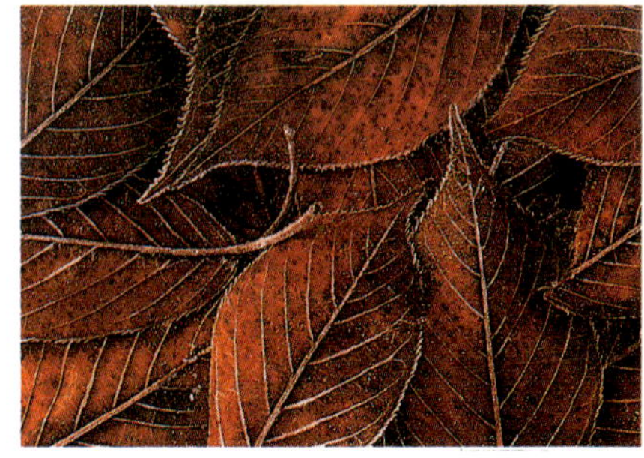

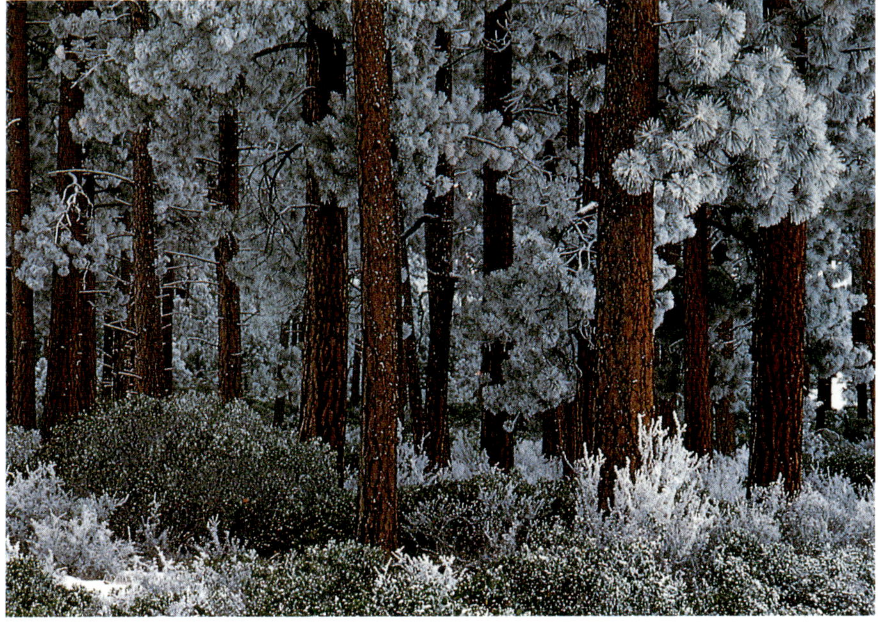

◀ TEXTURAL CONTRASTS

Snow photographs excite by changing the familiar into the unfamiliar. Though this study of a pine forest has a strong vertical element, its character lies not in the composition, but in textural contrast: the flaking bark, filigree-like snowy undergrowth and, especially, the snow-laden pine needles, whose outward growth is transformed by snow into a series of miniature fireworks.

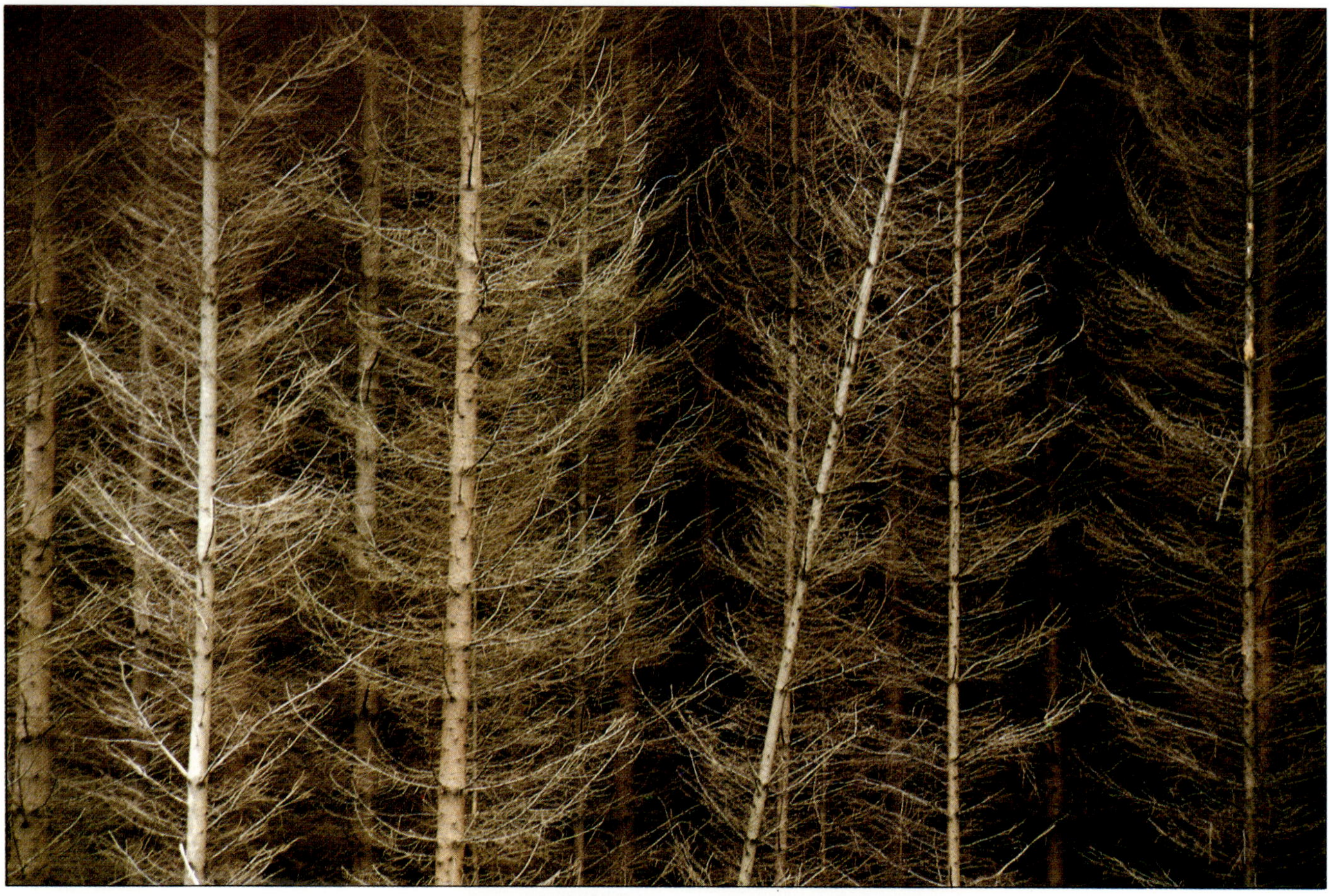

▲ **RHYTHM AND SCALE**
Here, formal rows of commercially grown forest trees have their rhythm broken by a single leaning nonconformist. They were taken with a telephoto lens from a clearing at the forest's edge. Because you can't see their crowns and bases, the trees become curiously ambiguous in size – and there's no other reference to scale to guide you.

The trees take on a delicate quality and become almost fern-like. Ranks of ghostly trunks in the background add to the sense of mystery.

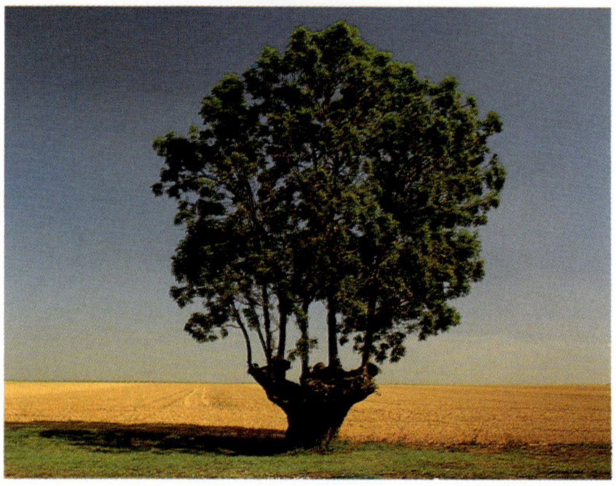

◀ **NATURAL CURIOSITY**
Heavily pruned trees, like this gnarled ash, often have an appealing sculptural quality. Here it's strongly captured in a no-nonsense landscape.

The photographer deliberately placed the subject in the centre. The low horizon throws the tree's upper limbs into profile against the sky, and its shadow and ghostly hint of a tractor path in the cornfield add off-centre interest.

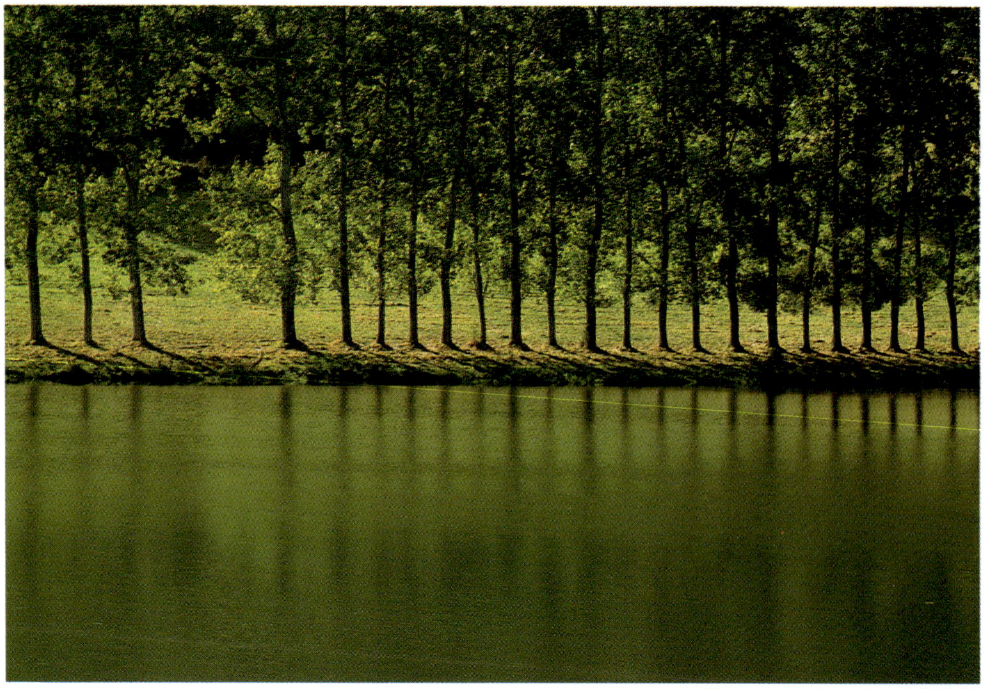

◀ **MISSING A BEAT**
An otherwise unmemorable subject is made interesting by the break in rhythm – one missing tree in a row makes the others visually stronger. The horizontal river bank divides the image exactly in half, emphasizing the artificial quality of straight line planting.

For a similar image, keep your camera vertical, and wait for wind to ripple the surface of the water and enhance the reflection of the trees.

A woodland scene

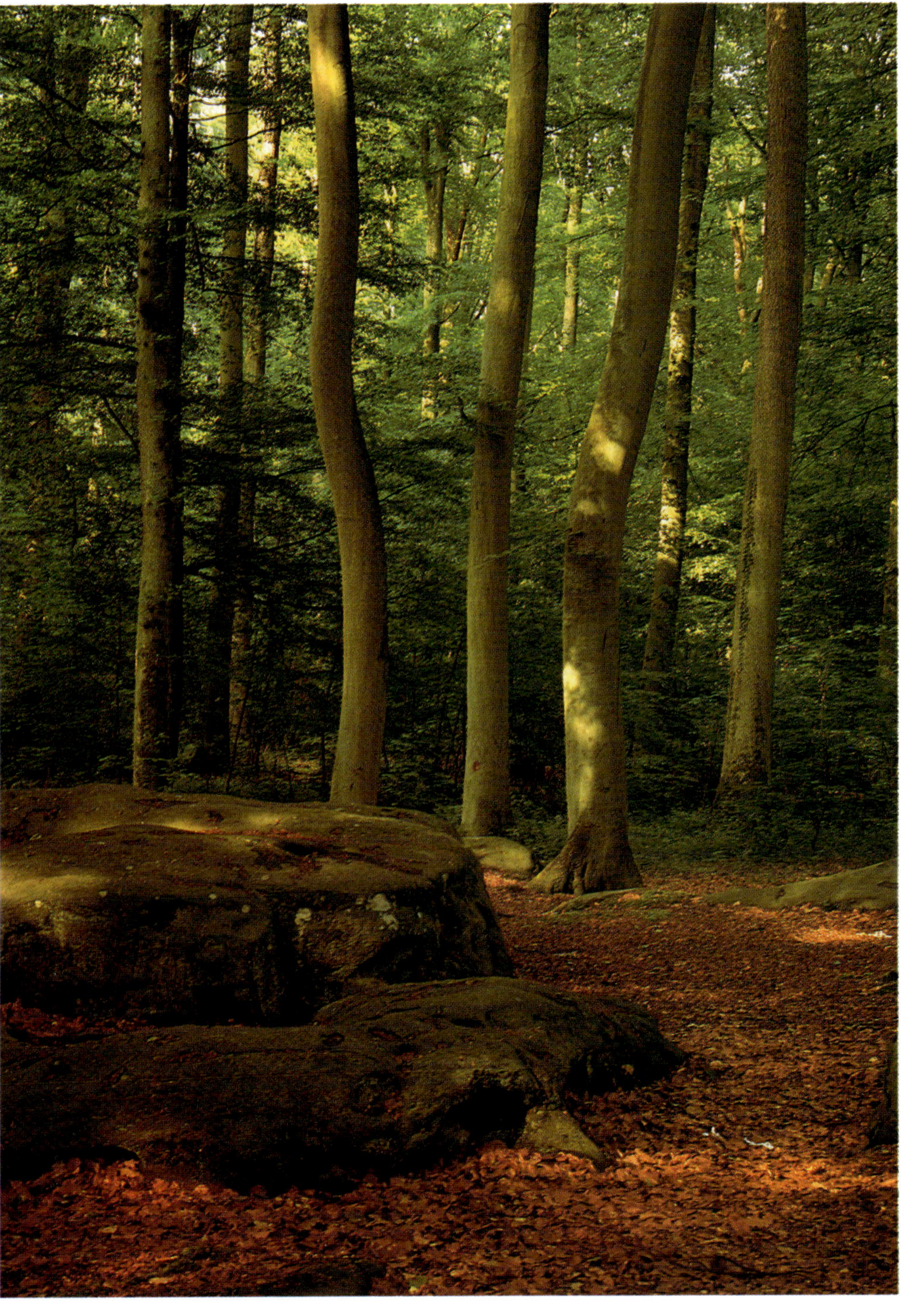

The set up

Mike and David were shooting in the Forest of Compiegne in Normandy, northern France towards the end of a fairly sunny June day. They took all their pictures in a small area around a rocky clearing on the edge of the forest. David used a Nikon F4 with a 35-70mm zoom lens, and Mike used a Nikon F801s with a 28-70mm lens. Both of them used tripods. There was no wind around to interfere with Mike's long exposures.

Shooting strong woodland landscapes isn't easy, because often a group of trees that's interesting to the eye ends up looking dull and messy on film. Mike Busselle shows David Jones how to find and photograph an attractive forest scene.

When I told Mike Busselle I wanted to do a woodland masterclass, he immediately suggested travelling to the Forest of Compiegne in Normandy, northern France. He'd been there before and had taken some lovely pictures, so we decided to sail over on the ferry and give it a go.

We chose a day early in June, when the weather was likely to be sunny but the forest would still be green. When we arrived at Compiegne, Mike began to look around as we drove through the woods, and seemed to be searching for something specific. 'I'm after a tidy looking glade', he explained, 'that will allow some sun in and give us a lot of scope with regard to foreground interest and focal points.'

The perfect spot

Before long, we'd found exactly the sort of place Mike was looking for – an open glade with a nice group of lichen covered rocks surrounded

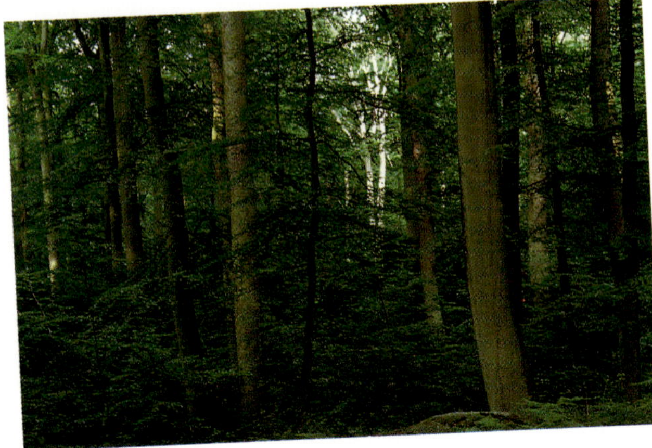

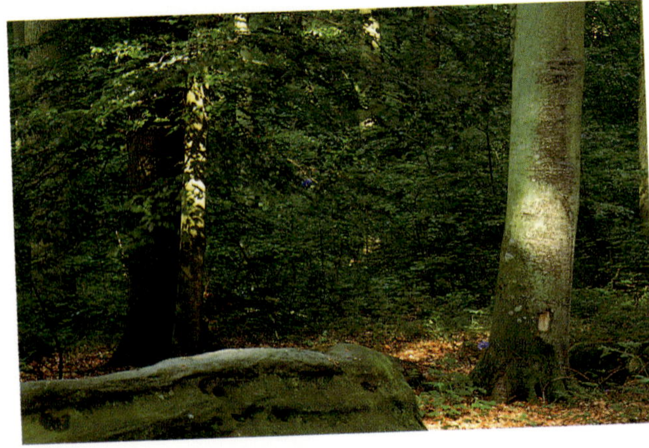

by tall, leafy trees. The weather was perfect, so as the gentle evening sun filtered through the thick, green canopy of leaves overhead, we set up our cameras and began shooting.

I was using a Nikon F4 with a 35-70mm zoom lens and Fuji ISO 50D professional slide film, and I began with a view into the woods beyond the glade. The scene looked lush and green to the naked eye, but without any sunny highlights to brighten it up, it ended up flat and colourless on film. The shot also suffered from a lack of any real focal point.

I tried to remedy these problems by concentrating on a couple of thick tree trunks and including a large rock in the foreground. The sun was drifting in and out of the clouds, so I waited till some sunny highlights hit the trees before I started shooting. It was a better shot but the composition was still messy, and the tangled overgrowth blocked off any clear view through to the trees behind.

A tidier picture

Mike began by looking around for a tidier looking piece of ground that offered a good view through the trees. He soon came across two distinctive trees that were growing very close to each other on a clear patch of the forest floor. He framed a lovely shot around them with sunlit trees receding into the distance behind, using a Nikon F801s with a 28-70mm zoom lens and Fuji

Velvia ISO 50 slide film.

Then he turned his attention to the glade. Because the canopy of leaves overhead was quite thick, the sun was only breaking through in patches, which created an attractive, dappled effect. By using the unusual group of rocks as points of interest, Mike was able to take advantage of the light in a series of imaginative and colourful photographs.

Around the rocks

He started by taking a wide view of the glade, with the lichen covered rocks in the foreground surrounded by a thick carpet of dead leaves. Then he closed in on one area of the rocks and took an upright shot that included two distinctive looking curved tree trunks. He zoomed in still further to take a low angle shot dominated by a colourful piece of rock in the foreground.

Mike used a warm up filter to accentuate the rich greens and browns of the forest, and a tripod to allow him to shoot the long exposures he wanted. But it was the light that made these pictures special – without sunshine they would have looked very different.

Feeling that he had now exhausted the possibilities of the glade, Mike decided to have one more look around before we left the area. Luckily, he discovered a dusty trail nearby, and finished the day's shoot by taking an evocative shot of it leading off through the thickening trees into the forest.

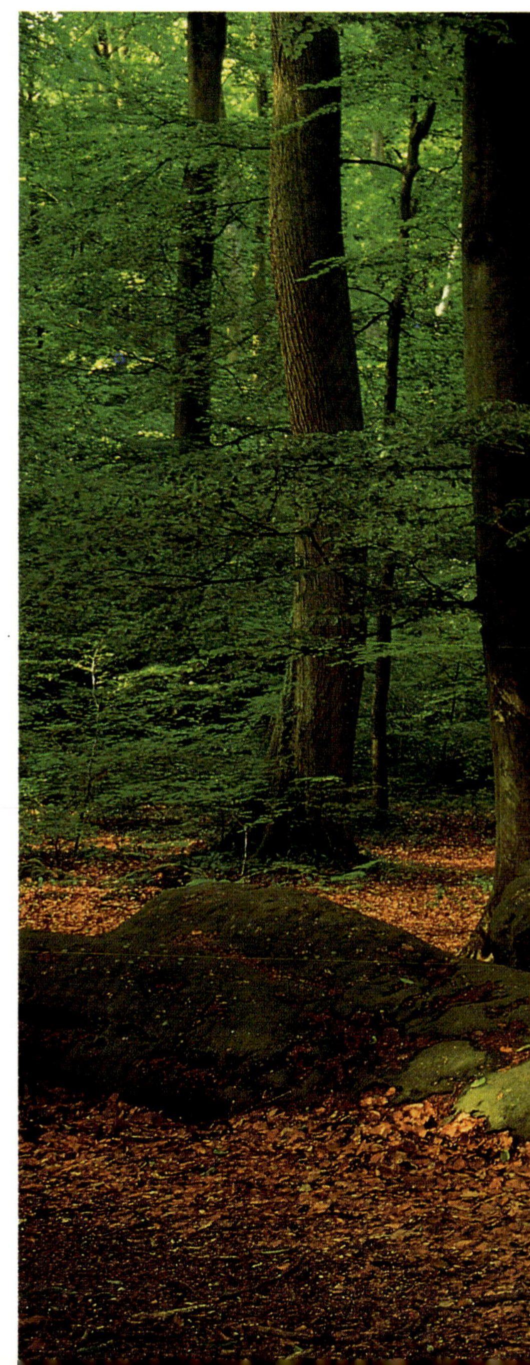

PERFECT
COMPOSITION

1 ▶ THROUGH THE TREES
Mike found a clearer stretch of
forest for his first shot. The two
distinctive looking tree trunks make a
strong focal point, and the lack of
undergrowth on the forest floor means
there's an attractive view through the
trees behind.

2 ▼ DAPPLED LIGHT
He then turned towards this glade,
where the strange formation of rocks
gave him a series of unusual woodland
shots. The rocks look very strong in
the foreground, and the dappled
sunlight really adds to the atmosphere.

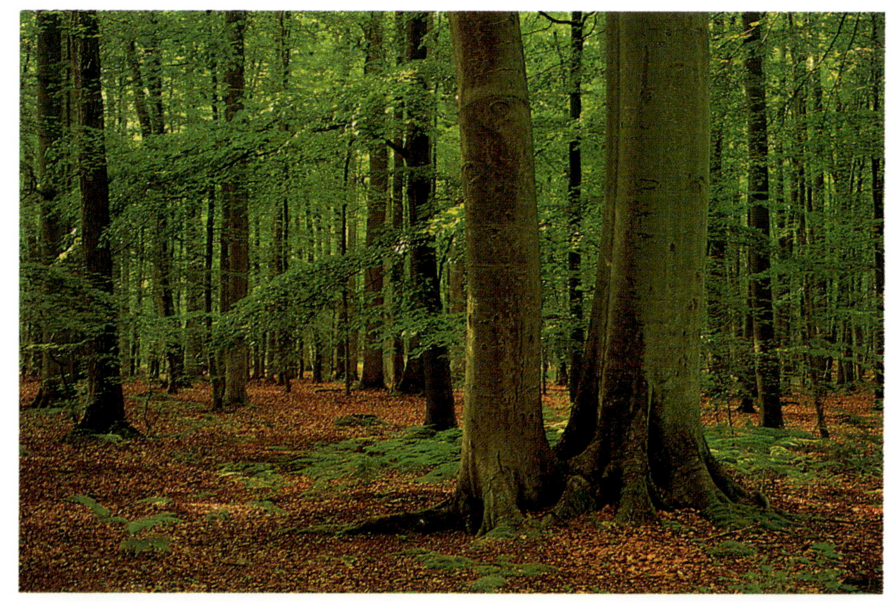

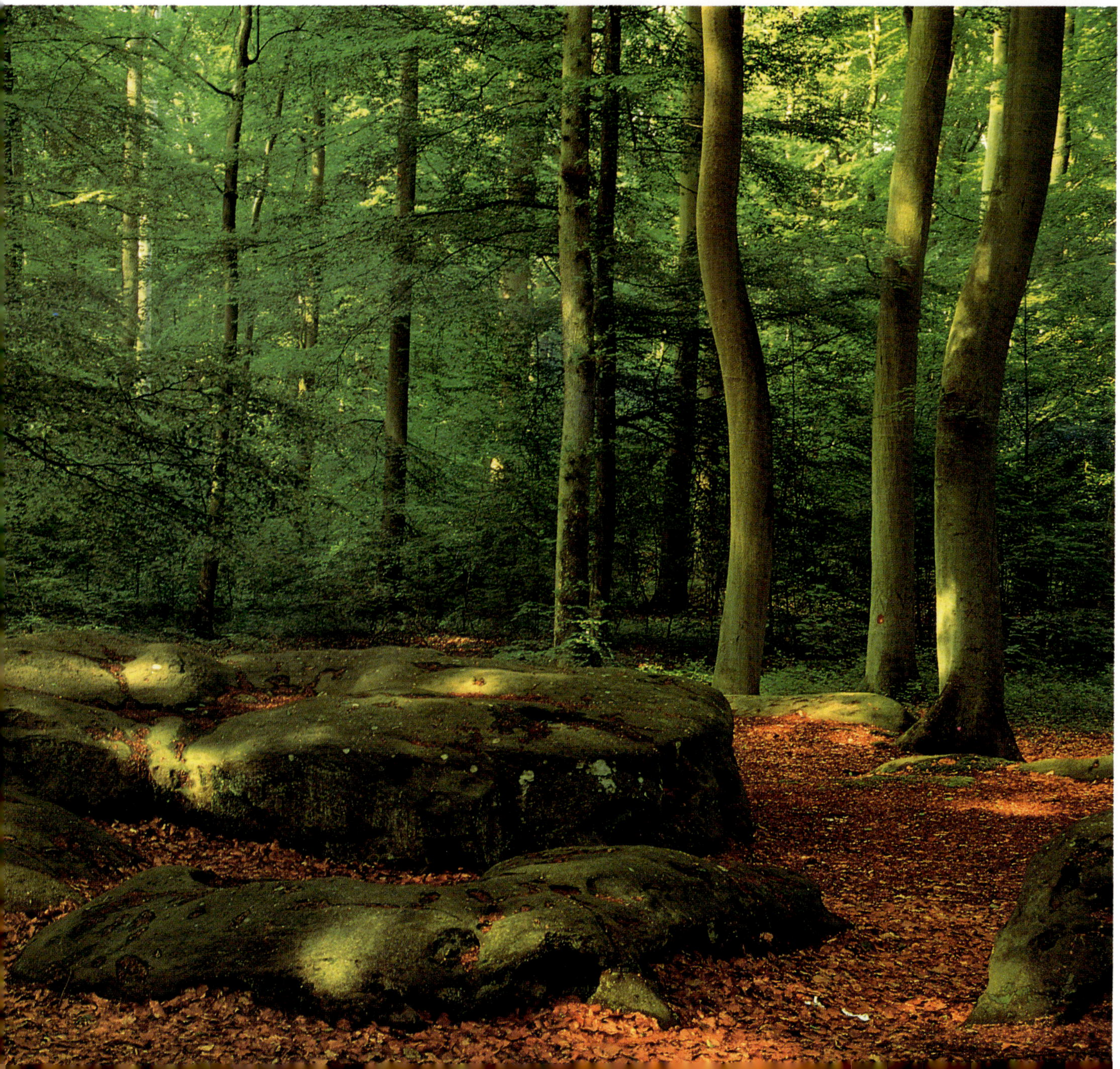

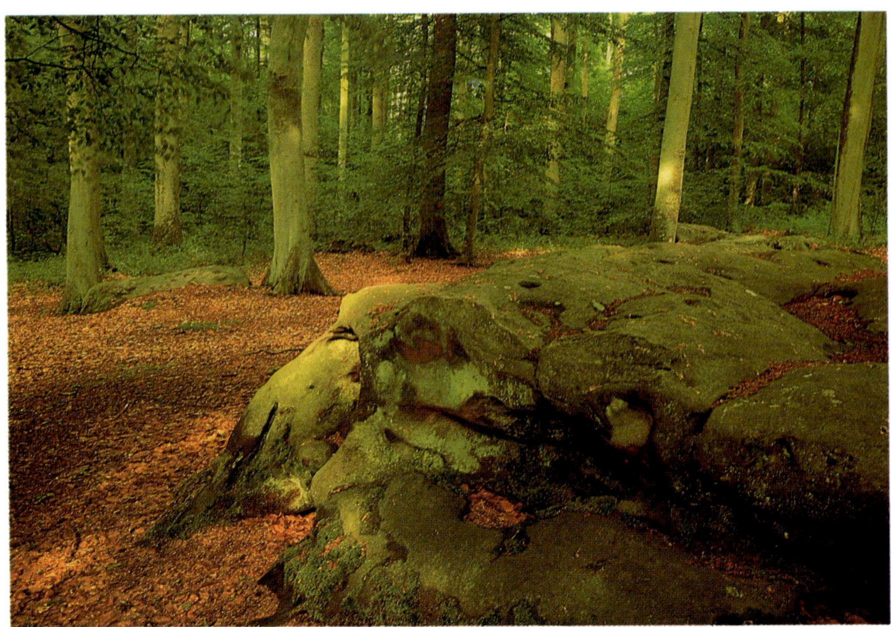

3 ▲ ROCKS AND TREES
To obtain a more dynamic picture of the rocks, Mike zoomed in on one of them so it filled almost half the frame. The different shades of lichen on the rock contrast nicely with the brown carpet of leaves on the forest floor below.

4 ▼ THE LONELY TRAIL
Mike found a dusty forest trail near the glade, so he composed this peaceful shot of it leading away through the tall trees. By this time the sun was a bit less intense, so there's a soft, even light on the branches overhead.

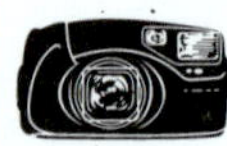

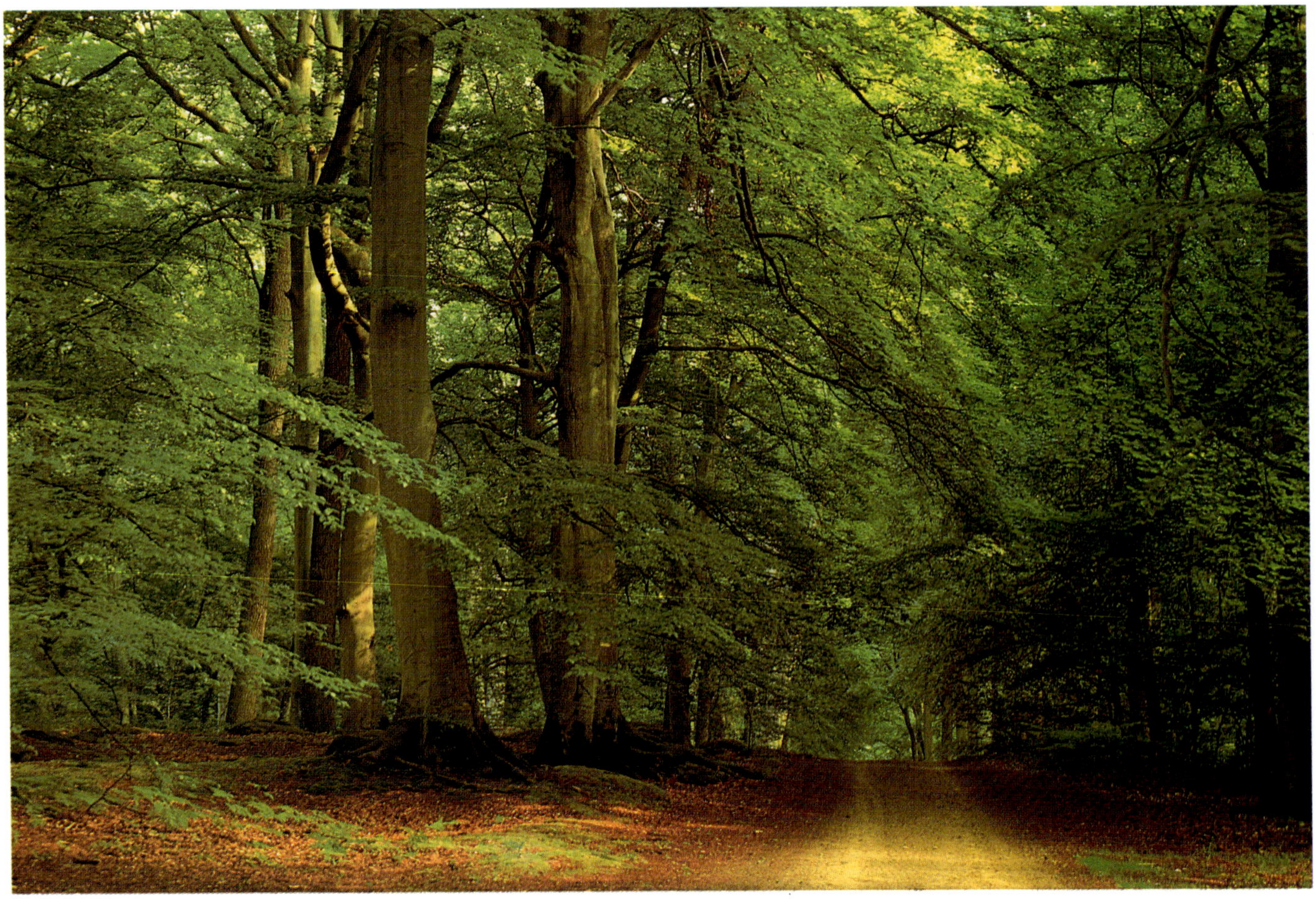

Compact tip

Without the benefit of inter-changeable lenses, compact cameras can sometimes record woodland as a jumble of leaves and branches. To make sense of the trees, try to shoot in a clearing as Mike did. This will allow you to put some distance between the camera and the nearest trunk, and you'll have more light in a clearing than you will in thick forest.

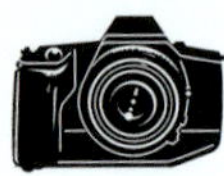

SLR tip

Though normally used for photographing buildings, perspective control or shift lenses can be very useful in woods and forests. A shift lens allows you to move the horizon down without tilting the camera up. This means you can reduce the amount of foreground in the picture without making the trees appear to slant towards each other at the top of the frame.

Clive Boursnell – Country gardens

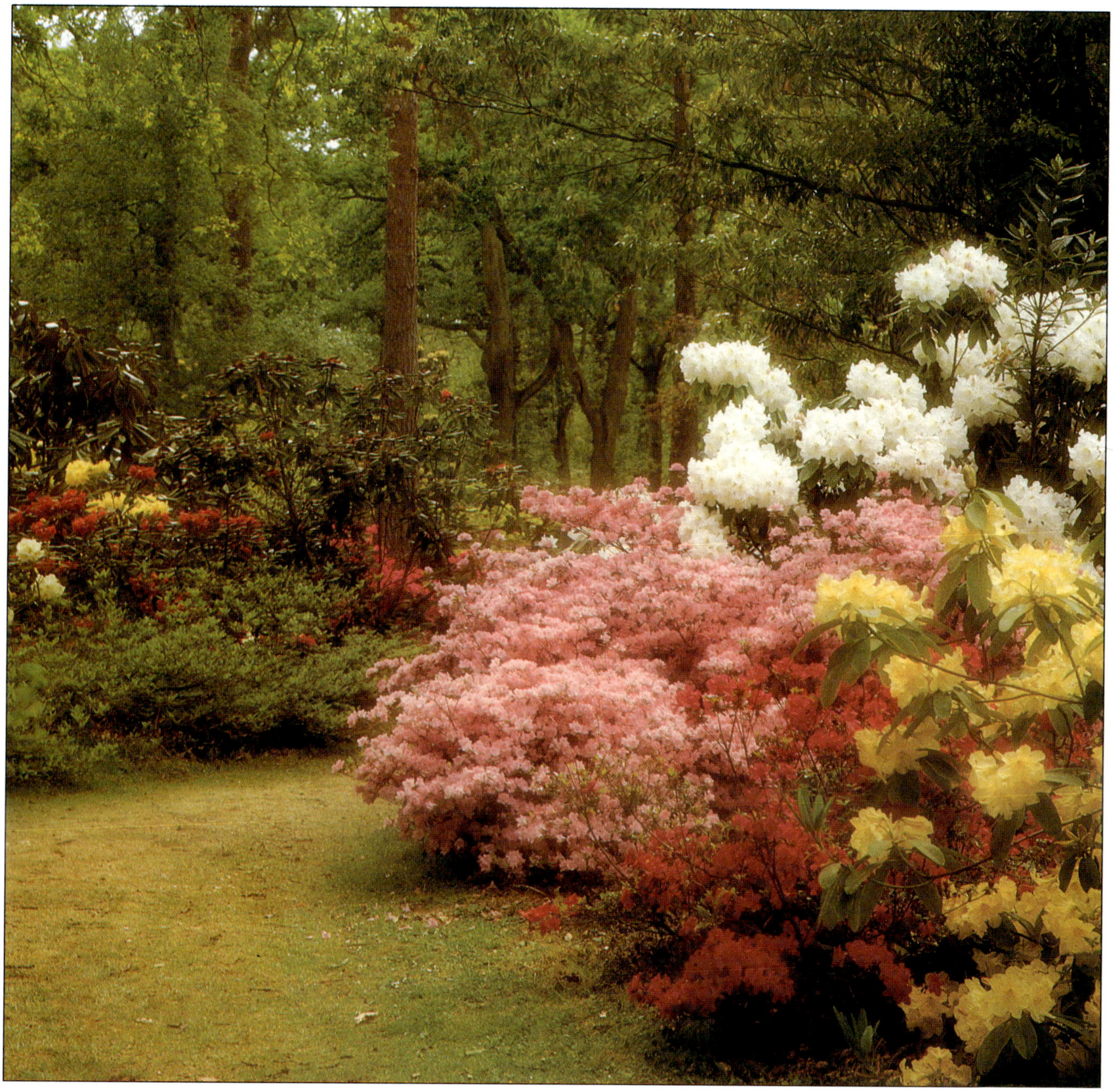

"I took this early on a grey, overcast day. Dull conditions like this are perfect for photographing flowers, because the contrast levels are low and you get far better colour rendition. Sun would have killed the picture." Taken on a Hasselblad 500CM with a 150mm lens on Kodak EPP slide film at 1/15th sec and f11.

Gardens are landscapes too: self-contained landscapes, where part of the work is already done for you because everything has already been designed to look good. Many great gardens are open to the public, or you may even be able to shoot your own handywork.

Clive Boursnell is a totally dedicated photographer who sets himself very high standards. When he's working on a large garden he often spends weeks on end getting the views he wants to photograph exactly right. He avoids four poster beds and fancy hotels, preferring the cold comfort of his camper van. 'I do most of my best work very early in the morning', he explains, 'so by camping on the spot I make sure I don't miss anything special in the early hours.'

'I try to arrive at a garden with a totally open mind', he says. 'When I come across a view that I like, I use the sun to work out what time of day it will look best at. You've really got to obey the light with this sort of photography. If the sun's too high or the light's too harsh, don't take the picture. Go and photograph some

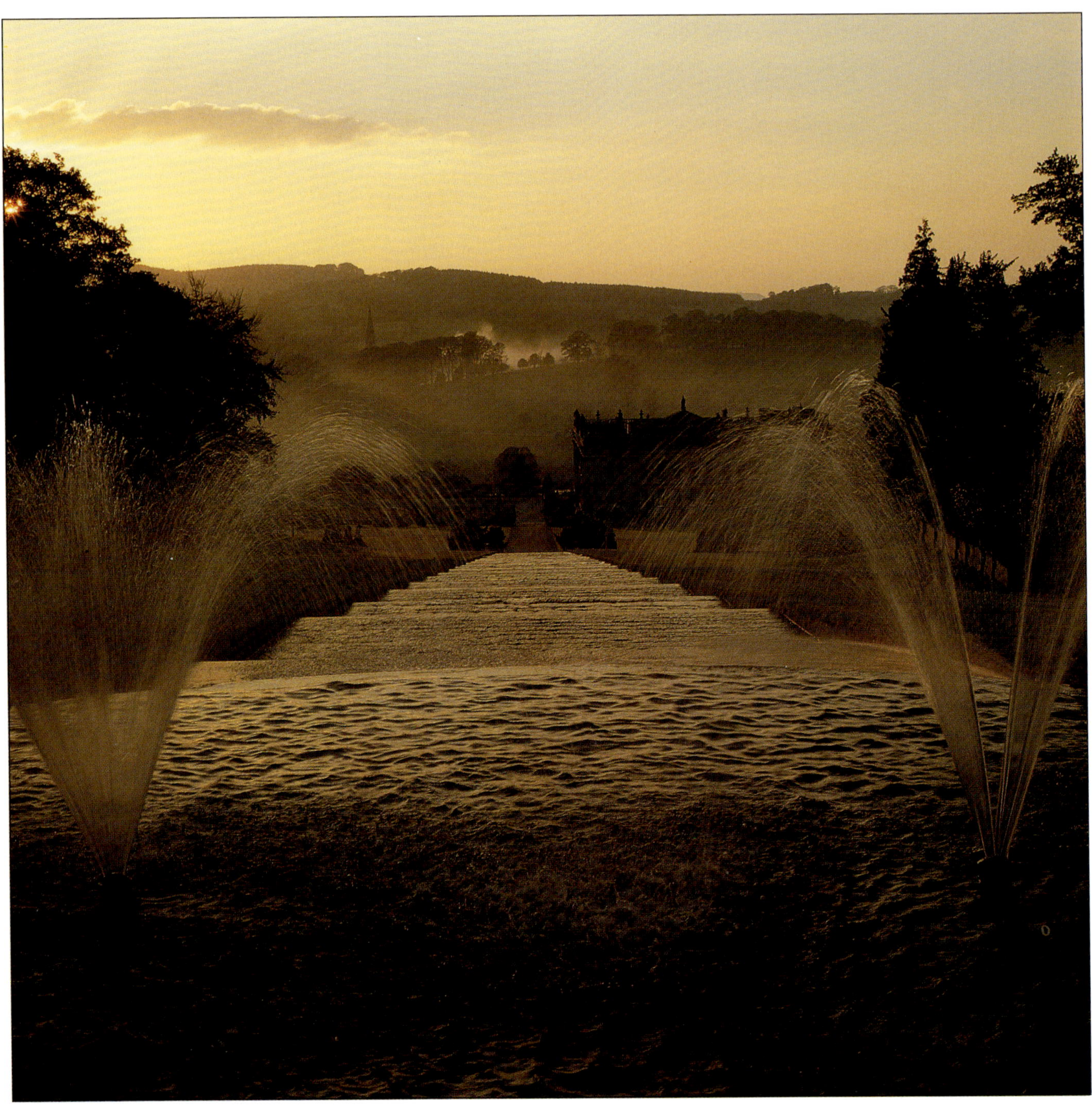

other subject if you can, and come back to the first one later in the day.'

'Early morning is definitely my favourite time for taking pictures', says Clive. 'Gardens can look really special at four or five in the morning, especially if there's low sun and a bit of mist about. Evenings can also be good when the sun's low again, but when the sun's high and the sky is blue I just don't bother. Dull days are often ideal for photographing plants and flowers, because you get a really delicate, soft light.'

Equipment and cropping

Clive uses a Hasselblad 500CM medium format camera for all his garden work, and likes to do all his cropping in the camera. 'I'd feel as if I'd failed if I had to crop a photograph after I'd taken it', he explains, 'so I always try to compose very carefully before I start shooting. When I've set a picture up I usually take a Polaroid beforehand to make sure the composition's nice and tight. I try to make sure that there's no excess space in my pictures, no one area that doesn't add to the overall effect.

No tricks

'I occasionally use a soft focus filter to add to dull day shots, but otherwise I'm a bit of a purist when it comes to filters', he admits. 'I'm only interested in photographing what's actually there. I don't mind enhancing it a little, but using trick filters to distort a garden scene does not appeal to me at all. I try to work with nature and use subtle changes in light and weather to produce the effects I want.'

"This was taken in the gardens of Chatsworth House in Derbyshire. I tried a morning shoot from the bottom of this lovely cascade, but I wasn't happy with it so I moved up to the top and waited for sunset. Warm twilight complimented the view perfectly."
Taken on a Hasselblad 500CM with an 80mm lens on Kodak EPN ISO 120 slide film at 1/15th sec and f11.

"The rest of these pictures were taken at the Rothschilds' rhododendron garden at Exbury near Southampton. I'd noticed this fallen plane tree before and noted it as a subject that might look good early in the day. I went over to it at a quarter past four one misty morning and found this."
Taken on a Hasselblad 500CM with a 50mm lens on Kodak EPP ISO 100 slide film at 1/15th sec and f16.

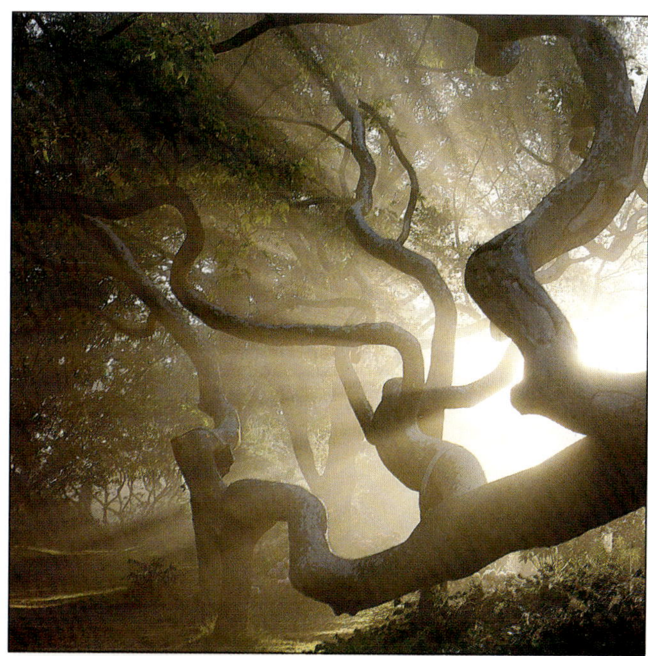

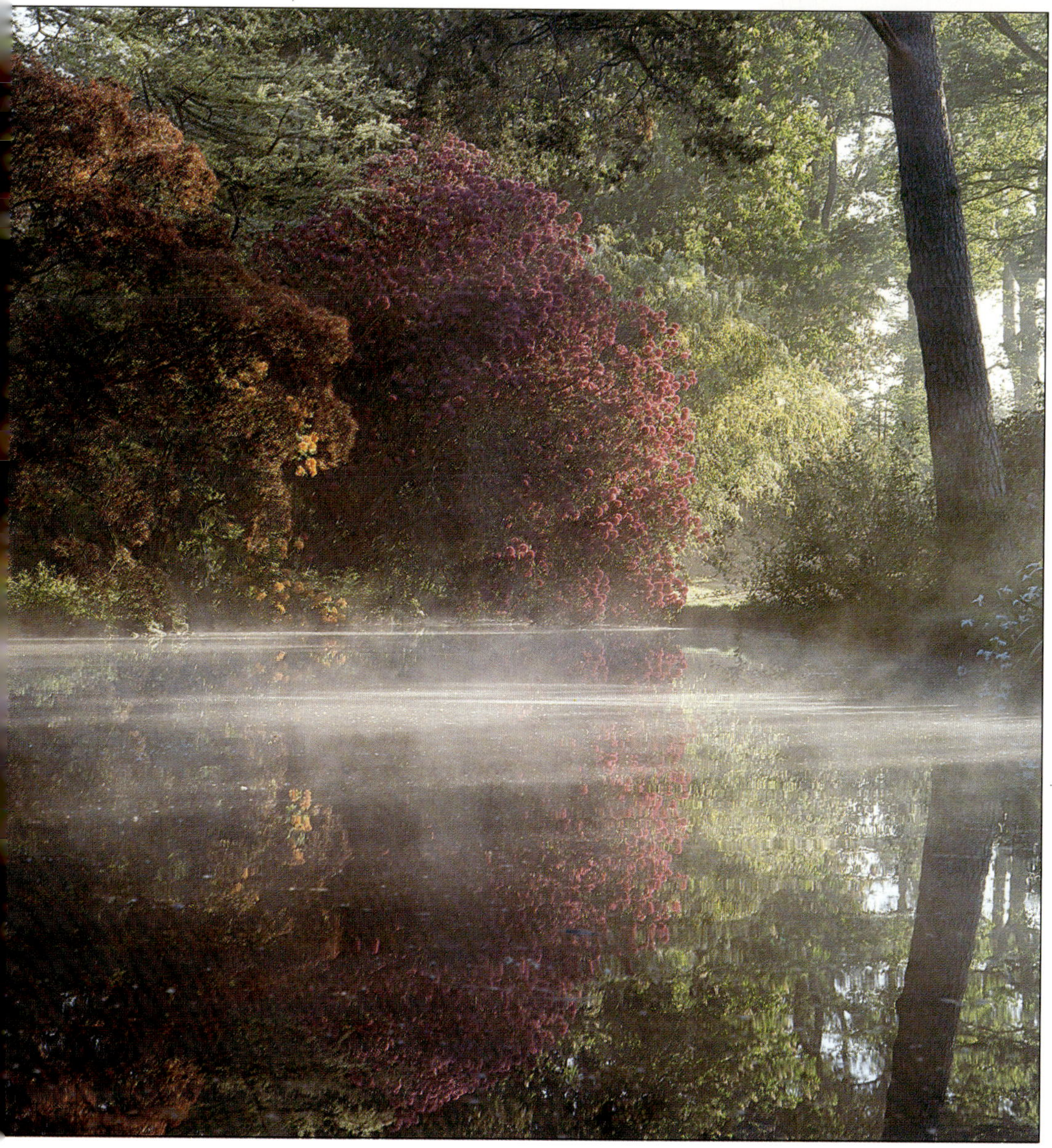

"This is another shot that I saw first in bad light and decided it would be worth looking at again early in the morning. I worked out roughly where the sun would come up and realised it could be of great help. The mist on the water was an added bonus."
Taken on a Hasselblad 500CM with a 150mm lens on Kodak EPP ISO 100 slide film at 1/15th sec and f11.

You can do it

'The easiest way to instantly improve your garden pictures', says Clive, 'is to get up early in the morning – and I mean early! In the summer months the sun comes up as early as 4am, so you've got to get up earlier still.

'When you do, you'll be amazed how different your garden can look at that time of day. As the sun comes up the light changes subtly all the time, and those variations can really bring a view to life.'

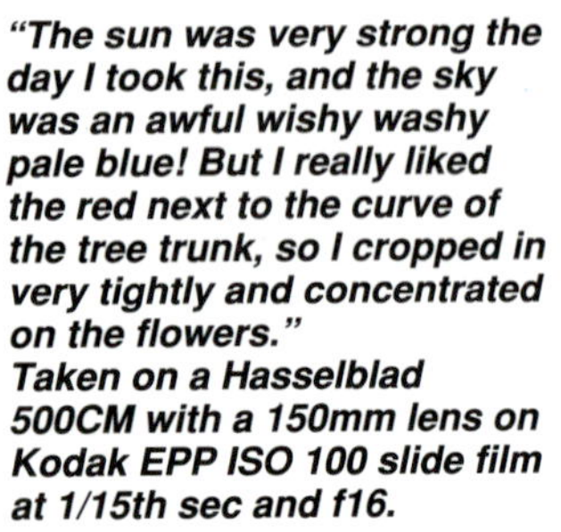

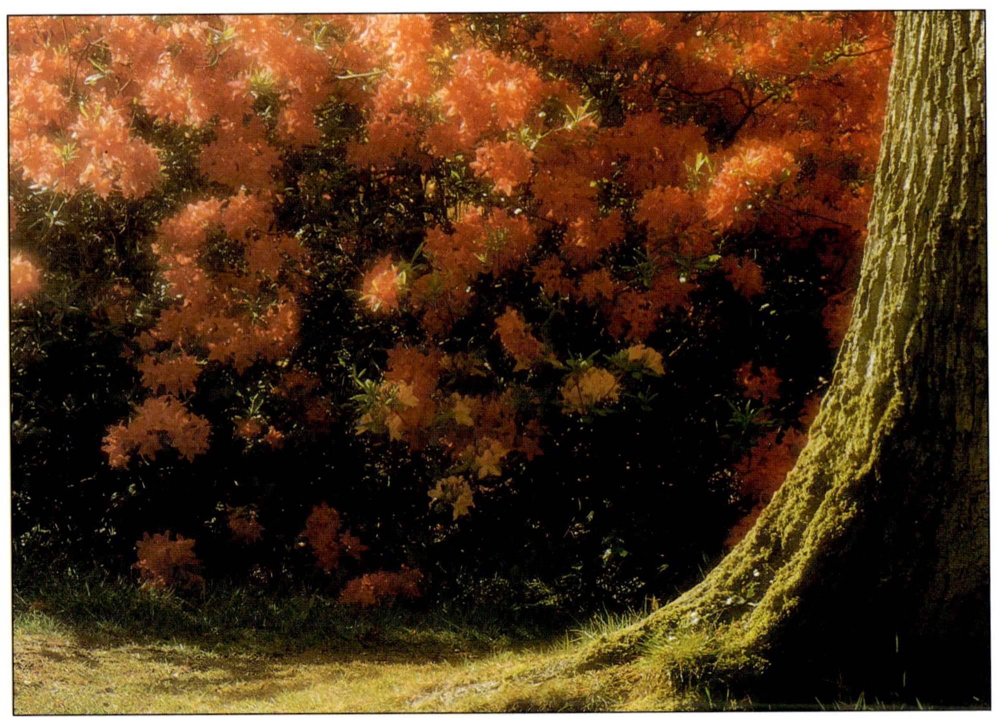

"The sun was very strong the day I took this, and the sky was an awful wishy washy pale blue! But I really liked the red next to the curve of the tree trunk, so I cropped in very tightly and concentrated on the flowers."
Taken on a Hasselblad 500CM with a 150mm lens on Kodak EPP ISO 100 slide film at 1/15th sec and f16.

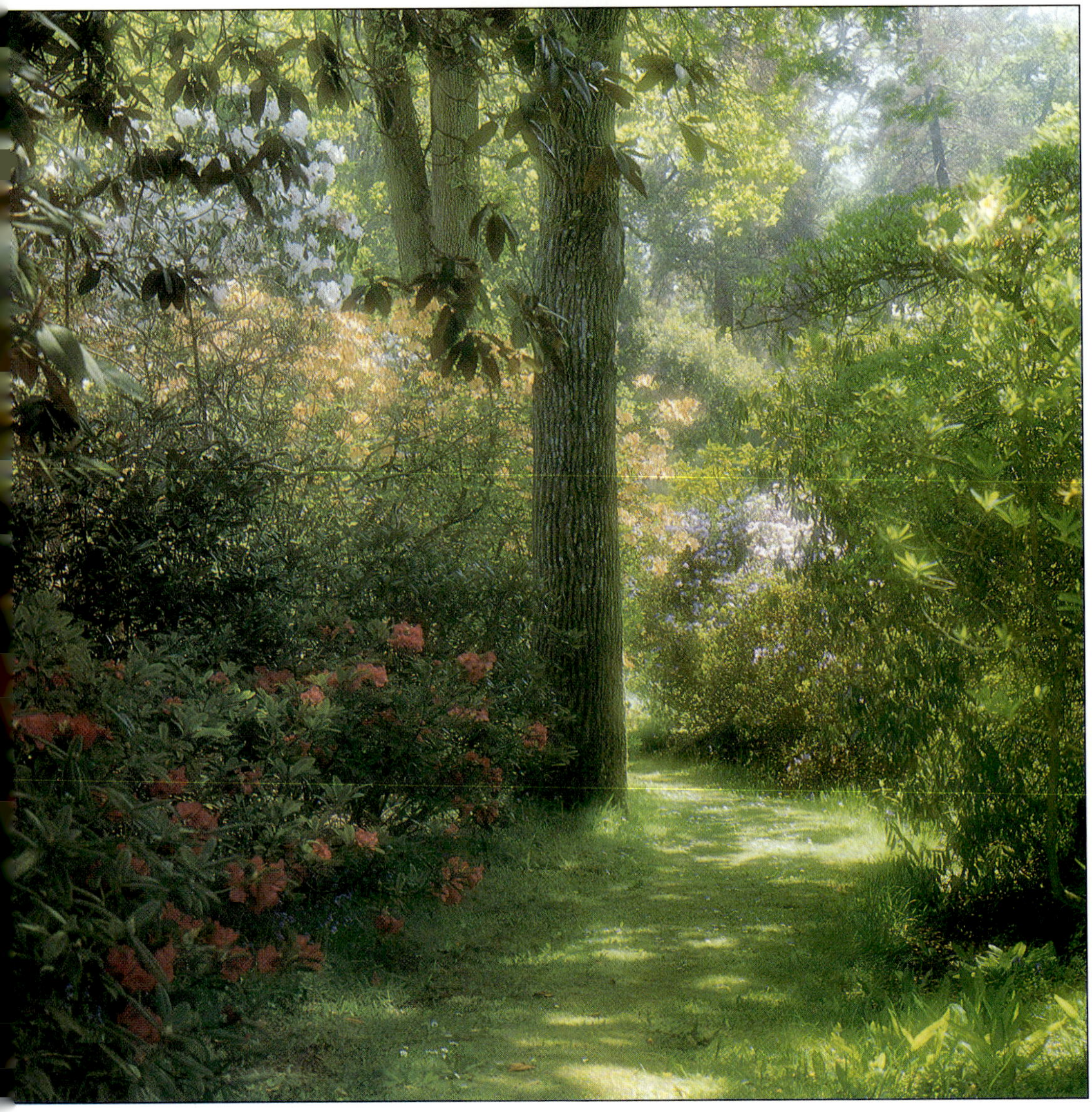

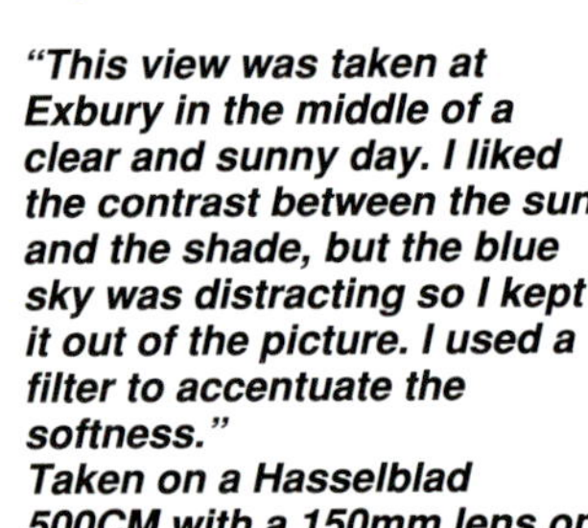

"This view was taken at Exbury in the middle of a clear and sunny day. I liked the contrast between the sun and the shade, but the blue sky was distracting so I kept it out of the picture. I used a filter to accentuate the softness."
Taken on a Hasselblad 500CM with a 150mm lens on Kodak EPP ISO 100 slide film at 1/8th sec and f22.

Technical details

'When you've got dense foliage and lots of colour in a shot', says Clive Boursnell, 'only a very strong sky is worth including in the frame. A light blue sky will kill a garden picture if you're not careful, because it can be very distracting without adding anything to the overall effect. It tends to lead the eye out of the frame, which is the last thing you want to be doing.

'I tend to frame my closer garden shots very tightly and try to keep the sky completely out of them.'

Spring flowers

Like trees, flowers are an essential part of many landscapes; so why not concentrate on the flowers, and make a feature of them? Buds bursting into bloom are sure to provide you with inspiration.

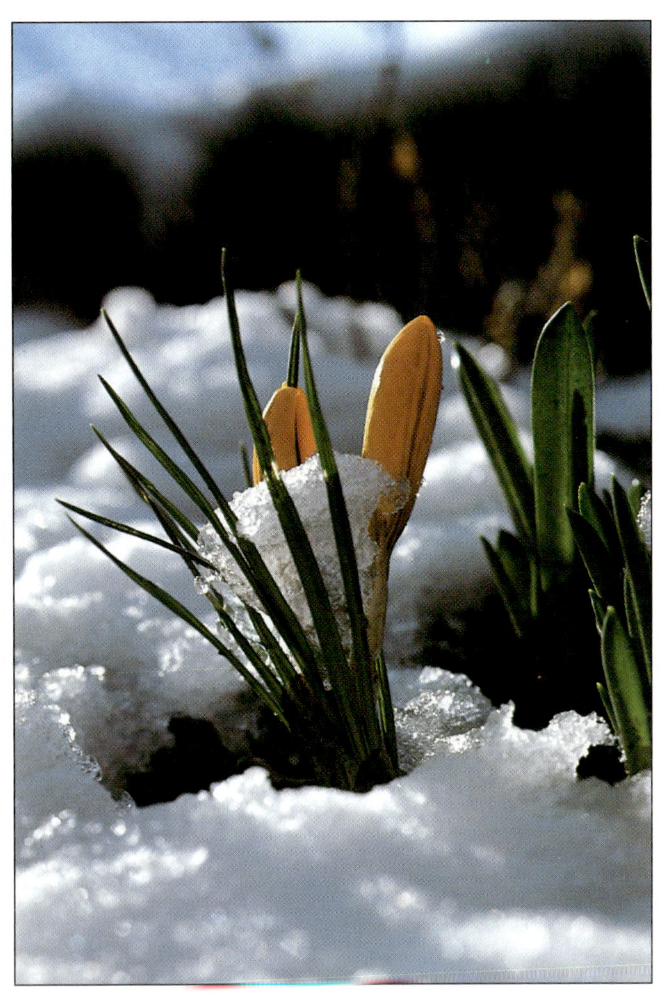

You don't have to travel far to see spring flowers – even roadside verges can be awash with colour. Take advantage of pretty pastel shades and a varied assortment of petal shapes. Shoot hyacinth bulbs growing indoors or pick flowers from your own garden and arrange them in a simple vase.

A straightforward vista of a garden in bloom makes an attractive but rather boring shot. Instead, try shooting an almost abstract image of flowers completely filling the frame – or a wood overflowing with colour, with a bright carpet of flowers and blossom on the trees.

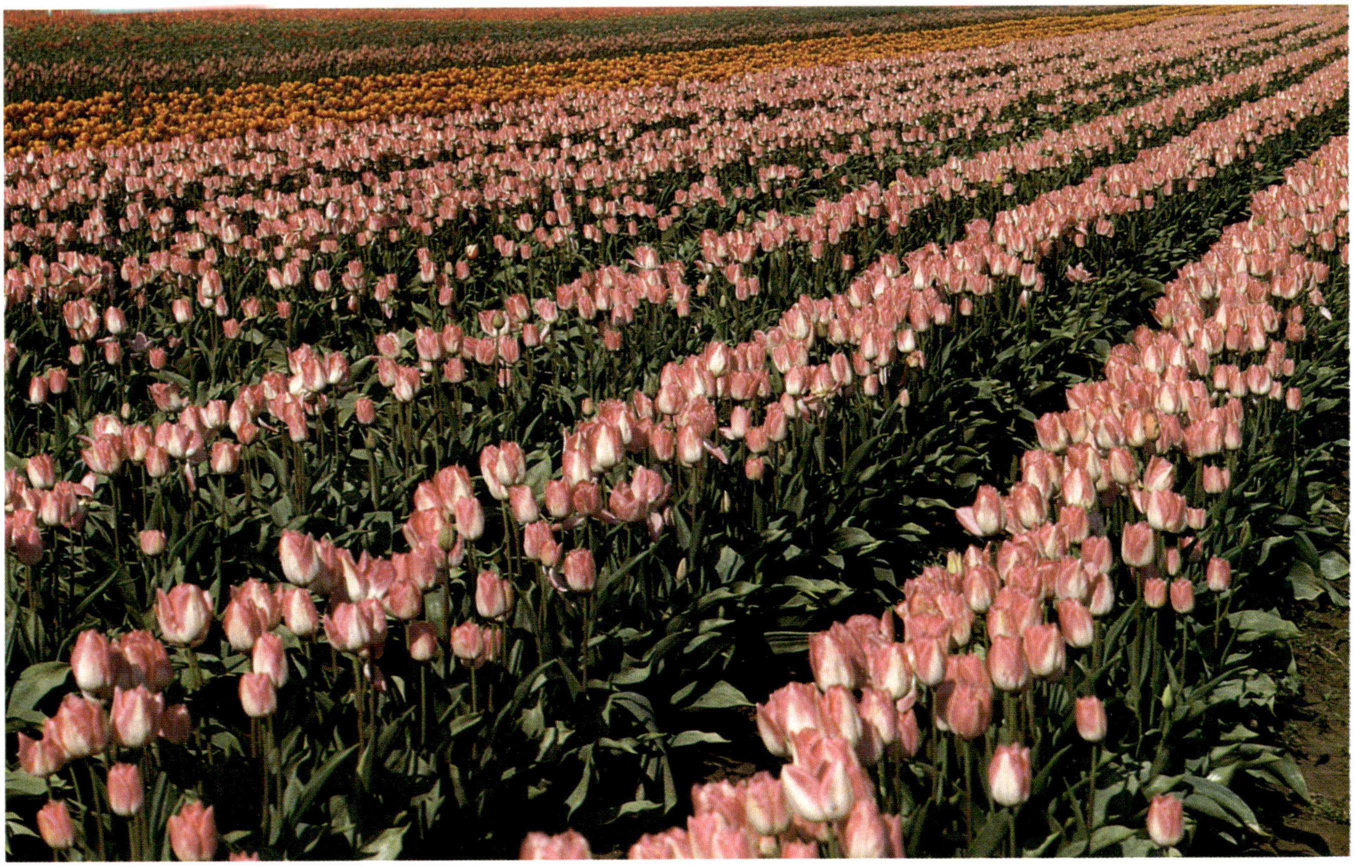

▼ FORMAL ROWS
Take advantage of formal, commercially grown rows of flowers to create graphic shots. Here the lines of carefully planted tulips lead your eye into the top right of the picture. The angle chosen by the photographer arranges the rows on the diagonal, making them look less static than a horizontal composition.

▶ BREAKTHROUGH
To many people, a crocus bursting through the ground is a sure sign that spring's here. Venture out into the snow and you'll be rewarded with shots like this one. A shaft of sunlight just outlining one side of the petals provides the finishing touch and shows it's worth waiting for a gap in the clouds.

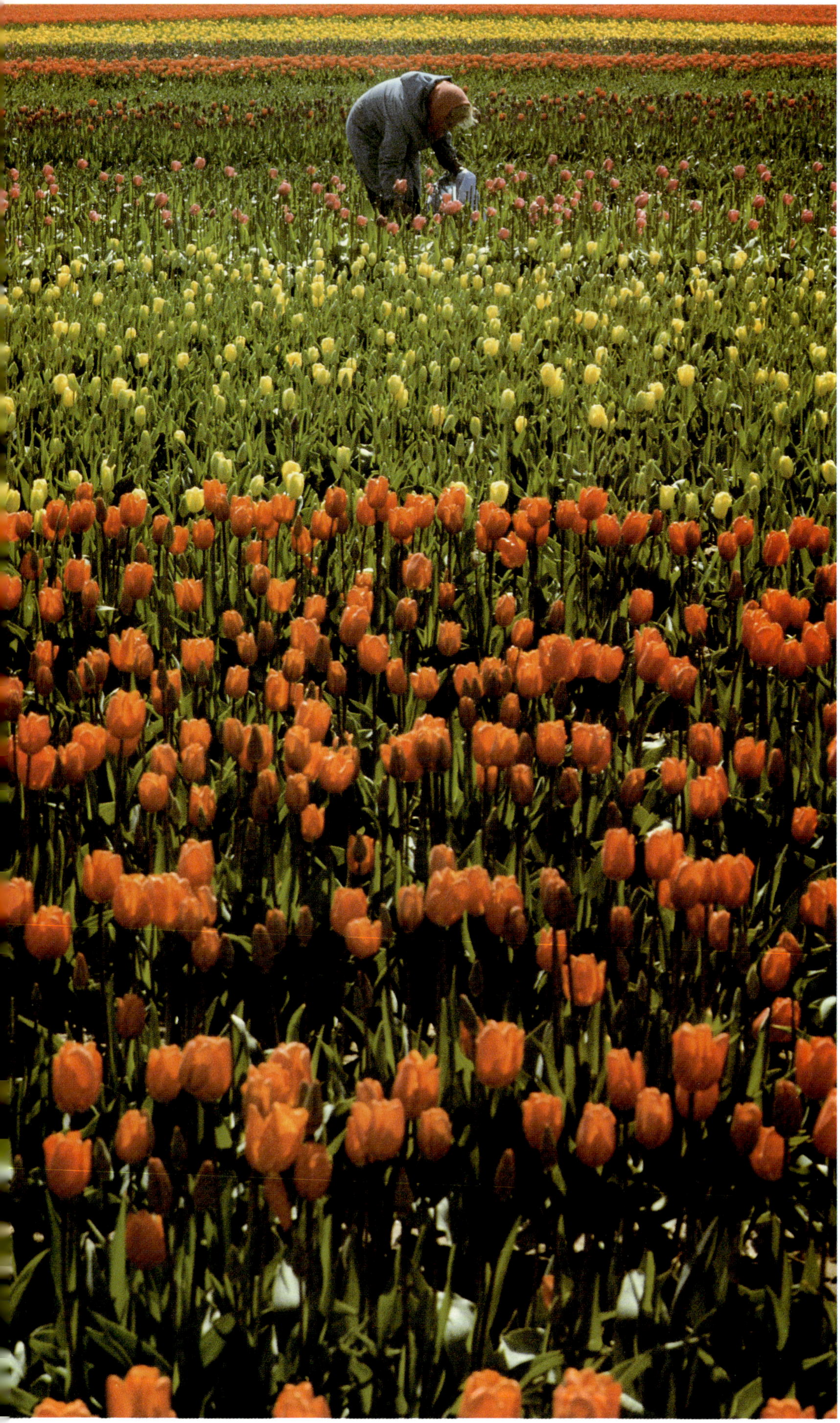

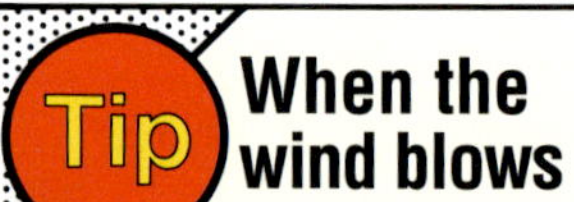

When the wind blows

For maximum sharpness, wait for a lull in the wind before taking a shot of flowers. If this is impossible, use your body as a windbreak.

Alternatively, construct a cardboard 'tent' before you go out. For close-ups, place it carefully around your chosen bloom as a shield from gusts of wind. Leave enough room to get your camera into position.

In poor light, a burst of flash makes an alternative to chancing long exposures, which can cause blur.

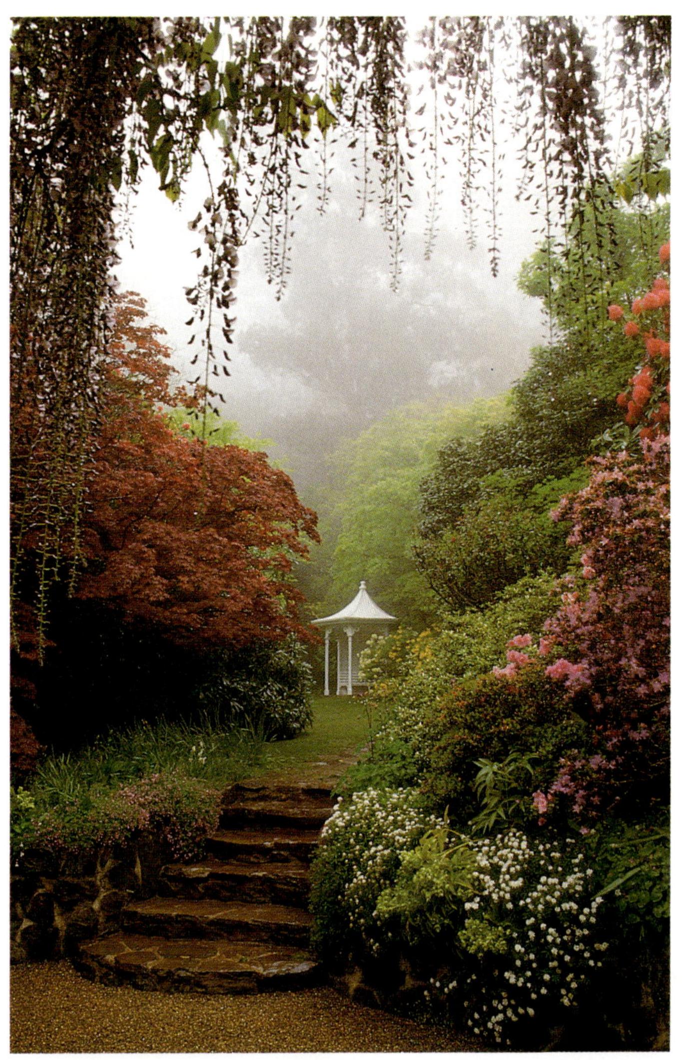

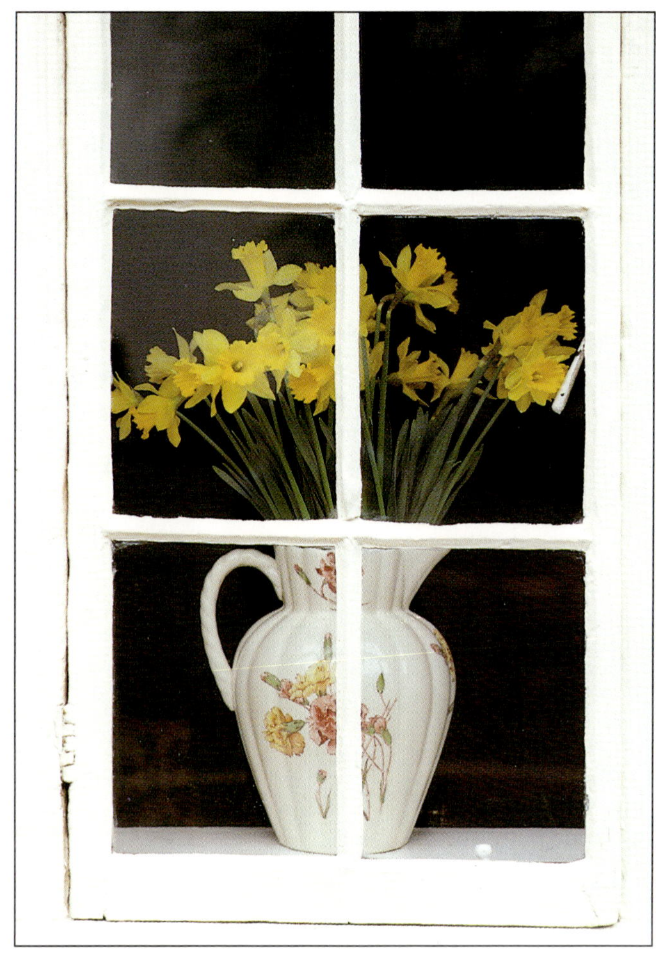

▲ WINDOW ARRANGEMENT

Here the window perfectly complements the simple vase of daffodils, and frames it at the same time. The jug's handle breaks up the composition's symmetry to increase interest. To reduce annoying reflections the photographer moved around until a dark area behind her was reflected in the glass.

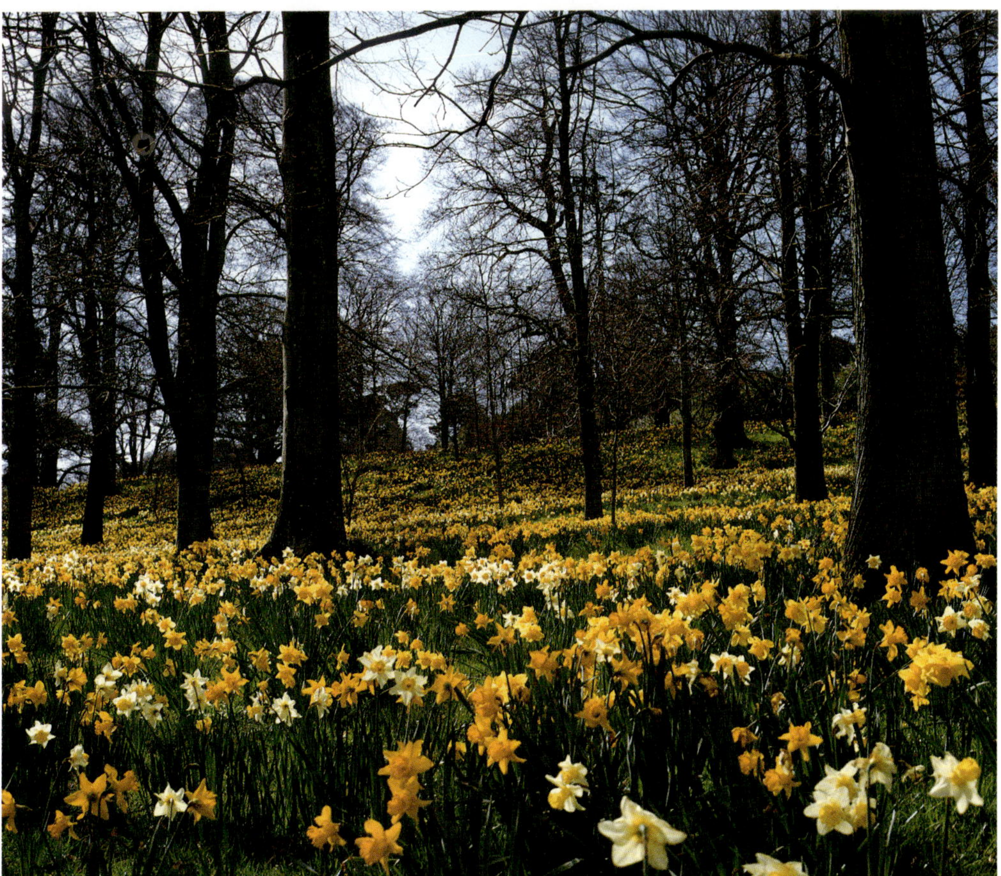

◄ YELLOW CARPET

Even bare branches can be photogenic, if there's a carpet of flowers underneath. Here the bright yellow provides a striking contrast to the darkness of the trees.

Before leaves appear on the trees, light levels in dense woodland are surprisingly high, so you can make use of fast shutter speeds or slow film for brighter colour. Here the photographer metered for the daffodils to bring out the yellow.

 TREAD CAREFULLY
For a really eyecatching shot, fill the whole frame with a few close-up specimens. Choose an overhead viewpoint if the inside of the flower is even more colourful than its outside petals. Crouch down over the flowers, using a small aperture for maximum sharpness from petal tip to stem. Make sure you don't crush any flowers in the process, though!

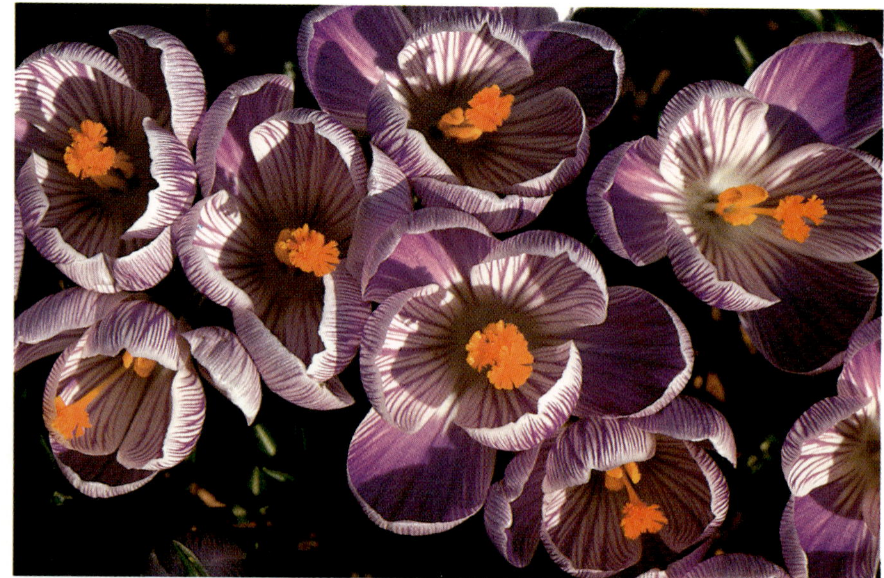

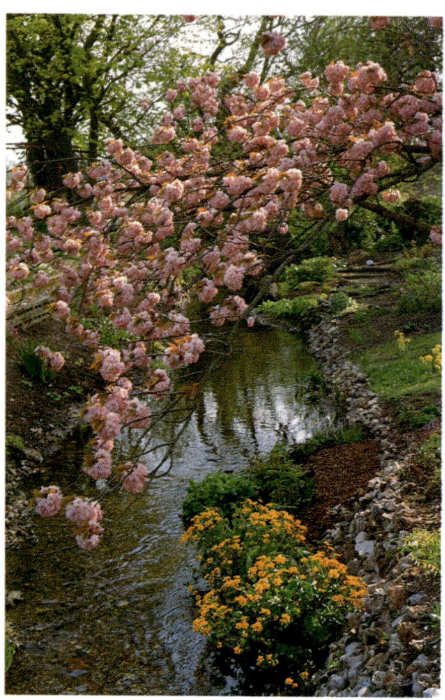

▲ **THE WHOLE VIEW**
When spring's well underway, look up and you're sure to see frothy blossom on the trees. But you must be quick – blossom is this full only for a couple of days, and a storm can knock every petal to the ground. So to catch a particular tree at its best, visit daily.

For a shot that cries out 'Springtime', use a wide angle lens to fill your frame with a mass of colours. Here the stream provides a perfect setting.

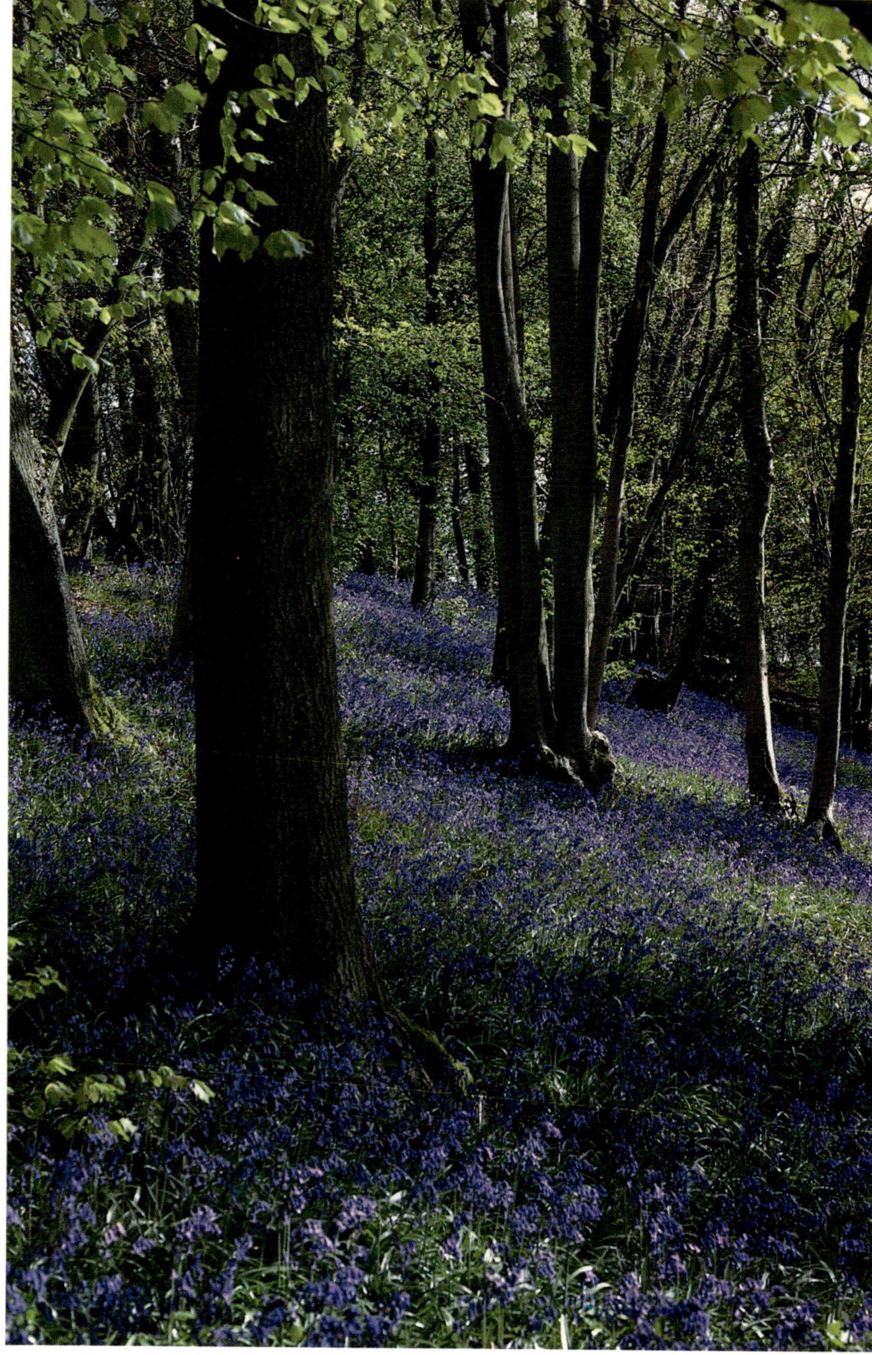

► **HIDDEN BLUEBELLS**
A bluebell wood is the essence of spring in Britain. If you chance to be abroad in spring, make the most of your new surroundings and take pictures of its flowers – often a total contrast from what you're used to.

A carpet of brilliant blue flowers makes a spectacular photo, but you'll need to watch your exposure. As spring turns to summer, the canopy of foliage drastically cuts light levels. You'll find more light at the edges of woodland, so it's a good idea to concentrate your picture taking near paths and clearings. Take a lightweight tripod just in case you need to use a long shutter speed.

Take to the water

"Landscapes" doesn't mean that you photograph only land. As we have already seen, you also photograph the sky; and the third of the elements along with earth and air, is water. Try a harbour, for example.

Try both formats – a vertical frame is ideal for photographs composed around a tall mast, while a horizontal shape lends itself more to boat 'profiles'. Alternatively, concentrate on photogenic details like coils of rope on the quayside, glossy or rusty hulls and sculptural features.

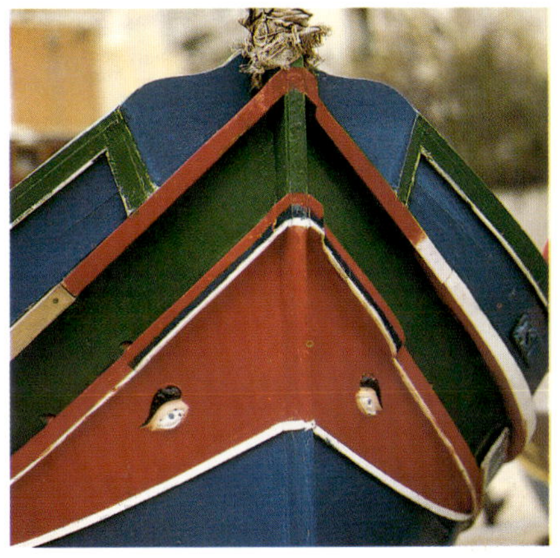

▲ DECORATIVE DETAIL
Regional differences in boat decoration make a fascinating subject for the camera. Take a closer look and you may be rewarded by ornamental touches, like the eyes on this boat, which can be a whole theme in themselves.

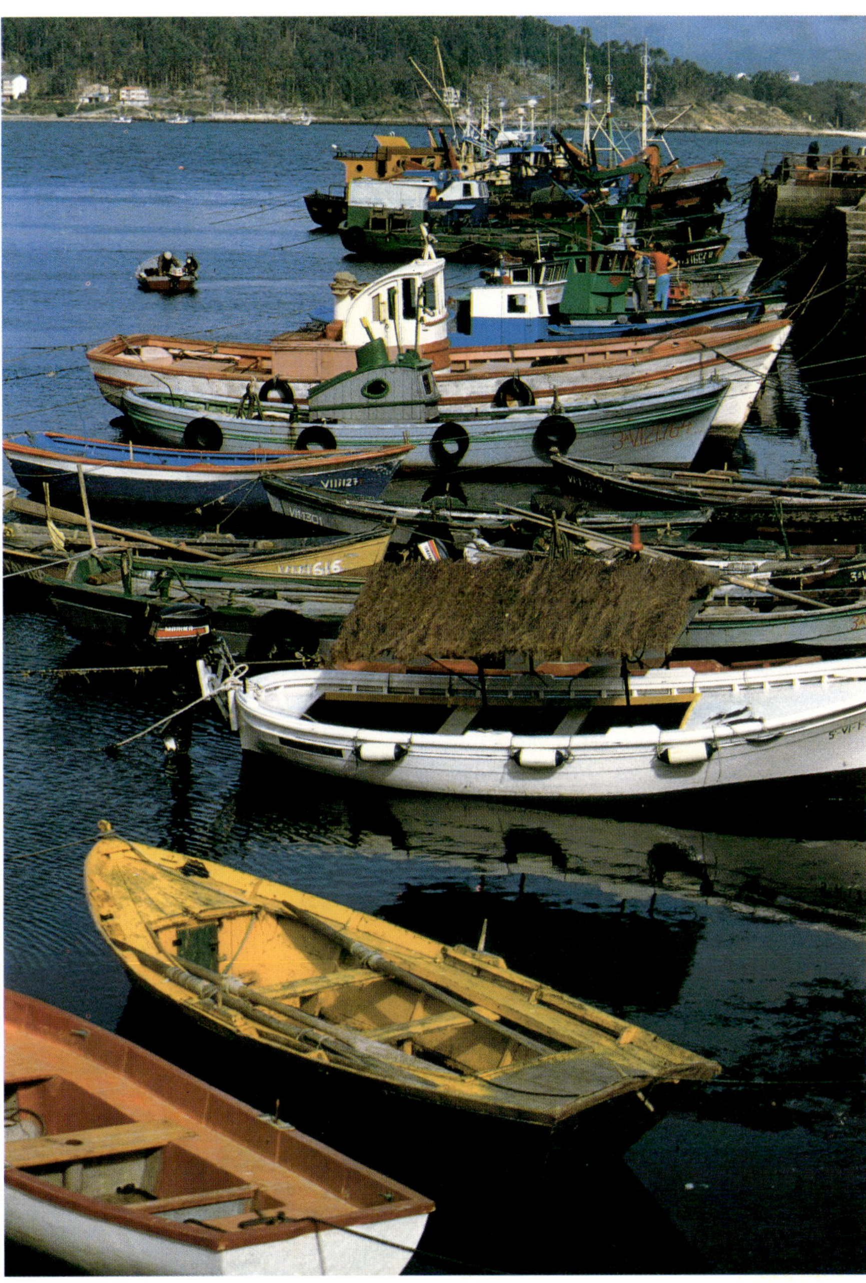

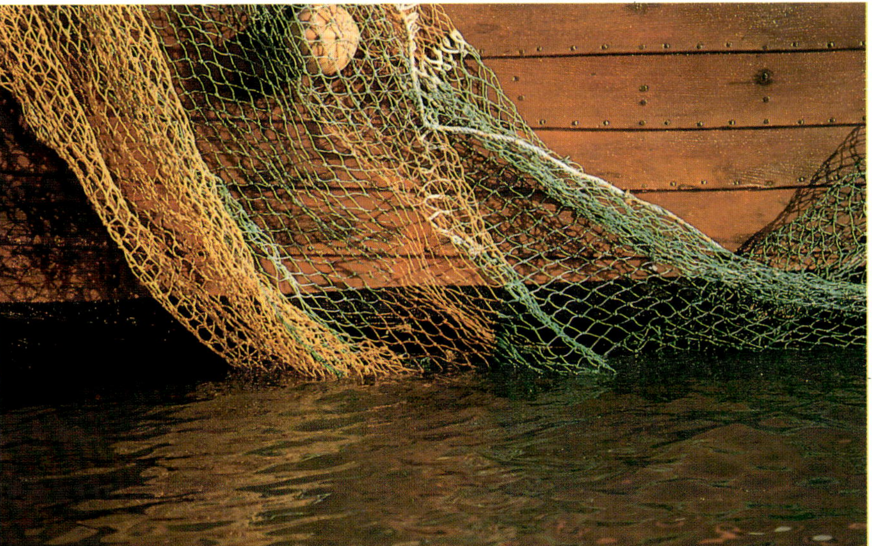

▲ FOREGROUND INTEREST
Photographing a line of boats emphasizes their similarities – or highlights their differences. One effective way to do this is to stand at the end of a quay and frame the rows of moored boats. Use a vertical format so boats stretch from front to back of the picture.

◄ KEEP IT SIMPLE
Most boats are festooned with ropes, wires, rigging and sails. Though orderly to the sailor, the photographer sometimes has to concentrate on one aspect to prevent a chaotic picture. Sunlight gives this one an extra twist, with every fibre in the net being matched by a shadow.

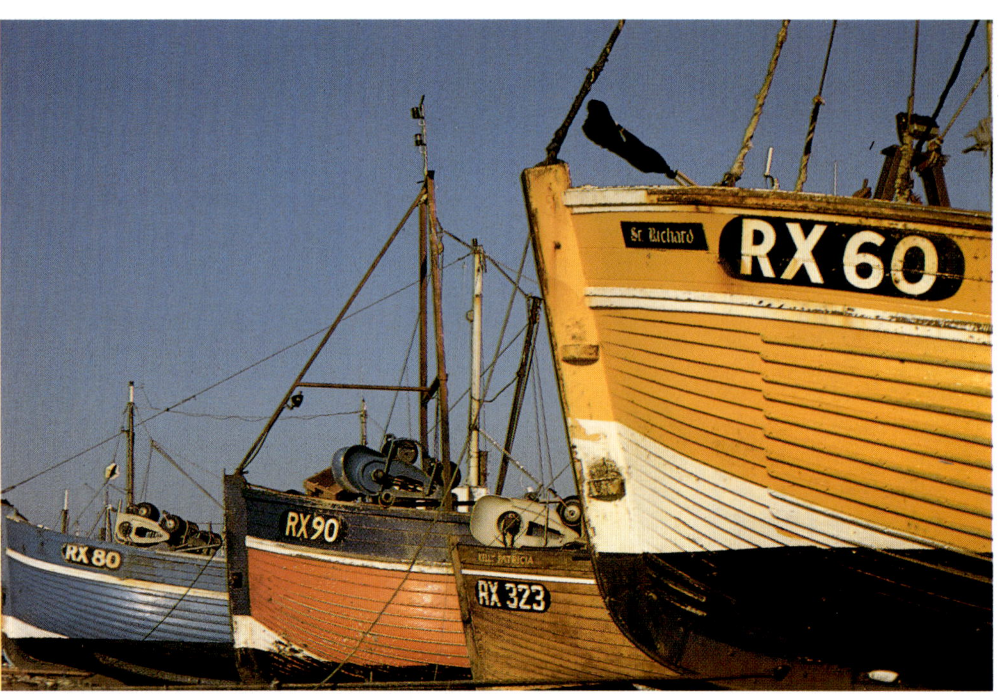

▲ COLOUR MATTERS

Most boats are repainted annually, and for photographers the sparkling colours of newly painted fishing smacks are a visual bonanza. If your camera takes filters, use a polarizing filter to enrich colours. On an SLR or compact with through the lens viewing, look through the viewfinder and rotate the filter in front of the lens until the colours are at their deepest.

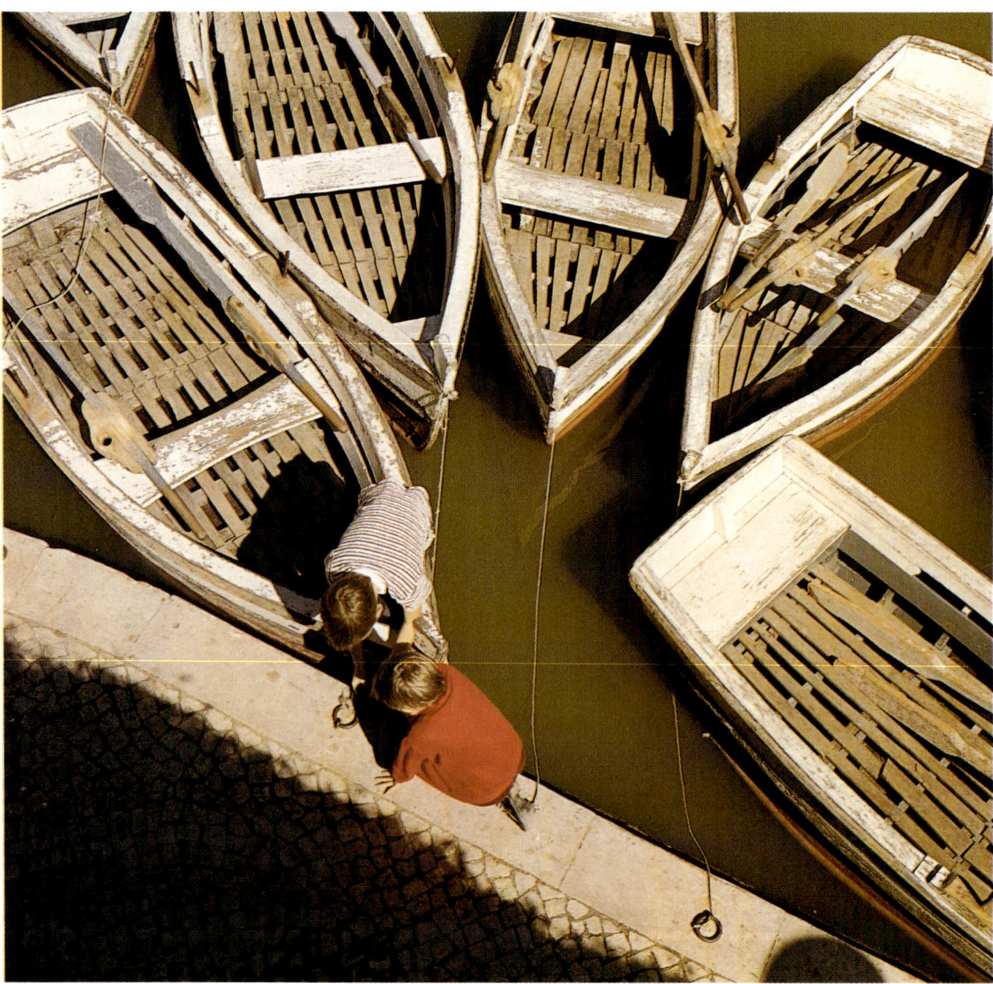

◄ BOYS 'N' BOATS

Wharfs and riversides often provide high viewpoints from which you can see waterside action. Here the downward pointing camera stresses the converging lines of the boats' bows, drawing the eye to the children, who provide the focus of the picture.

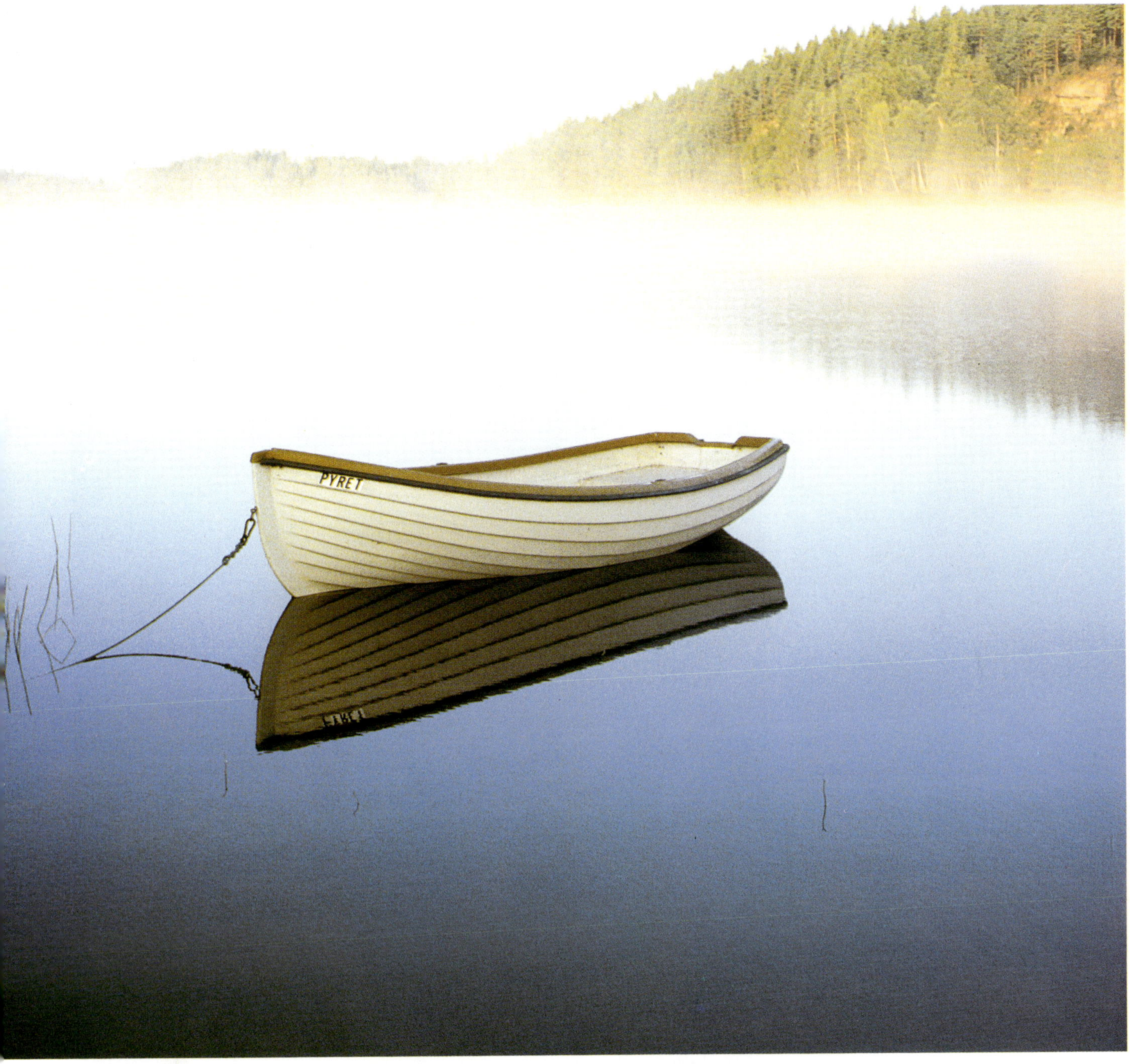

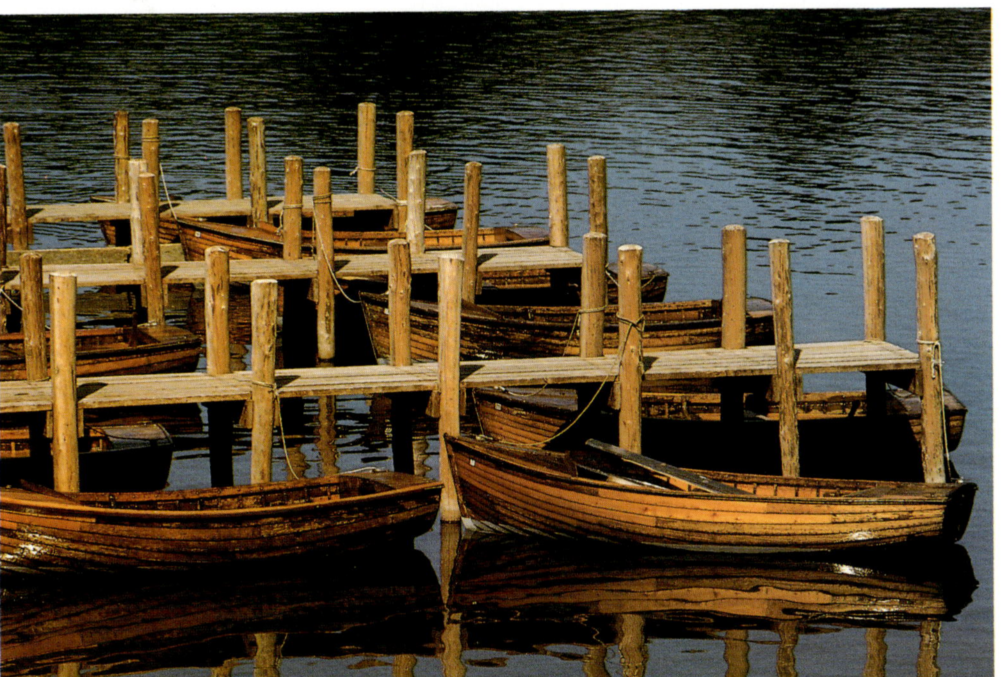

▲ MISTY LAKE
At dawn the air is still, and all is quiet and peaceful. Reflections are mirror-like and the sun's rays haven't yet penetrated the mist. With the help of a wide angle lens, the skiff is framed against a background graded from the deepest blue of the sky's reflection in the glassy water to the pure white of the distant mist.

◀ AT THE JETTY
Sunlight and water alternately darken and lighten the varnished woodwork. Keeping the sun behind the camera emphasizes the subtle shifts of colour and play of light.

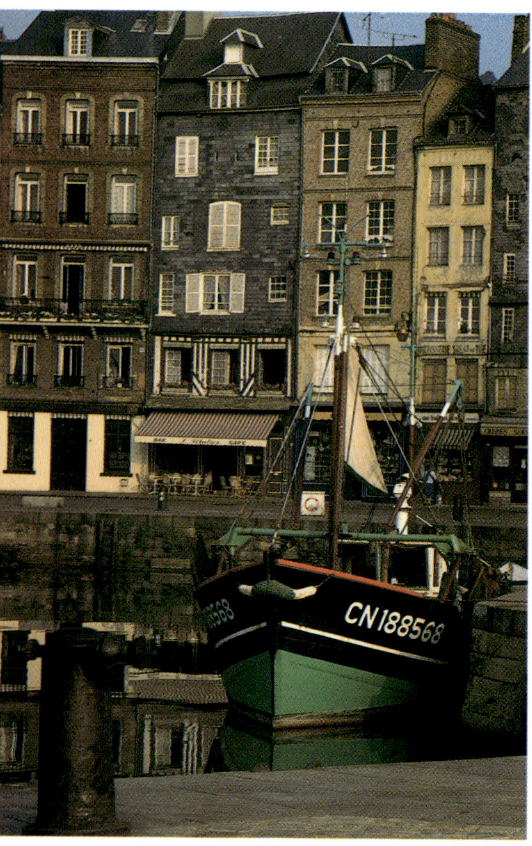

▲ IN PORT

Including a ship's dockside surroundings gives nautical images an extra dimension and lets you set the scene. The photographer chose a distant viewpoint on the far side of the harbour and fitted a telephoto lens to frame the fishing boat against the quayside cafés beyond.

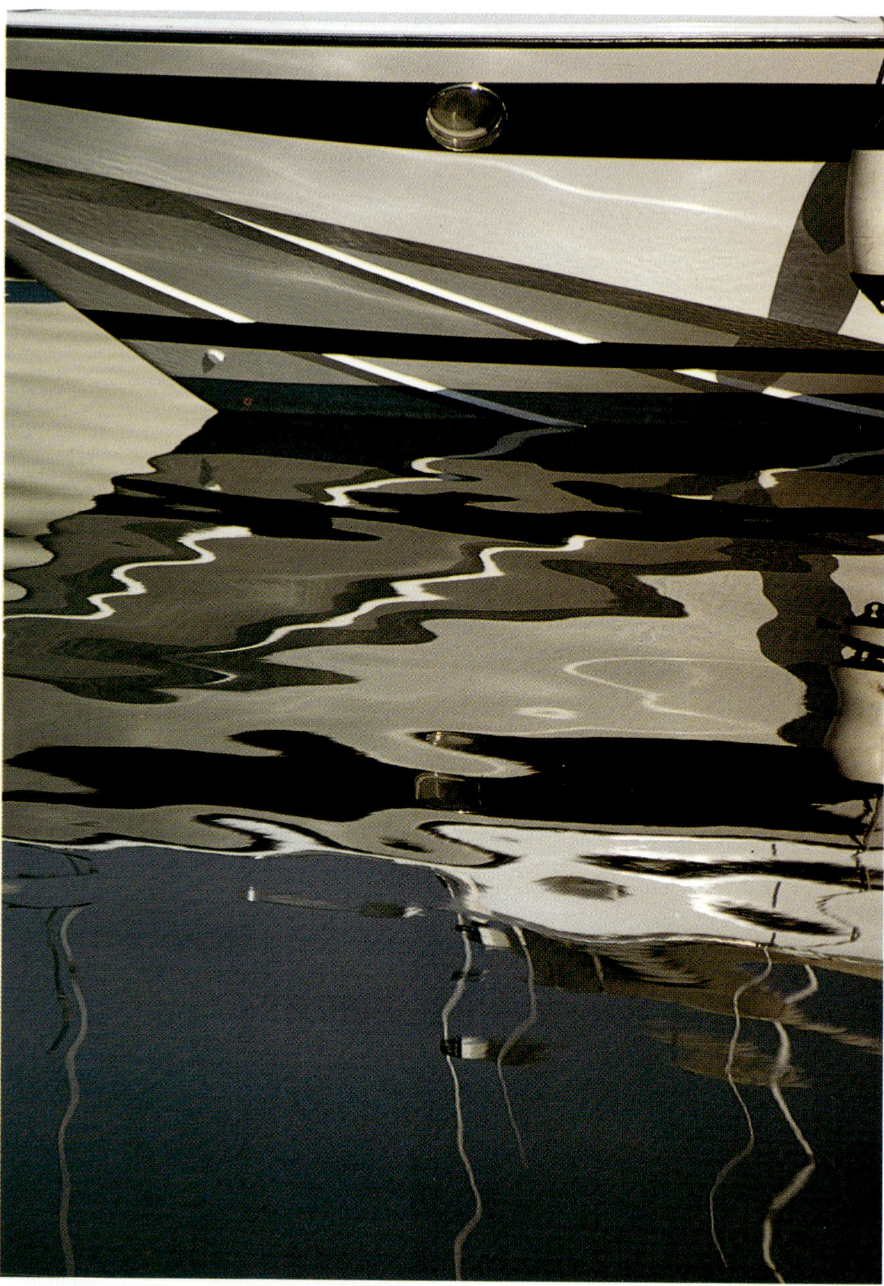

▲ REFLECTIONS

Moving water both distorts and breaks up the reflections of floating boats. Close in on the reflection alone for an abstract image, or include the hull to provide a hard edged reference point.

◀ EMPTY VESSELS

You don't have to stop photographing boats just because they're hauled out of the water for the winter. Here shadows formed by the weak winter sun bring out the shape of the hulls and texture of the paint flakes.

Seascapes

If you want to create powerful landscapes, exploit the photographic qualities of the ocean – at home or abroad.

1 Exposure

Especially on a sunny day, watch your exposure. It's easy to fool the camera meter if the sea forms a large part of the picture, because water reflects light.

Bracket your shots in half or third stop intervals, to make sure that you don't underexpose the photograph.

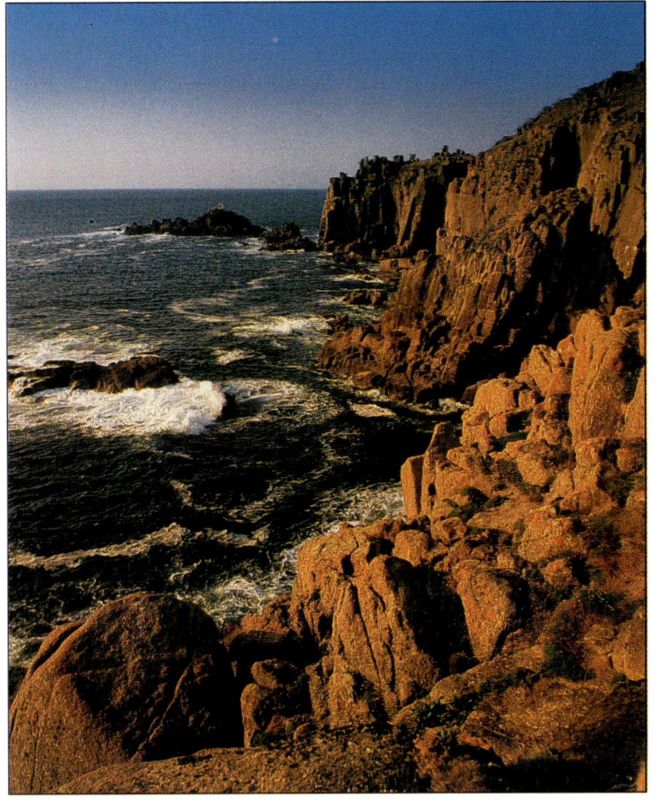

▶ *Interesting rocks provide foreground detail in this shot of Land's End, Cornwall. The low sun gives the rocks a lovely warm colour.*

2 Timing

Be aware of tidal movements. It's no good arriving to photograph a lovely aquamarine sea and finding that the tide's out, because you'll have a wait of several hours until it's full tide, and even longer if the tide is halfway out and ebbing.

Wherever you decide to shoot from, make very sure that you aren't cut off by the tide.

If you're on holiday in an unfamiliar country and you have limited time, get hold of the local tide table. The times of high and low tide may also be printed in the newspaper. That way you can decide when to be at the scene for the best photographs.

▼ *For a holiday shot to be proud of, remember to take a polarizer with you for blue skies and arrive when the tide's far enough up the beach.*

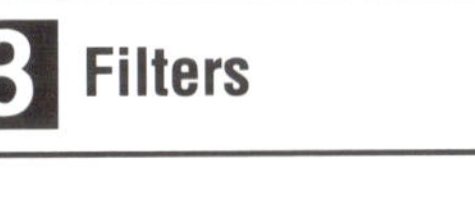

3 Filters

Deep blue sea and sky make the best known seaside landscape. Fit a polarizer to maximize the sky's blueness – but remember that it will also reduce any reflections in the water.

While the sun's rising or setting and creating highlights on the water, why not try a starburst filter? It will turn every point of light into a glittering star.

This effect looks especially effective if you can include a silhouette of, say, a figure or a boat in front of the pink or reddish toned water.

Graduated filters are also worth trying. For example, if the sky looks washed out, a blue grad will add colour to the sky and darken it. It will also reduce any difference in contrast between land and sky, making it easier to expose correctly.

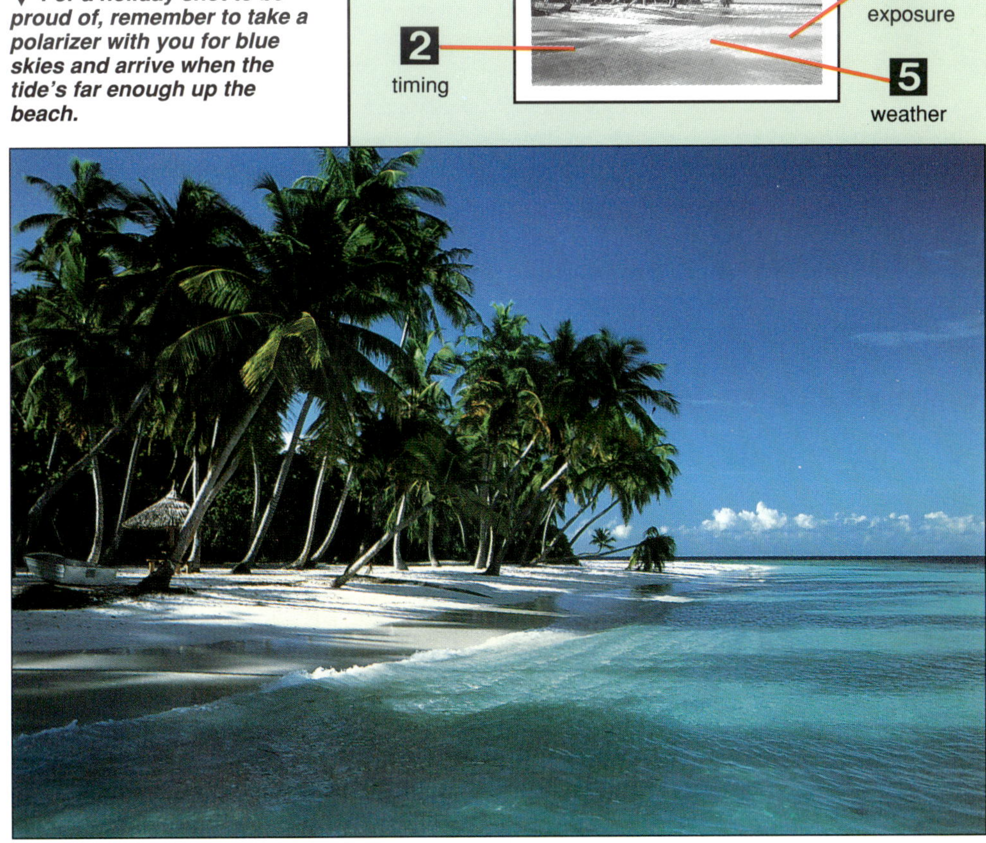

"

Composition

When you are taking a straightforward seascape, it's easy to end up with no obvious focal point, so that your eyes roam around the picture looking for a detail to rest on.

Subjects that could take on the role of focal point could be anything from a brightly coloured windsurfer or boat, to a pier jutting out to sea.

Try to avoid bisecting the shot with the horizon. An unequal split, perhaps based on the rule of thirds, usually works best. Include more of whichever element – sky or sea – is the most interesting. But an equal split works if there's a focal point in both areas.

Why not try including some foreground detail in the seascape, too? Use a wide angle lens and a wide depth of field to include the water rushing over seashells or the white, foamy crest of a wave against blue sky.

Rocks or palm trees can be used to frame the sides of the picture effectively.

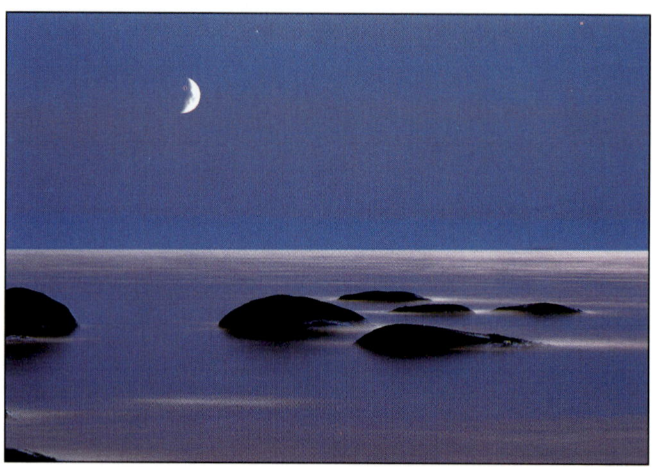

▲ *The long exposure used here gives a mysterious, unworldly look to the sea.*

5 Weather

For gorgeous blues, choose a bright sunny day. But if you're after something more dramatic, stormy weather is ideal.

A foaming ocean that's throwing up huge waves, with a black, threatening sky, makes for a really dramatic picture. Include a windswept figure looking out to sea or a small boat tossing in the waves for a sense of scale.

People being showered with spray make good subjects – but make sure that your camera is protected from salt water. Encase it with a clear plastic bag that has a hole cut for the lens. Fit a UV or skylight filter to protect the lens from spray.

▼ *The photographer waited until the waves were at their highest before shooting, setting a shutter speed of 1/500th sec to capture the churning water and spray.*

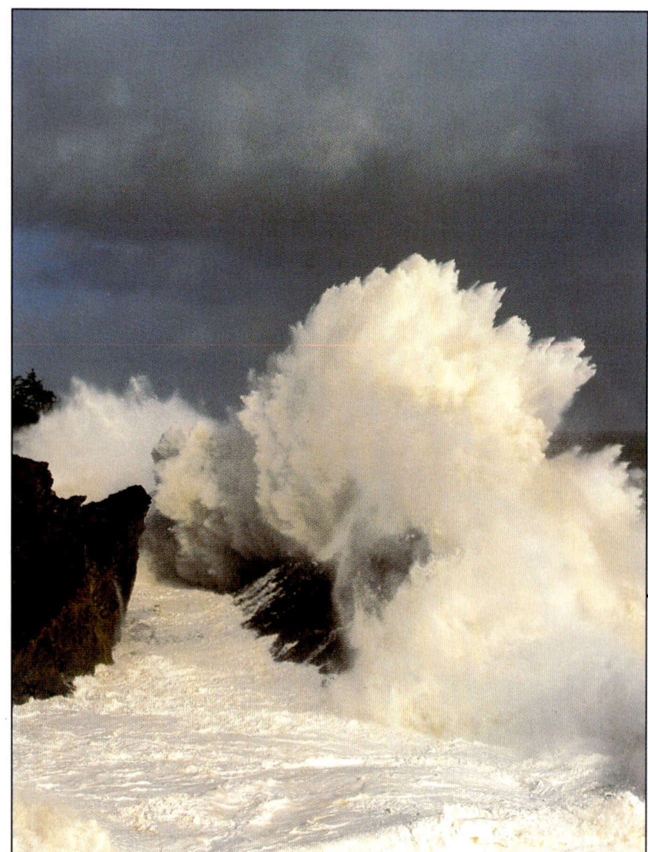

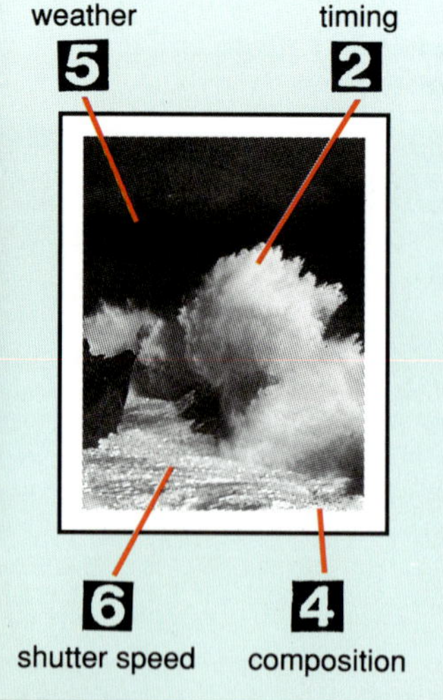

Camera: SLR.
Lens: anything from 24mm to a telephoto, depending on the shot.
Film: ISO 50-100.
Camera support: a tripod is useful, especially when you are shooting at dawn or dusk in limited light, or want to set a narrow aperture for maximum depth of field.
Filters: polarizer, starburst, graduated.
Time of day: for high tide, look at local tide tables. Sunrise and sunset give the scene a lovely warm tone.
Weather: depends on the effect you want. Deep blue sky reflected in the sea makes the water a lovely shade of blue. For drama, shoot in stormy conditions.
Note: protect your equipment from sea spray – keep it in a plastic bag with a hole for the lens to poke through. Make very sure you aren't cut off by the tide if you're shooting in inaccessible places.

6 Shutter speed

Where you want to capture individual droplets of water, use a shutter speed of 1/250th sec or higher.

On the other hand, if you want to make the water look ghostly, choose fast moving currents and set a shutter speed of below 1/8th sec.

Riverscapes

For endless variety in your shots, you can't beat a river. Rain or shine, there's always something worth photographing on and around the water.

Use the river's character and the time of day to guide the mood of your photograph. For example, on a busy river, shoot manoeuvring boats and people having fun feeding birds from its banks. At sundown, on the other hand, you could capture the peaceful atmosphere when still water provides a mirror-like reflection of trees and moored boats.

Shooting on a sunny day means the water takes on a deep blue colour. If it's a miserable day, you can still shoot the grey water – look for brightly painted boats or flowers near the river bank to liven up your photos with a splash of colour.

Foreground interest turns a good shot into a superb one. Walk along the river bank before you take out your camera so you find the most photogenic spot. Use a wide angle lens and a small aperture for maximum depth of field, and if it's a sunny day you may be able to get away without using a tripod. Compose the picture as a vertical, and keep the horizon close to the top of the frame to take in as much foreground as possible.

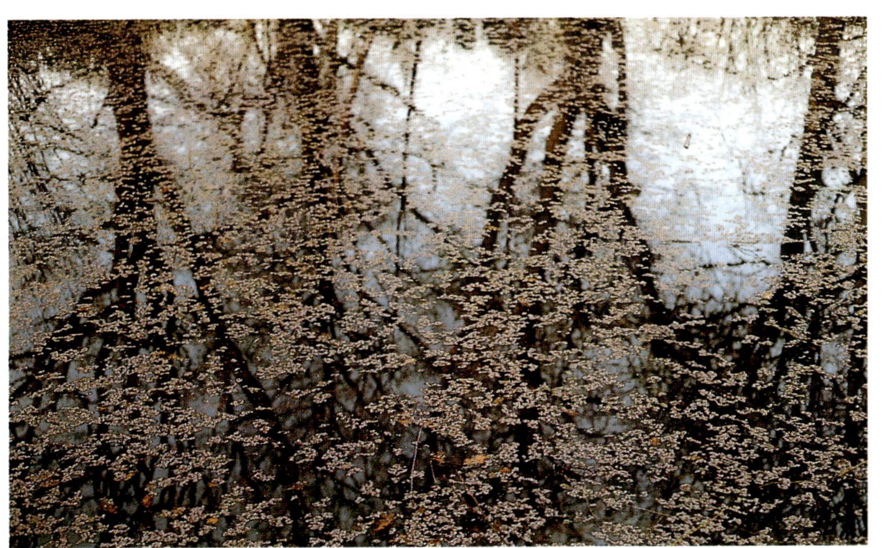

◀ **PINK CONFETTI**
In some stretches, rivers can be almost static, allowing you to capture undistorted reflections of trees and buildings on the river bank. Here, the photographer focused on the veil of blossom, leaving the reflections slightly blurred. This creates a serene mood in the picture. You can easily focus both manual and autofocus cameras on subjects lying on the water, but an autofocus camera may not be able to cope with the reflections underneath.

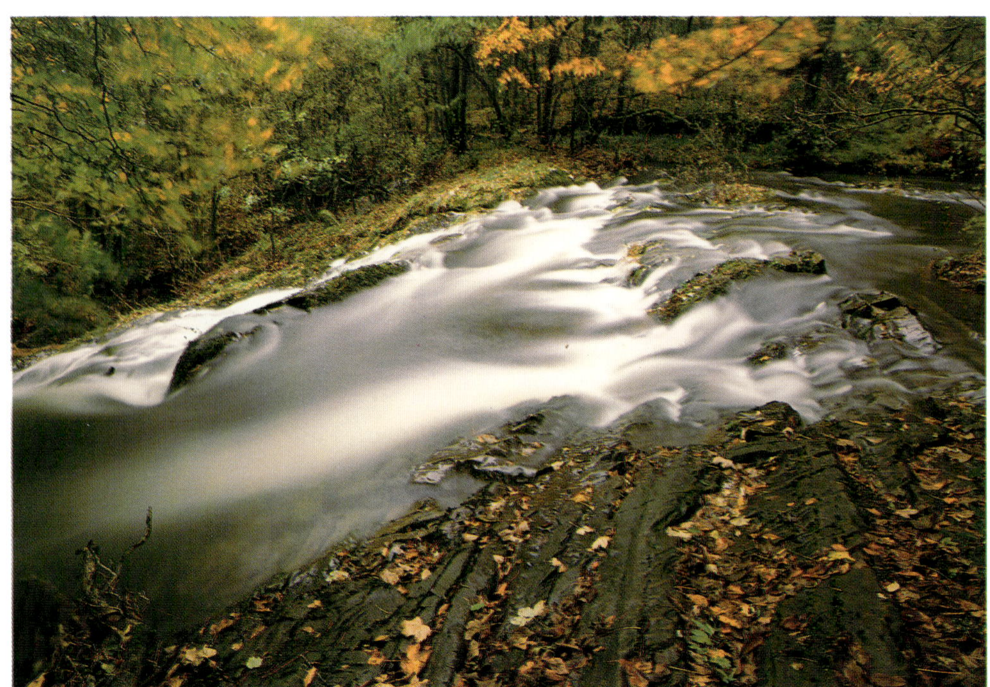

◀ RUSHING WATER

Where there's a river you may find a nearby waterfall, or at least a fast flowing tributary. A slow shutter speed makes the water take on a wispy appearance. Watch out if you're scrambling on wet rocks – it's easy to slip and damage both yourself and your camera.

▼ TOUCH DOWN

Rivers offer great chances of wildlife shots. If you're very lucky, you can capture a bird landing on the surface of the water. A fast shutter speed keeps the swan sharp, while a slow shutter speed blurs movement for a more action packed shot. You need fast reflexes for a picture like this one!

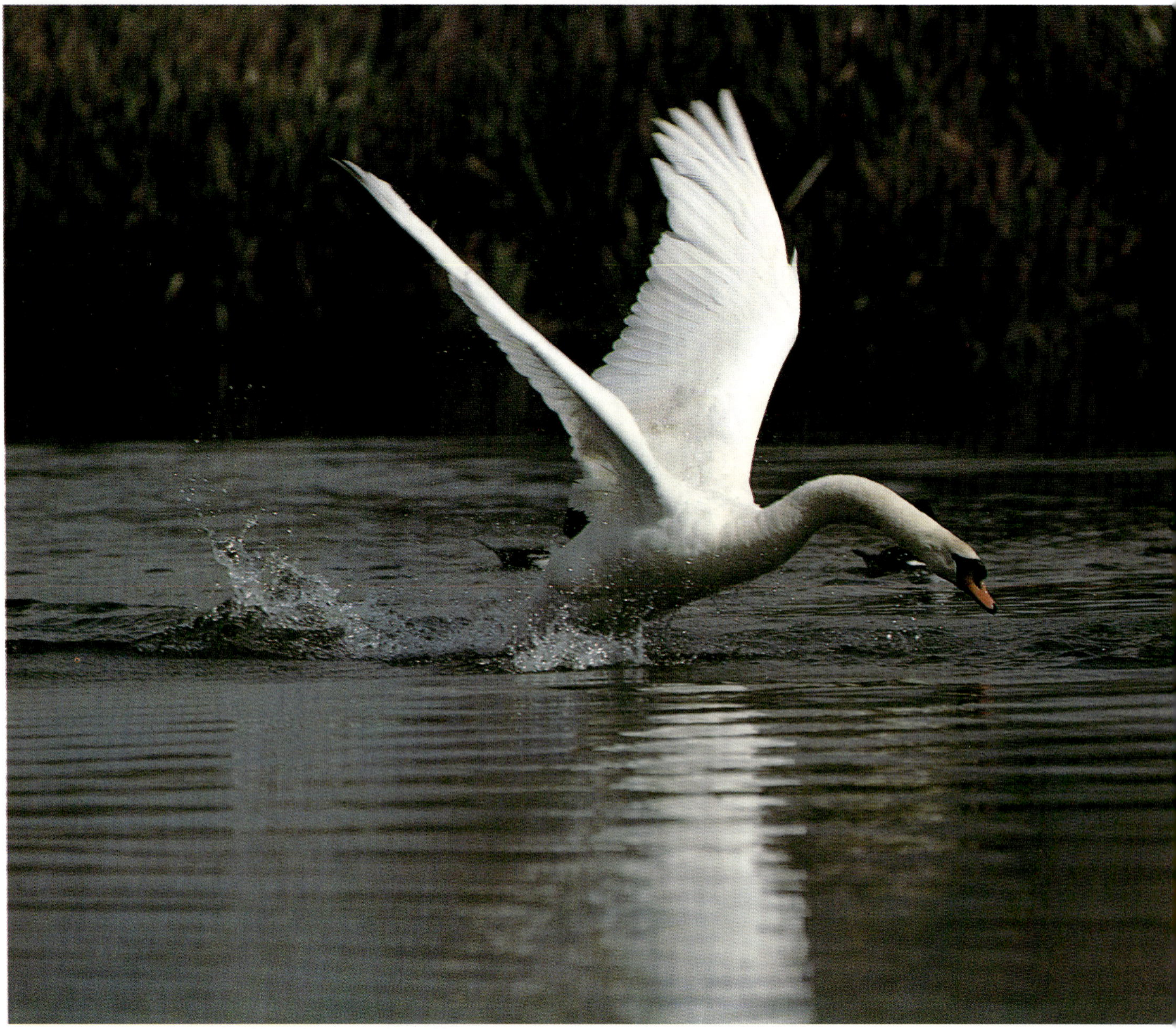

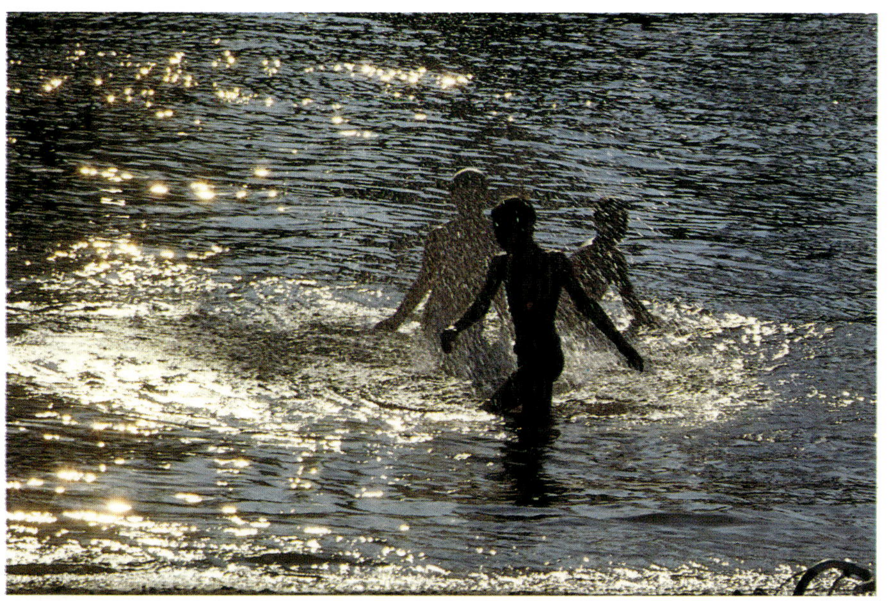

◀ SPARKLE
Sunlight dancing on the water makes for a sparkling photograph. This image may remind you of the sea, but in fact the children are having fun in the shallows of the River Thames. The bright sunshine lights the spray of water droplets and creates a sense of liveliness.

▼ CAREFUL EXPOSURE
River estuaries look picturesque at high tide, but low water exposes areas of mud. Check tide tables for the best time to visit – or try to catch the sunset, which washes the mud with a golden glow. If you want to avoid silhouettes when you're taking sunsets, wait until the sun is very low in the sky. If necessary use a graduated neutral density filter to cut down on excess brightness from the sky. Take a meter reading from the foreground and expose for that.

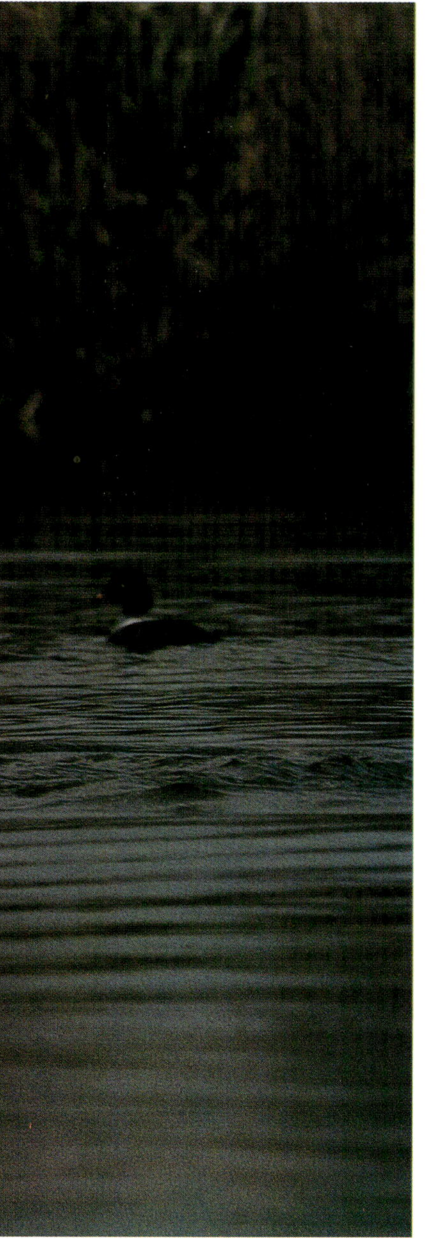

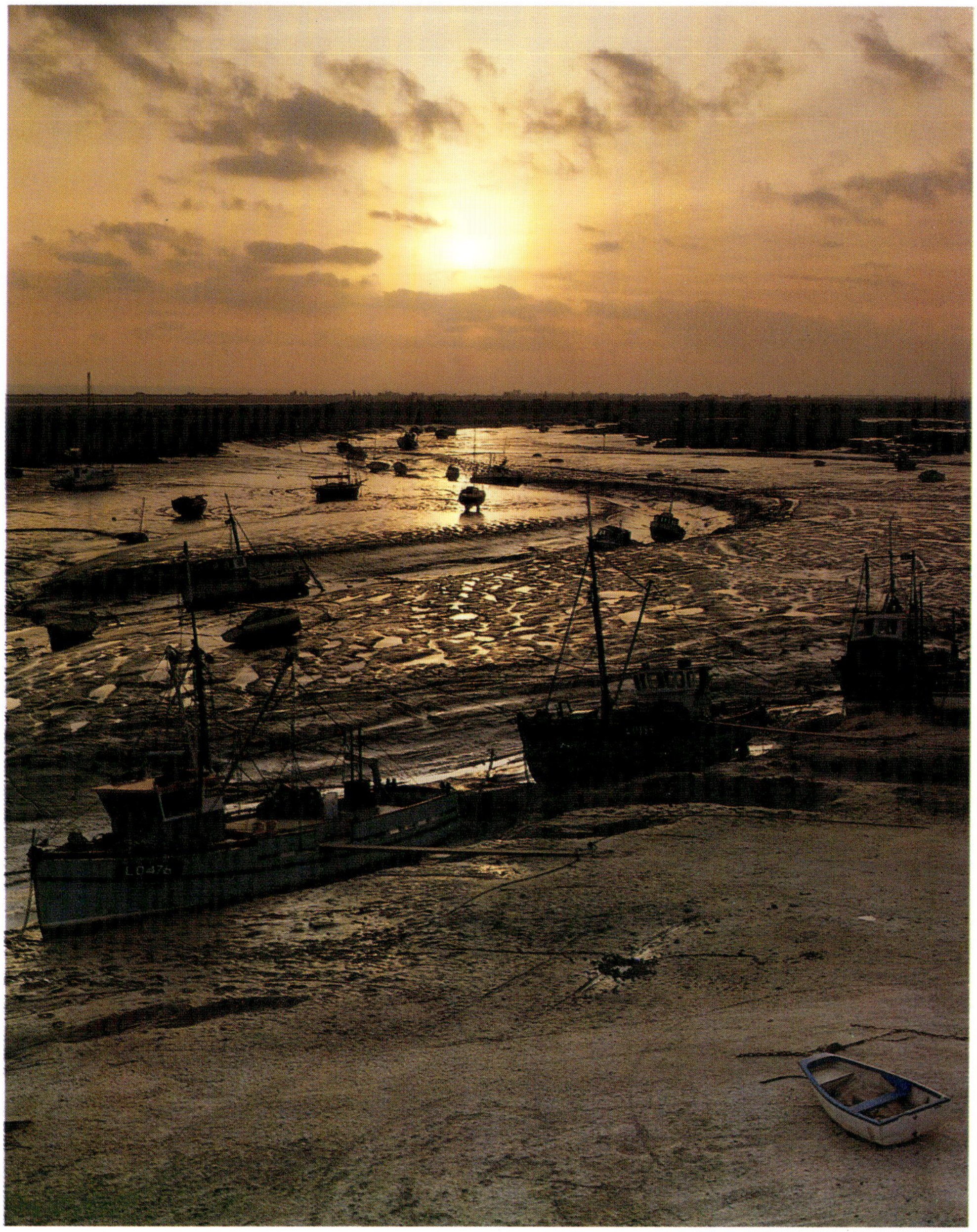

▶ BRANCH OUT
Try using natural features to frame your river scene, particularly when the midday sun is at its harshest. Here the curving branches and backlit leaves provide the interest, and serve to blot out the pale sky and deep shadows cast by the high sun. The photographer took a meter reading from the leaves so that the branches are silhouetted.

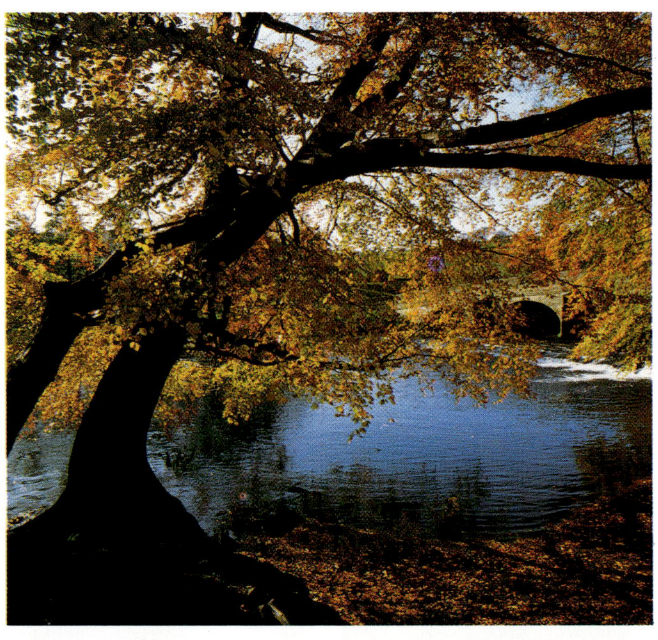

Watch your metering

The reflective qualities of river water make it a challenging subject to meter correctly. When it mirrors a shadow or deep blue sky, water can appear pitch black, and you'll need to cut exposure by one or two stops to portray it realistically.

But when the water reflects sparkling sunlight, take the reverse approach. Give at least a stop more than your camera's meter recommends.

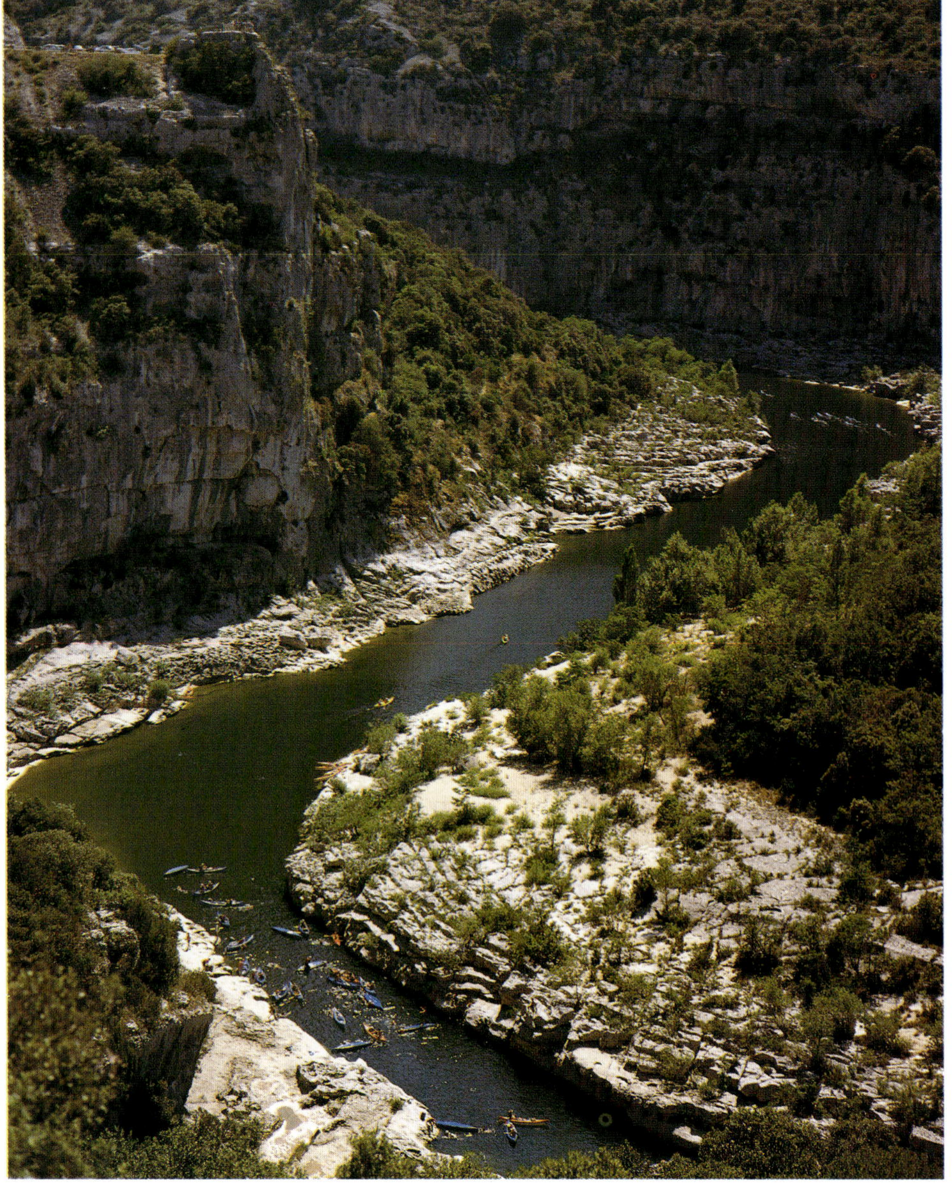

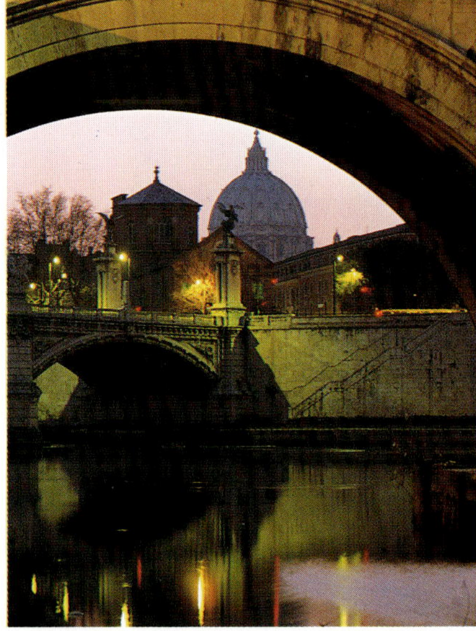

▲ ON REFLECTION
This view of Rome would have been perfectly acceptable without the bottom third of the image, but the street lights' reflections provide the finishing touch by balancing the buildings. The photographer stood on the bank and framed the scene so that the bridge almost appears to touch the dome's spire. He shot at dusk so that the street lights were of a similar brightness to the fading sky.

◀ RIVER BENDS
Changing your viewpoint can dramatically alter the appearance of a river. Shoot from low down on the bank for close-ups of river life, or back off and, as here, stand way above the water to turn it into a curving pattern. Here the winding path of the water leads your eye into the picture, as your gaze drifts down river with the canoes. Choose a day with good visibility for a haze-free shot.

Moving water

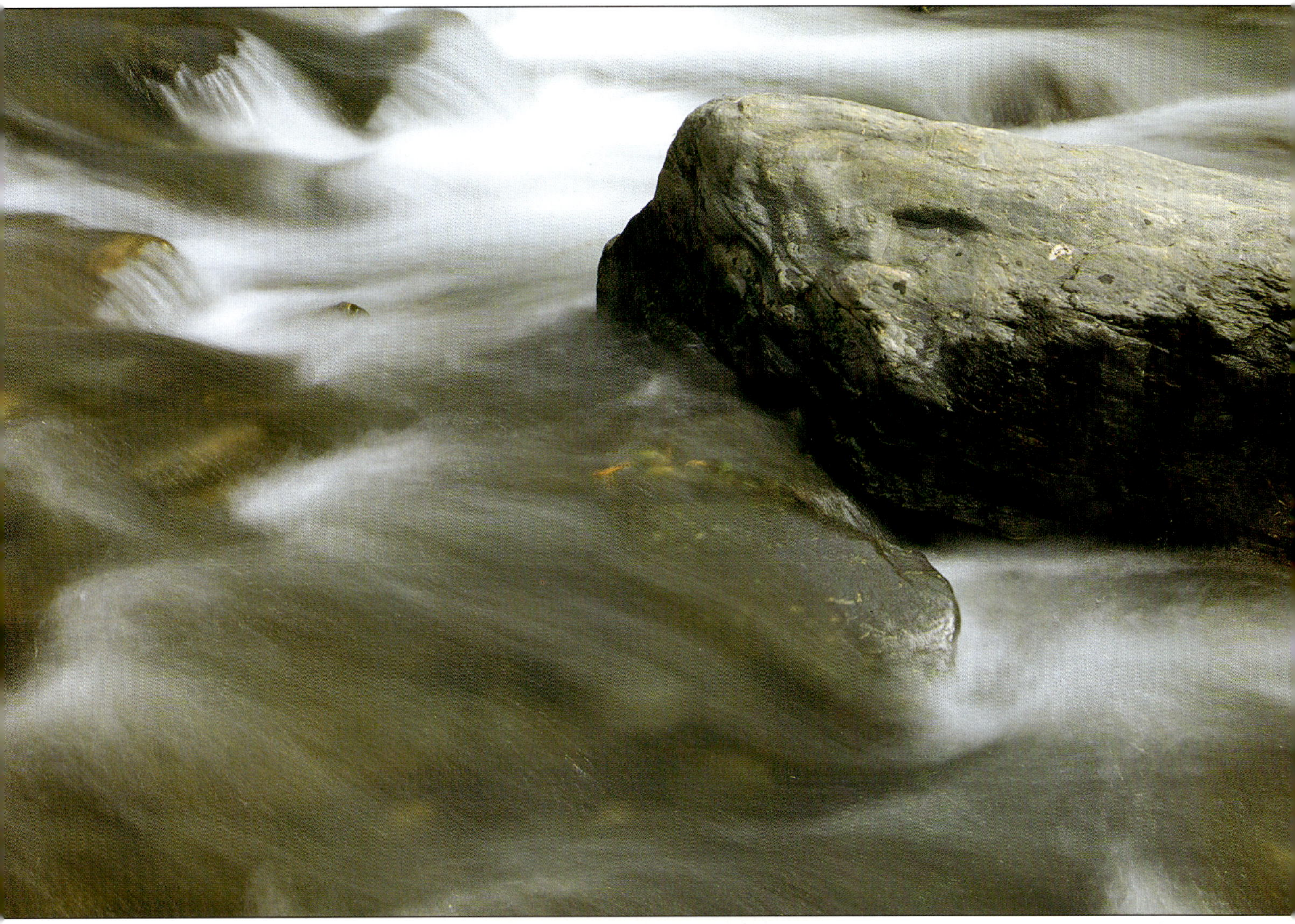

On a long exposure, fast-moving white water blurs and creates attractive patterns while anything solid in the frame remains sharp. In this shot the sunlight has made the rock really stand out against the foam.

With a little technical know how, a fast-moving river or stream can produce spectacular results on film. Mike Busselle introduces David Jones to the art of long exposure.

I've tried shooting moving water before and have never been happy with my results. What appears as a smoothly flowing stream to the naked eye becomes a messy, splashing torrent on film. But fast-moving water can actually be accentuated in a photograph, so I asked Mike Busselle to join me on this masterclass and show me how.

We came across this idyllic stream in the mountains above Malaga in southern Spain. It was a clear, fast-running mountain stream

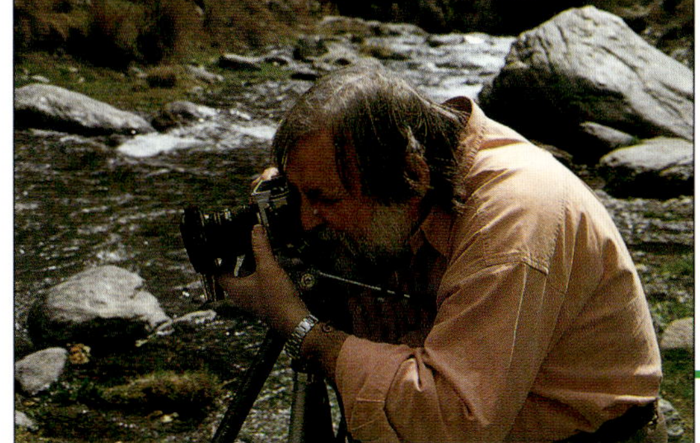

peppered with rocks and stones, and it suited our requirements perfectly. 'The rocks can come in very handy', Mike explained, 'because they make good centres of interest in a moving water shot.'

The wrong approach

The weather was in our favour as well – it was warm and sunny with only the occasional cloud in sight. I started shooting first, using a Nikon

The set up

Mike and David were photographing a fast-flowing mountain stream in Andalucia, southern Spain on a sunny spring morning. There were plenty of rocks in the water to add to the shots, and low banks on either side allowed Mike to get as close as he liked. David hand held his camera and stuck to fast shutter speeds. Mike used a tripod and shot long exposures.

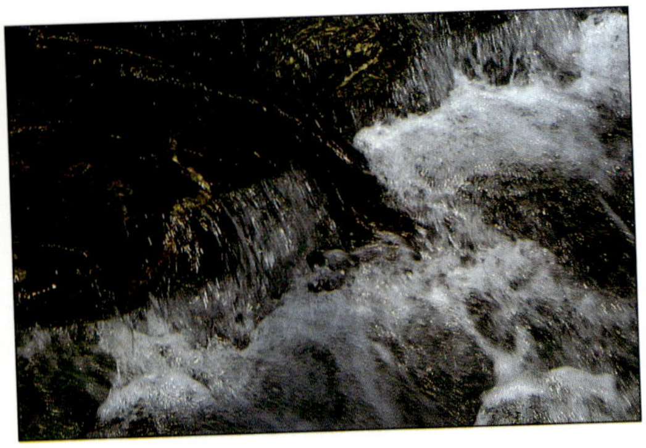

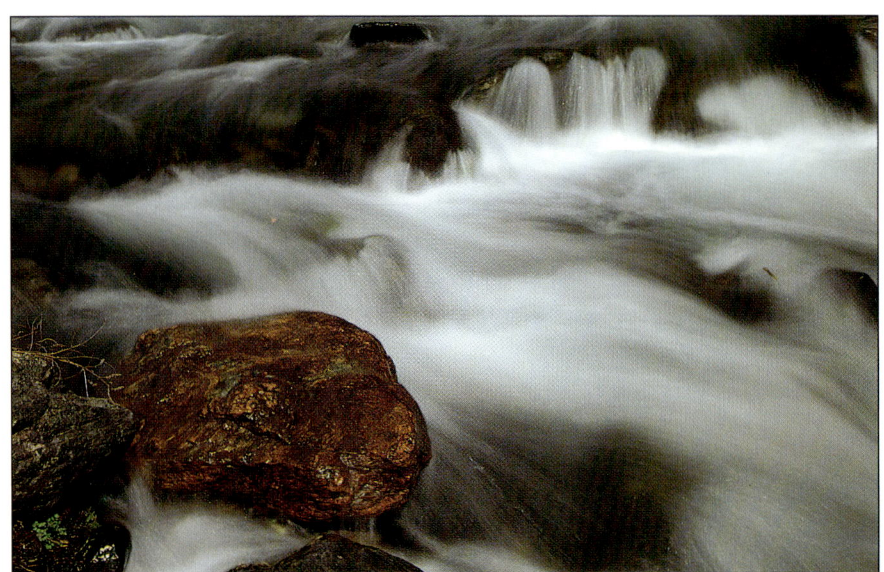

▲ *David saw this unusual looking rock at the edge of the stream and moved in to take a close-up of the water running over it. But on a shutter speed of 1/125th sec, the foam looks messy and uninteresting. A wider shot on a much longer exposure would have been far more effective.*

F3 with a 50mm lens and Fuji ISO 50 colour slide film. Following Mike's sound advice, I found a large rock and framed my shot around it.

Believing that the torrent of sparkling water was bound to make a lively enough picture, I simply took an exposure reading with the camera and started shooting. I bracketed slightly to be sure of a good exposure and shot a whole roll on one scene.

But it was a waste of good film because all my exposures were too short to be effective. I shot most of my pictures on a shutter speed of 1/125th sec, which left the water looking messy and indistinct. I found out later that only on exposures of a second or longer can you achieve the beautiful special effects I was searching for.

Using long exposure

Mike had a careful look at the stream before deciding where to start. He settled on a distinctive looking rock near the bank with plenty of fast-moving water around it. Then he loaded his Nikon FE2 with Fuji ISO 50 slide film, attached a 28-70mm zoom lens and mounted it on a tripod.

Shooting downwards towards the water, he stopped the lens right down and took a series of one second exposures. 'On a long exposure the moving water creates lovely smooth patterns as it shoots through the frame', he explains. 'You have to close your aperture

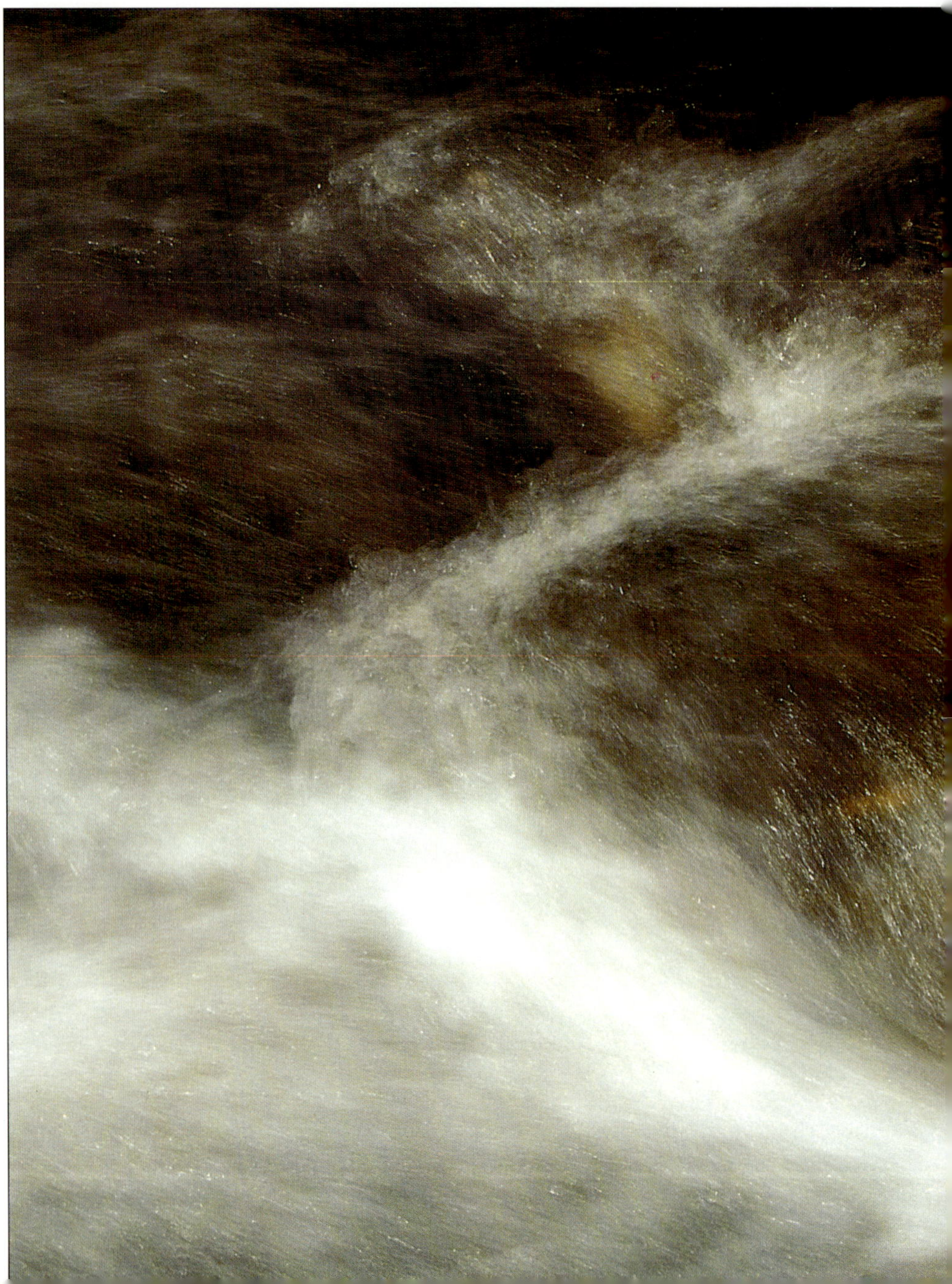

1 LONG EXPOSURE

Mike started by concentrating on this rock by the side of the river. He took an exposure of one second with the aperture closed right down to f22 to avoid overexposure. That was easily long enough to create the blurred effect on the fast flowing water that he was looking for.

2 MULTIPLE EXPOSURE

He then focused on a rock in midstream and tried shooting it on multiple exposure instead. By using eight short exposures on one frame he achieved the same blurred effect as he had with longer shutter speeds. He used a polarizer to cut out any reflections.

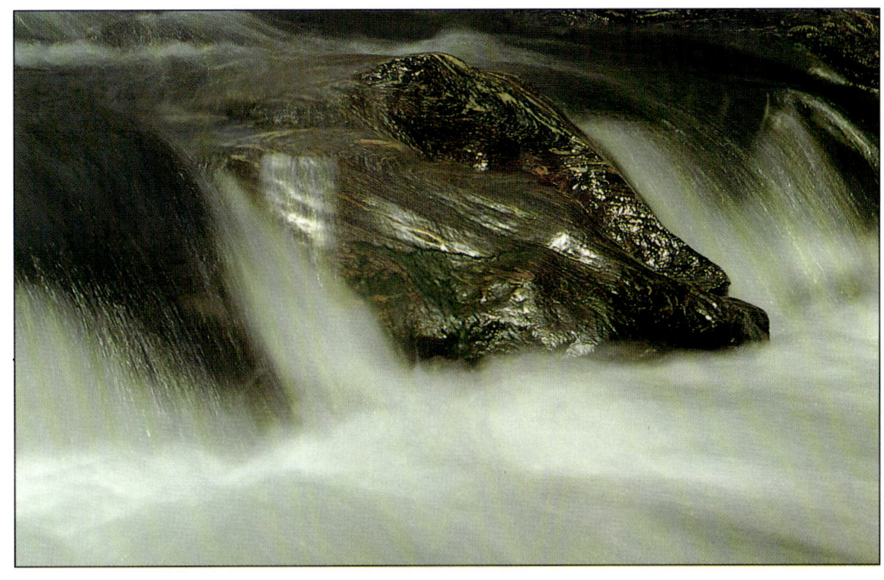

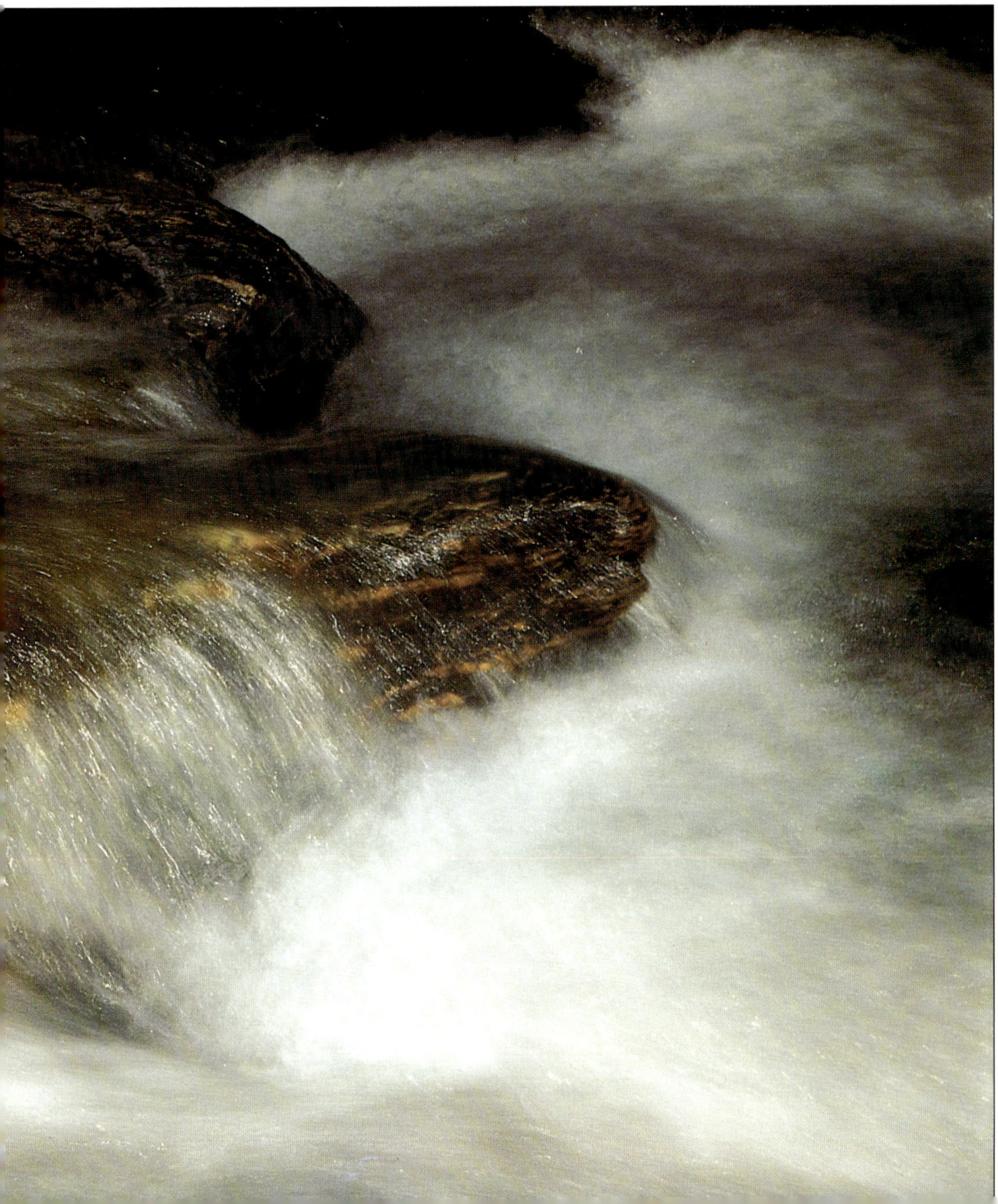

3 A DARKER SHOT

Mike then tried taking a multiple exposure of a group of rocks in a shaded part of the river. This meant taking eight separate short exposures on one frame. He has succeeded in capturing some beautiful patterns, and there's more texture in the highlights here and a less smoky effect than in a long exposure.

4 A TOUCH OF COLOUR

For his last shots Mike reverted to long exposure and tried putting some colour in the shot. Using two polarizers on the lens produced a deep blue tinge on the image that gave it a very cool feel. He exposed for two seconds because the two filters let less light through.

Using multiple exposure

'If you're trying a multiple exposure', says Mike, 'the first thing to do is calculate the overall exposure you want. Say for example you want to end up with an exposure of 1/30th sec at f16, then you divide your shutter speed by eight and shoot eight exposures of 1/250th sec at the same aperture setting (f16) on the same frame. This will give you the same basic effect with moving water as a long exposure but without any risk of reciprocity failure or colour cast.'

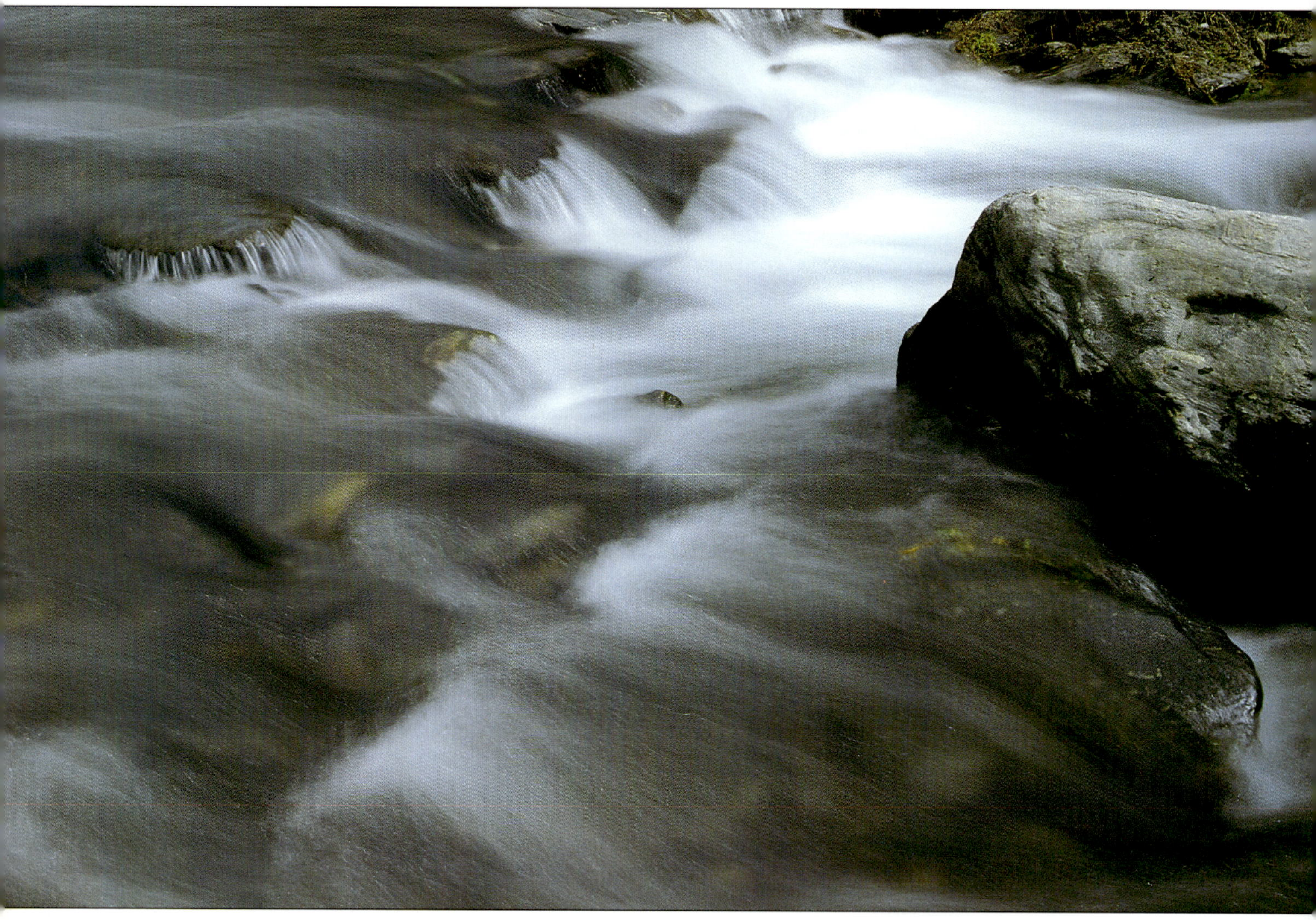

down to avoid completely overexposing. Because the sun was shining I used a polarizer to cut out any reflections on the water.'

An alternative

When he'd shot off a roll of long exposures he decided to try an alternative. He focused on a rock in midstream and began taking multiple exposures of the same scene. He switched to the Nikon F801 for these shots, because it can work out and shoot all the exposures automatically.

'A multiple exposure has the same effect on moving water as a long exposure', explains Mike. 'The only difference is that with multiple exposures you tend to get more texture in the highlights. The advantage is that with long exposures there's always a risk of reciprocity failure and colour cast problems, but that can't happen with multiple exposure. In this case they worked out very well.'

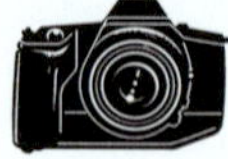

SLR tip

❑ A polarizing filter is very handy when photographing moving water. As well as preventing unwanted reflections on the water, it allows you to use longer exposures without overexposing. This is because it reduces the amount of light hitting the film.

Waterfalls

Waterfalls are among the most spectacular natural subjects, and the faster they flow the better they look on film. Mike Busselle and David Jones found plenty to choose from in the mountains of central France.

After looking long and hard for a suitable area in which to shoot this masterclass, Mike and I chose the Auvergne region in central France. It's a lush, green, mountainous area full of lakes and rivers, so there was a wide selection of interesting waterfalls for us to choose from.

We arrived in the region during one of the wettest Junes they'd had in years. There was widespread flooding, and many of the rivers had overflown their banks. This was good news from our point of view, because it meant that the waterfalls would be much more active than usual. In fact some of the falls we visited were so intense and fast flowing that the spray was a big problem.

A variety of locations

Rather than concentrate on a single waterfall, we decided to photograph a number of them and compare the pictures afterwards. The first fall we visited was situated in a small, wooded valley and could be reached by a narrow path on its right that offered us a number of different viewpoints. The early morning sky was overcast, but Mike told me that this was actually preferable to sunshine.

There was a wooden bridge about 15 metres from the falls, and we both began by setting up there. I was using a Nikon FM on a tripod with a 35-105mm zoom lens and Fuji ISO 50D colour slide film. I took a series of shots from this viewpoint, but included too much foliage in all of them and didn't leave my shutter open for long enough to make the water blur into a really dramatic flow.

Different viewpoints

Mike made much better use of the opportunity. He was shooting on a

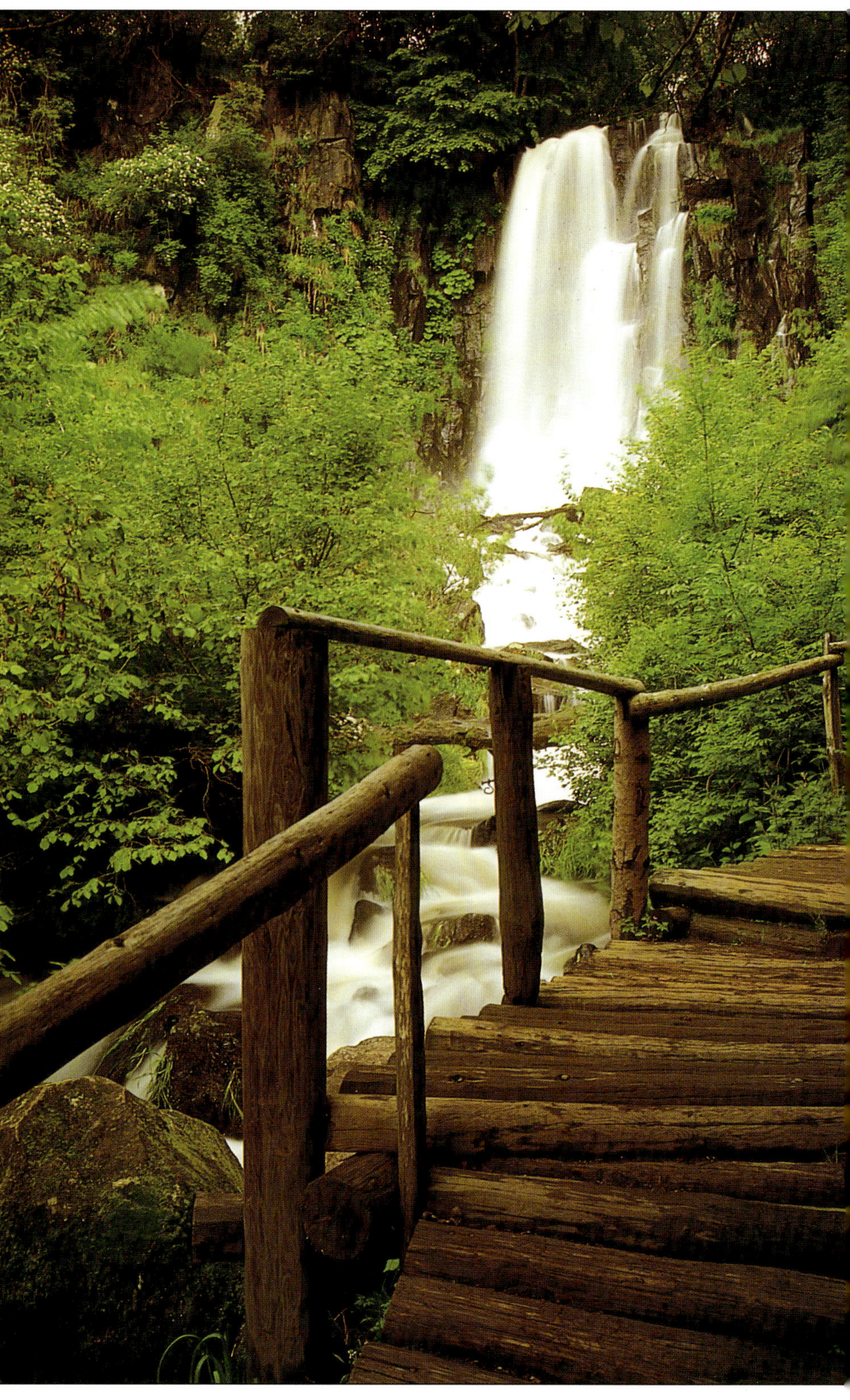

Nikon FE2 with a 28-70mm zoom lens and Fuji Velvia ISO 50 slide film, and began by including the bridge in the foreground of his first shots. Then he zoomed in to take a closer view with the fall itself in the background and enough water in the foreground to make the picture interesting.

▲ At the first waterfall they visited, Mike decided to pull back to include this attractive wooden footbridge in the foreground of a wide view. The overcast weather was perfect for capturing the moving water, and he used a Kodak Wratten 81EF filter to brighten up the rest of the shot.

While my pictures were a bit dark, Mike's exposure was perfect, and he used a Kodak Wratten 81EF filter to warm up the colours. For his last shot at this location, Mike moved right up to within five or six metres of the waterfall and shot across it from the right. It was an interesting viewpoint that clearly illustrates the waterfall's sheer power, but the grass between the rocks made the foreground look a little messy.

A raging torrent

A few miles up the road, we came across another waterfall that ran down the side of a rocky mountain. It was smaller than the first fall we had visited, but far more intense. In fact, by the time we had got near enough to photograph it we were covered with spray. I took quite a few shots but they were all ruined by spray on the lens.

Mike also found the spray a problem, but he was determined to shoot some film at this location because he thought the fast flowing

SHOOTING THE FALLS

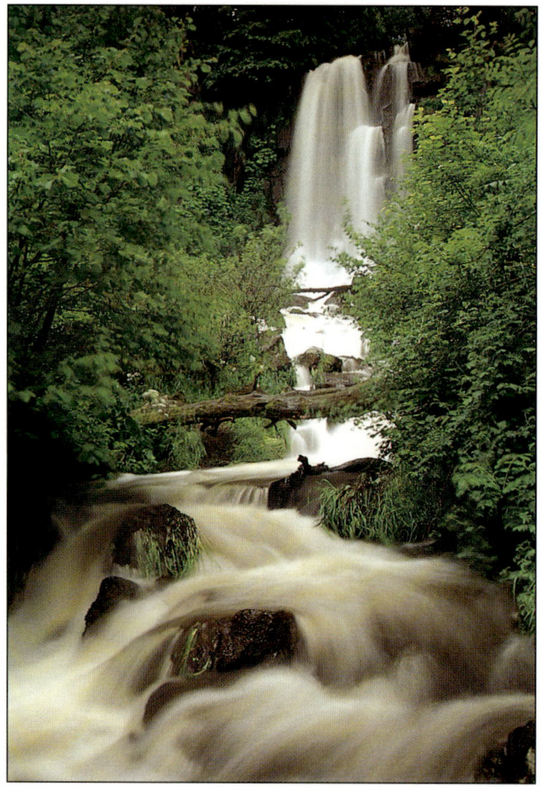

1 ◄ A DISTANT VIEW
Mike's first shot was similar to David's, but by bracketing he ended up with a much brighter picture. He made sure the fall was central in the background, and used a warm up filter to brighten up the leaves. There's plenty of moving water to balance up the picture in the foreground.

2 ▼ SIDE ON
Mike then moved up much closer to the waterfall and shot towards it from the right. This picture gives you a real sense of the fall's power, and the battered rocks make a very strong foreground. You can see how whole trees have been thrown down by the water from the mountains above.

The set up

Mike and David were photographing waterfalls in the Auvergne region of central France. They arrived during one of the heaviest rainy spells the area had ever experienced, so the waterfalls were flowing much faster than usual. The weather was cold for June, and the morning of this masterclass was heavily overcast, but the sun did come out around midday.

Mike photographed three different waterfalls to come up with an interesting combination of pictures. Both photographers used tripods, which are essential for moving water shots.

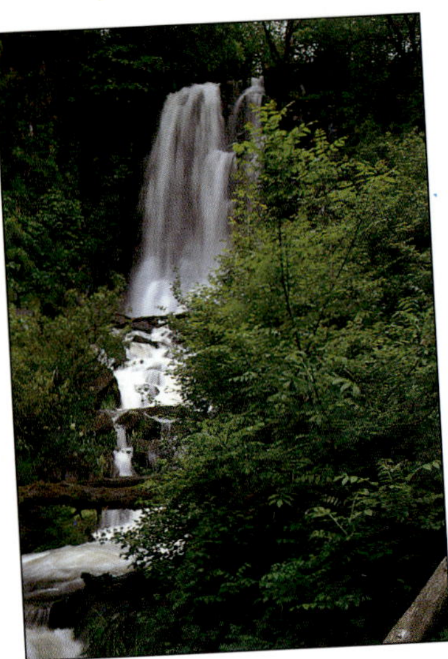

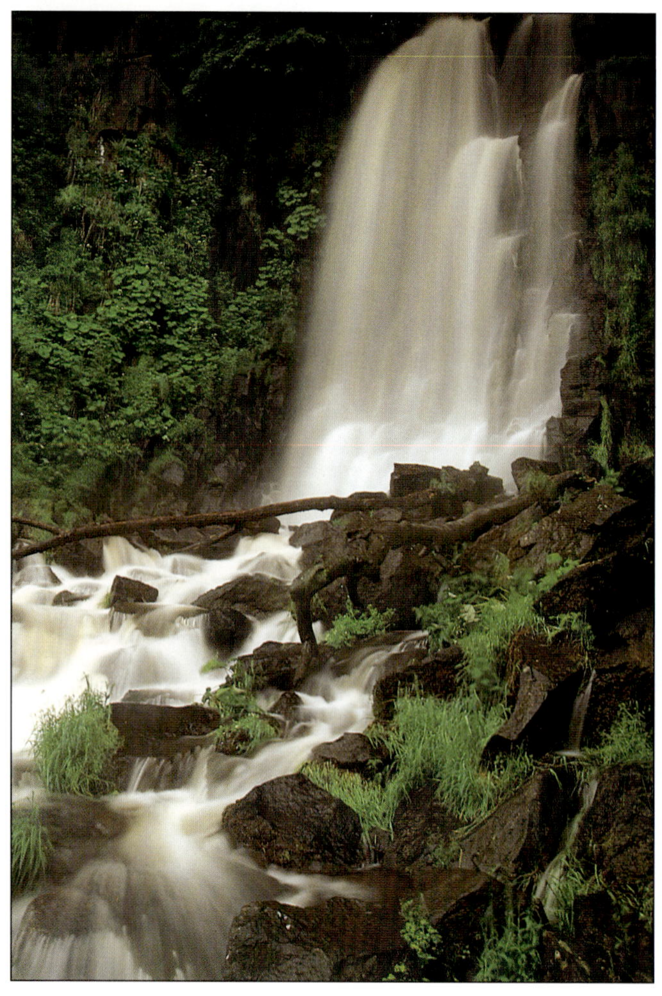

◄ *David used a slow enough exposure to blur the water in this shot, but he didn't compose it very well. There's so much messy greenery in the foreground that the waterfall is barely visible. All the foliage in the front of the frame has left the picture looking far too dark.*

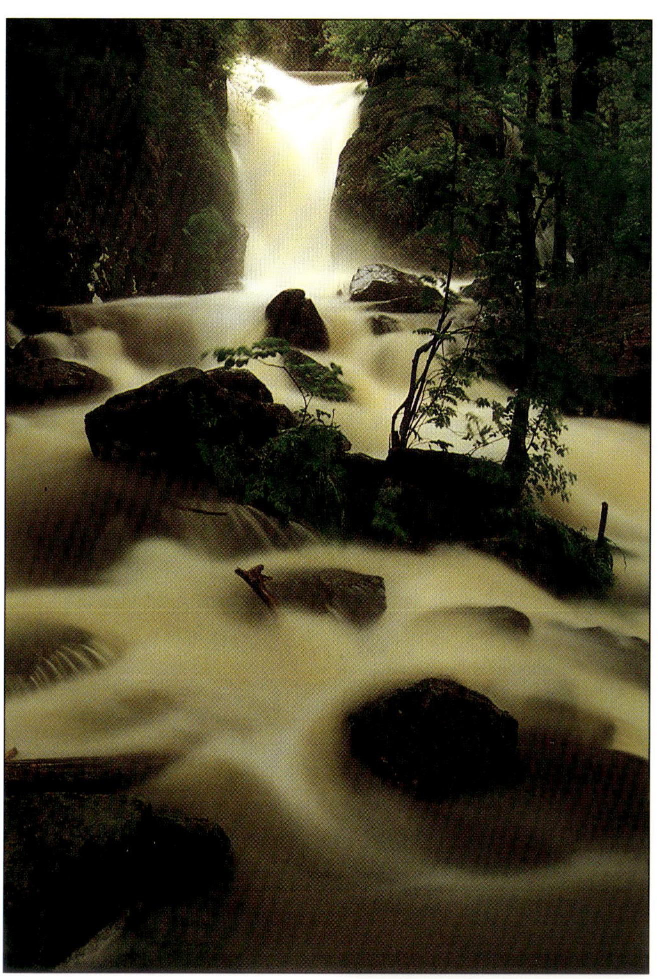

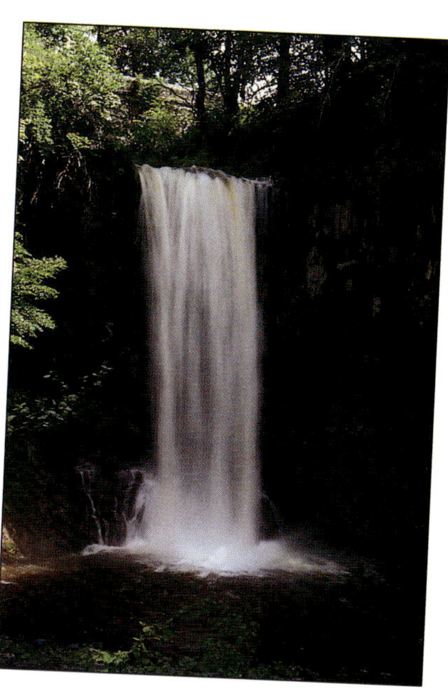

▶ *The last waterfall David and Mike visited was the most dramatic. The sheer fall of water looks very effective with a slow shutter speed, but unfortunately the centre weighted metering on David's camera was fooled by the brightness of the water and has underexposed the rest of the picture.*

Tip

Exposure lengths

The exposure length when shooting waterfalls will vary according to the conditions. If the fall's out in the open and the sky is bright you'll probably be unable to set a shutter speed slower than 1/60th sec with medium speed film. This blurs the falling water, but it will lack the misty softness that makes Mike's pictures so attractive. Add a grey 2X ND filter to set much slower speeds. Even a polarizer absorbs enough light to permit a speed of 1/15th or 1/30th sec. In wooded areas you should be able to set a speed of 1/4 sec or slower easily.

---

3 ▲ **ROUGHER WATER**
Heavy rain had turned the next fall they visited into a raging torrent. The water was so rough that all David's shots were ruined by spray on the lens. Mike wiped his lens between each exposure, and balanced his tripod half in the river so he could capture a good view of the fall itself.

4 ▶ **RAGING RIVER**
The faster water is flowing, the more spectacular it can look when blurred on film, so Mike decided to take a moving water shot of the river itself before he left. The rock and tree act as a focal point in the middle, and the river is running so fast it looks more like brown mist than water.

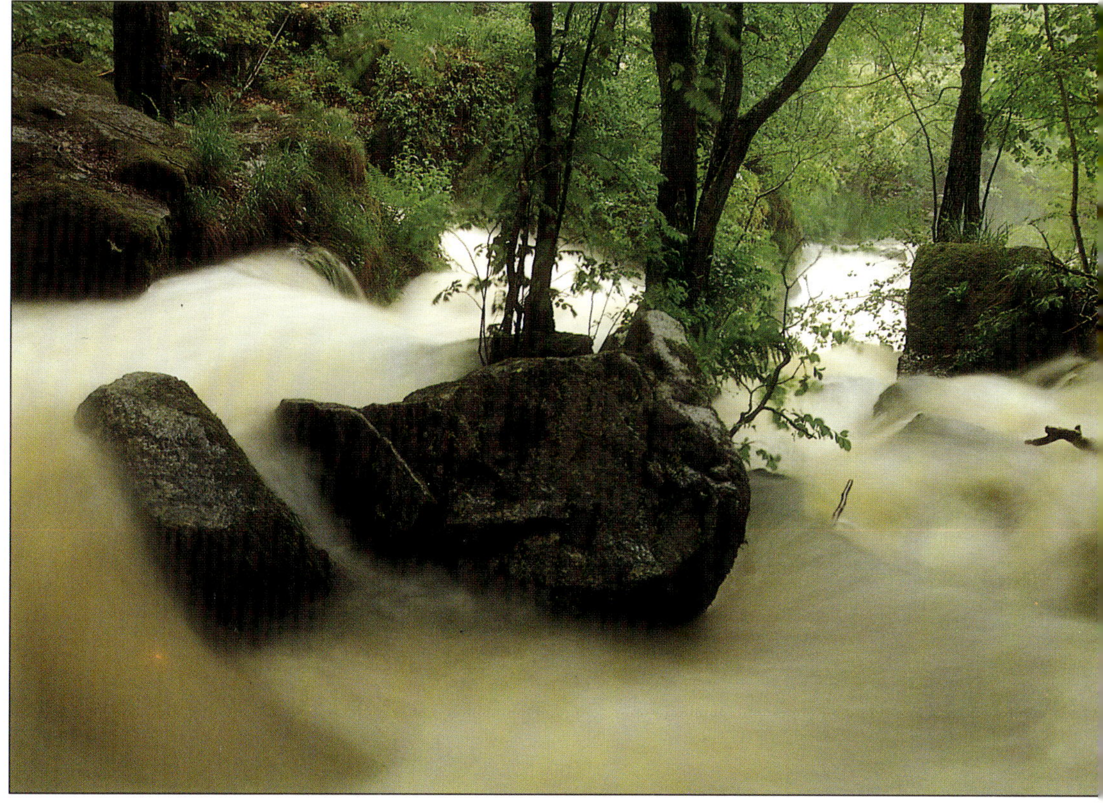

water would look spectacular on a slow exposure. He set up at the edge of the water as close as he could to the fall and took a series of one second exposures. He wiped his lens before each shot to make sure there was as little visible spray as possible. When he'd taken a shot of the water rushing through the rocks for good measure, we moved on.

The perfect fall

The next waterfall we came across was perfect for our needs – a clear, strong flow of water over a low cliff that was uninterrupted by rocks. By now the sun had come out, but for once it was a curse rather than a blessing. I was using autoexposure and unfortunately the combination of sunny highlights and bright water fooled my camera into underexposing the shot.

Mike solved these problems by cropping out as much sunlight as possible and bracketing manually to make sure he got the right exposure. The result was a lovely upright shot in which the smooth fall really stands out against the dark green background.

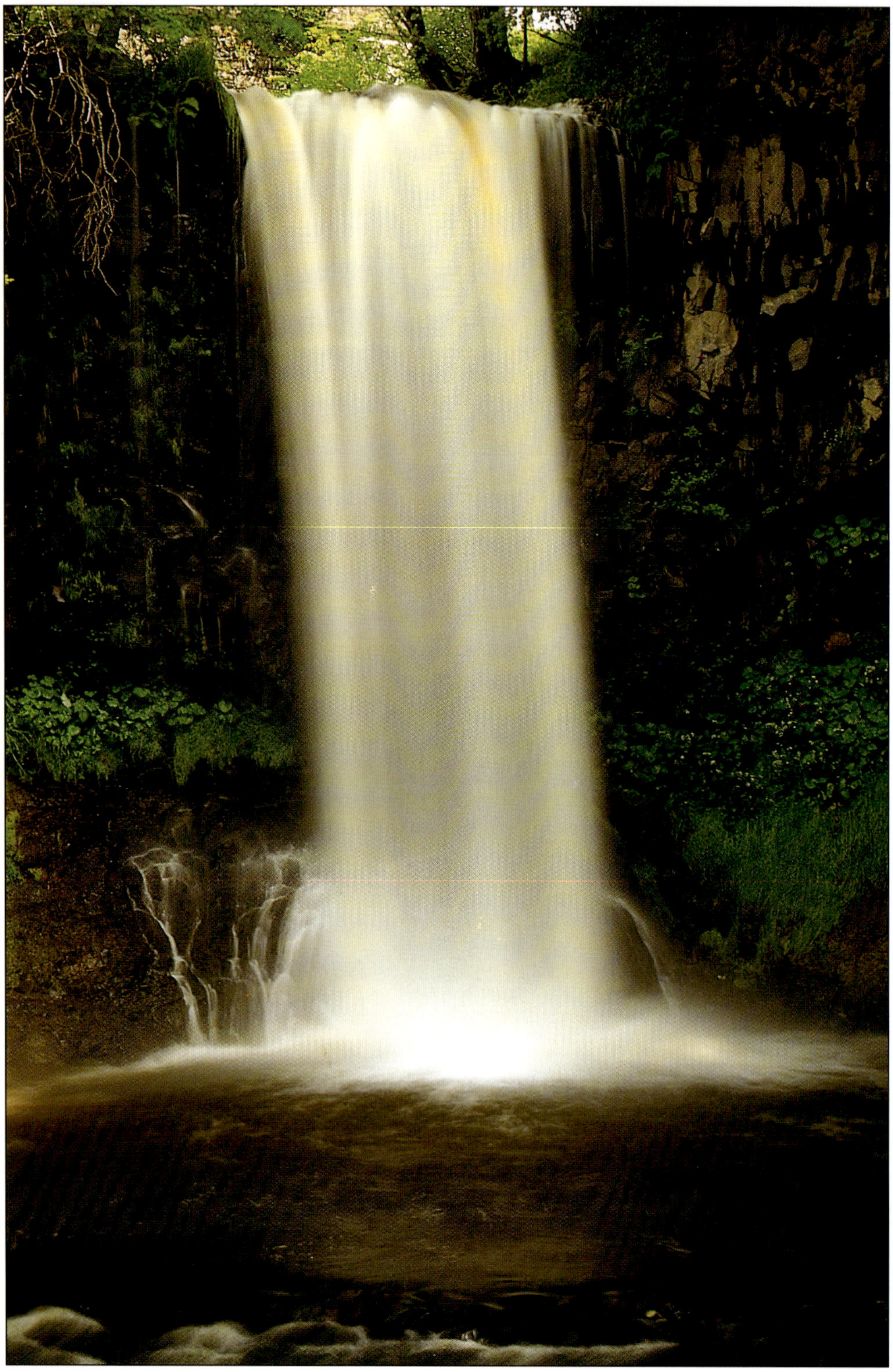

5 A SHEER FALL
The last waterfall they photographed was really spectacular. The flow of water looked beautiful when blurred by a one second exposure. The area behind the fall was very dark, so Mike exposed the film manually and bracketed very widely to make sure he achieved the right balance.

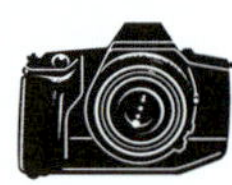

SLR tip

Even the most up to date automatic exposure systems are sometimes fooled into underexposing by water in the centre of the frame. Matrix or zone metering systems are unlikely to fall into this trap, but a centre weighted metering system like the one on the camera David used often will.

If your camera has such a system, avoid underexposure by taking another reading from a mid tone in the frame. Otherwise you can meter and bracket widely, as Mike did.

Lakescapes

Shooting a lake can be difficult in unfavourable weather conditions, but professional photographer Mike Busselle shows Steve Parker how, with a bag of filters and a keen eye, exciting results can be achieved.

Sunshine and deep blue skies add tremendously to landscape shots. How unlucky it was then that, as top photographer Mike Busselle and myself arrived at the shores of the lake of Chambron in southern France's Auvergne region, we were confronted by a grey overcast sky and a sun playing hide and seek behind the cloud formations. It didn't seem very inspiring.

I was all for going in search of a safer subject, but Mike was for staying. 'This', he told me, 'is going to be a challenge.'

We spent some time wandering round the lake to find an interesting view of the opposite bank. We took our time, hoping that the light would change for the better, but to no avail.

Eventually, Mike selected a position where one of the hills on the opposite bank sloped down to the level of the lake. A more distant hill sloped down in the opposite direction, giving a slight 'V' shape in the centre of the horizon. This, Mike informed me, looked more interesting than a flat horizon.

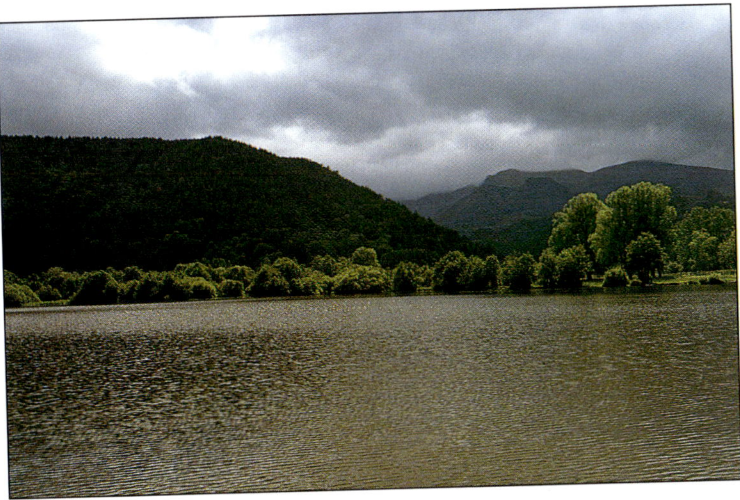

▲ *Steve's shot was from a reasonable location, but the angle of view of the 28mm lens was too wide. It caused him to include a lot of uninteresting subject matter on the left of the frame. Other problems include the dark slopes that are lacking in detail and the ripples on the water, which obscure the more interesting reflection of the hillside. As a result the shot is rather drab.*

1 WARMING UP

Mike's first shot eliminated a lot of Steve's mistakes. For a start, more accurate exposure unblocks the shadows, revealing more detail. The polarizer removes reflections from the foliage, while the graduated neutral density filter reduces the contrast between the sky and the rest of the scene. The 81C filter effectively warms up the whole scene. Mike set his zoom lens to about 40mm to crop in on the more interesting detail.

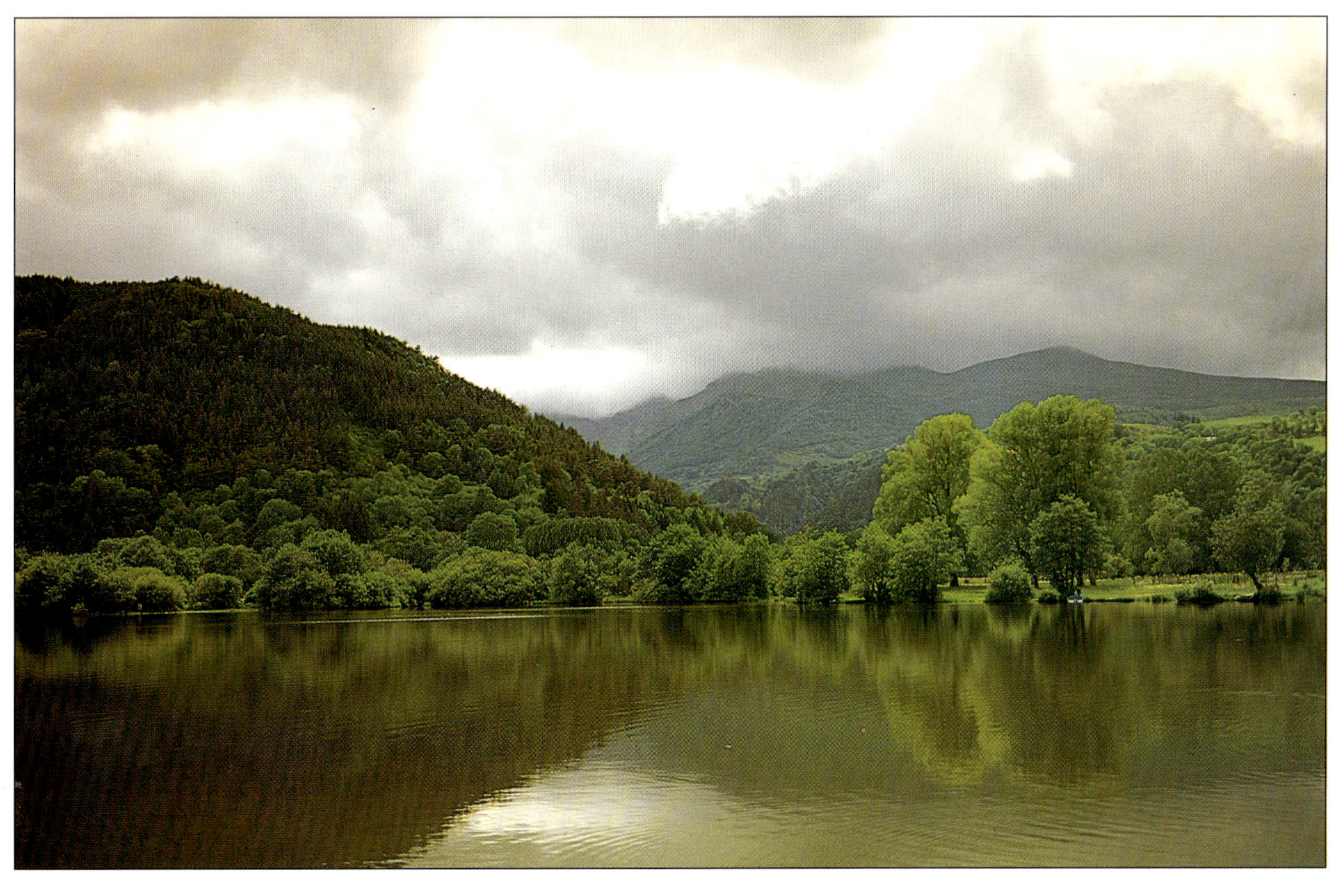

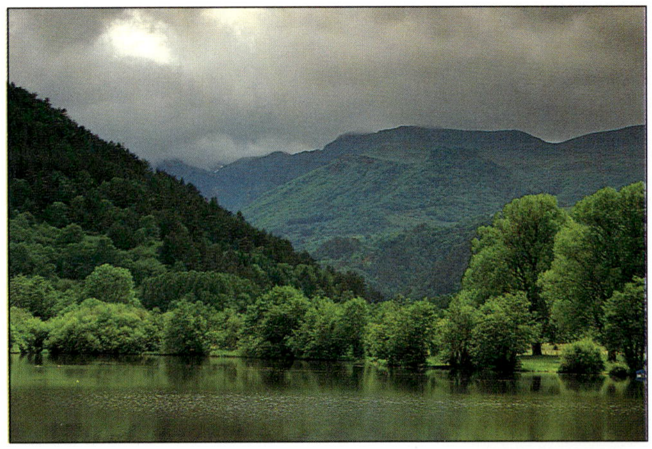

The set up

For these shots the set up was very simple. As the subject was a wide landscape, there was no call for any artificial light.

Mike and Steve walked round the shore until they found the view they wanted. If the sun had been stronger in the sky, they would have looked for a subject that wasn't in deep shadow, but as the sky was overcast, the lighting was fairly even.

Steve used an Olympus OM1 and Mike a Nikon F801s. Both shot on Fuji Velvia ISO 50 slide film.

The accessories in use were a series of filters (for Mike's shots) and an easily portable tripod used by both photographers.

2 ▲ ZOOMING IN
Mike wasn't totally happy with his initial shot. 'There's still too much irrelevant subject matter in the scene', he said. 'I'm going to crop in closer on the bottom of the slope. That's where the strong diagonals and the interesting trees are.' For this shot, Mike had the zoom set closer to its 70mm focal length than its 28mm wide angle setting.

3 ▶ PORTRAIT APPROACH
Zooming in lost the contrast between the land and the lake, cutting out the reflection of the hills in the water. Mike chose a solution Steve hadn't thought of — he concentrated on the same spot, but turned the camera round for an unusual portrait view.

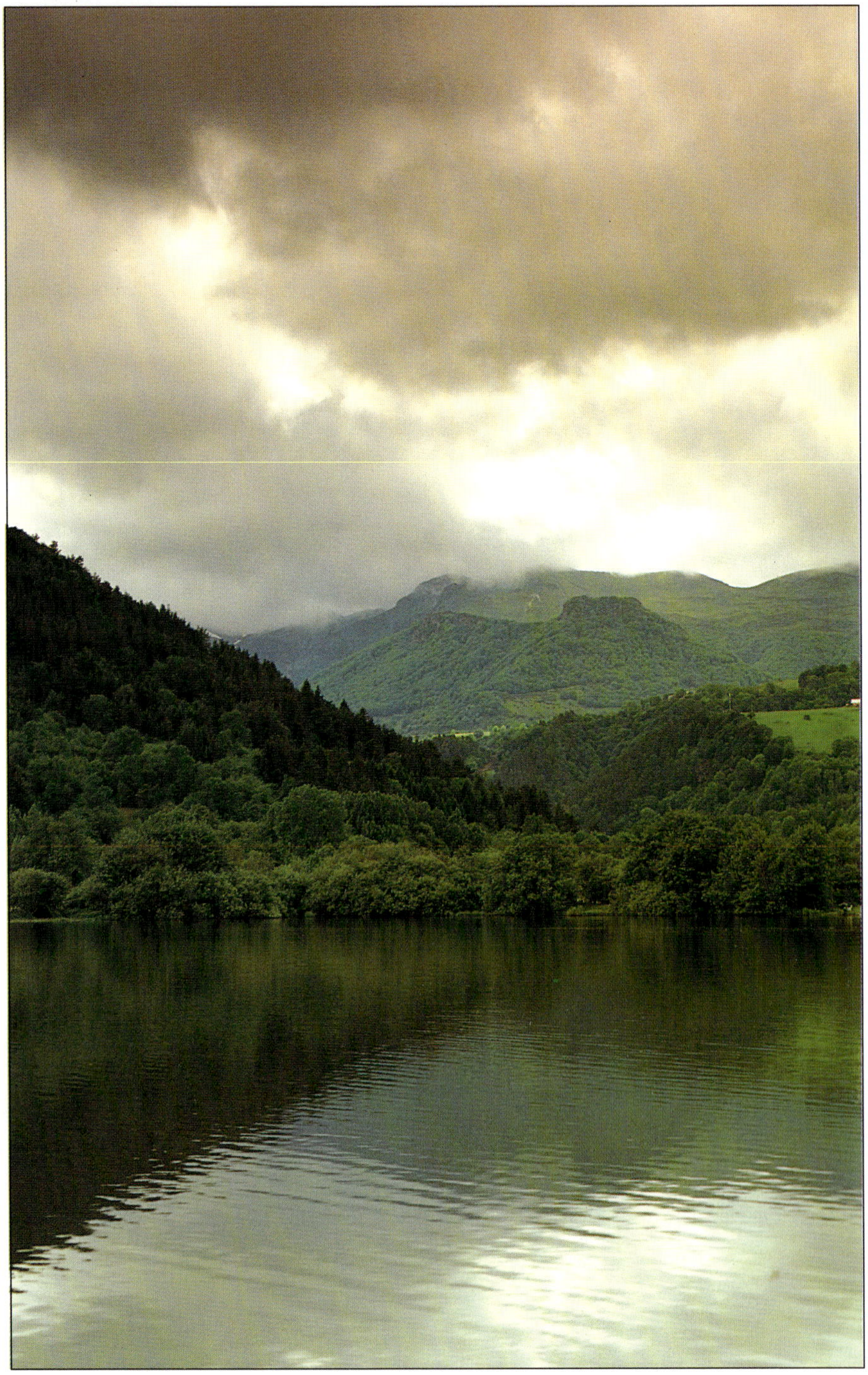

Rule of thirds

'I'll go first', I told him, removing my Olympus OM1 from its case. I had taken a number of landscapes before, and knew the secret lay in choosing a good wide angle lens to fit in as much of the scene as possible.

I fitted my 28mm f2.8 lens to the front of the camera and set about composing the shot. I borrowed Mike's tripod so that I could get the horizon straight. As we were both using slow film, Fuji Velvia ISO 50, the tripod also helped to keep the camera steady. This enabled me to use a narrower aperture without fear of camera shake.

I knew the rule of thirds was important, so I placed the horizon about a third of the way from the top of the frame to get a balanced shot. Mike waited patiently while I adjusted the tripod exactly, took a light reading and pressed the shutter release. I bracketed a little, to make sure that I achieved exactly the right exposure.

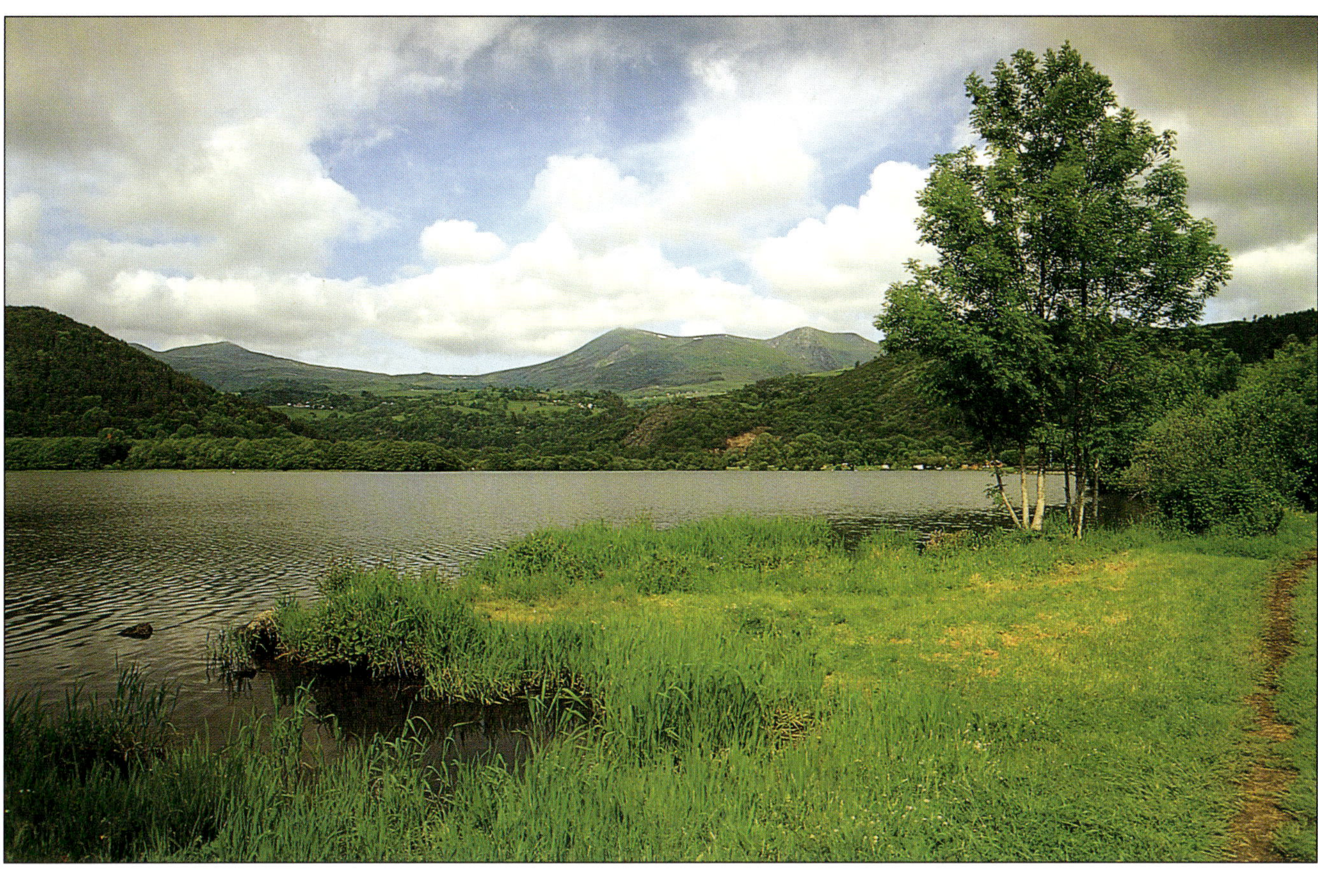

Changing composition

Mike left the tripod in the same place, and replaced my OM1 with his Nikon F801s. He was using a 28-70mm zoom, and I was surprised to see him zoom in slightly to around the 40mm mark.

'The whole of the left hand side of the frame is a bit similar', he explained. 'The V between the two hills is the most interesting part of the shot, so I want to crop in on that part of the frame.'

He tilted the camera down a nudge, and I asked him why. 'Rule of thirds', he said. 'It's not always useful, but in this case, I think it'll help.

'It would be tempting', he continued, 'to choose the horizon as the main line in this scene, but the strongest line is actually the one between the lake and the hills. As the background is more interesting than the lake, I'm going to place it a third of the way from the bottom of the frame.' I nodded.

Before taking the shot, he added a polarizing filter. 'Won't that get rid of all the light reflecting on the water?' I asked, thinking that the slight glitter on the water would add to the shot.

'We're shooting from a low angle', Mike replied, 'so it won't affect the reflections on the water. But it will cut out the reflections from the foliage to give more saturated colours.'

Mike also placed a Kodak Wratten 81C warm up filter over the lens. 'That'll bring out the greens and the yellows even more', he assured me.

'Anything else?' I asked. He went into his gadget bag again and pulled out a graduated neutral density filter. 'This', he replied 'will

4 FOREGROUND INTEREST
Mike decided the real problem with the shot was that, as the subject was so far away, there was not much depth in the scene. To overcome this, we picked up the camera gear and moved along the shore a little. This took us to a bend in the shoreline, from where we could shoot the opposite bank and include some foreground detail too. The strongest shape is the tree to the right of the frame, and Mike chose a composition that had all of the lines in the scene leading the eye to this spot from the left of the frame. To ensure sharp focus, Mike chose a wide angle setting and stopped down to f11. Despite the overcast sky, there was enough ambient light to allow this.

darken the sky and reduce contrast. By bringing the brightness of the sky and water more into line, we'll get better colour in both areas.'

After his initial shots, we moved to two more positions. Although Mike got some shots he liked, the light ran out before he could capture the picture he really wanted. Finally, we decided to come back on the following day at dawn, to see if the early morning sun would bathe the lake in our much desired warm glow. Happily, it did.

Neutral density grads

When choosing a neutral density graduated filter, you may wish to meter from the sky and ground, and choose a filter which reduces the difference between the two areas to two or three stops. Don't expect a neutral density graduated filter to totally eliminate the difference in brightness. Unless the sky is deep blue, it will look very stormy if it is the same tone as the ground.

5 ▶ GETTING IN CLOSE

Before we left, Mike wanted to try a couple more shots of different scenes on the lake. The lake of Chambron narrows at one end, and we found an interesting spot surrounded by trees with a large boulder coming out of the water. Mike removed the graduated neutral density filter, but kept the polarizer and the warm up filter fitted. It's the interesting shapes and bright colours that make this shot.

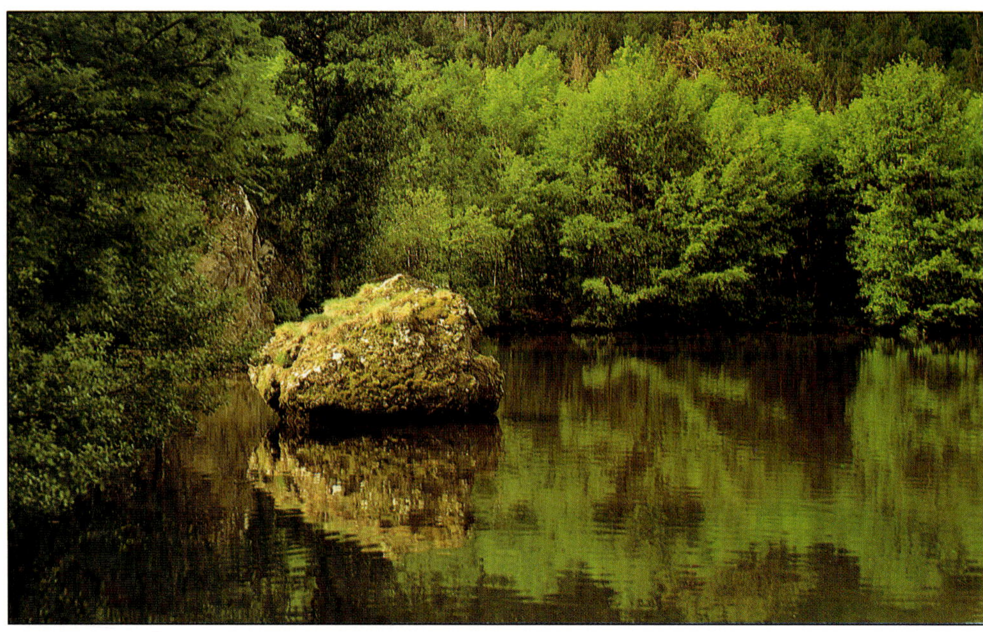

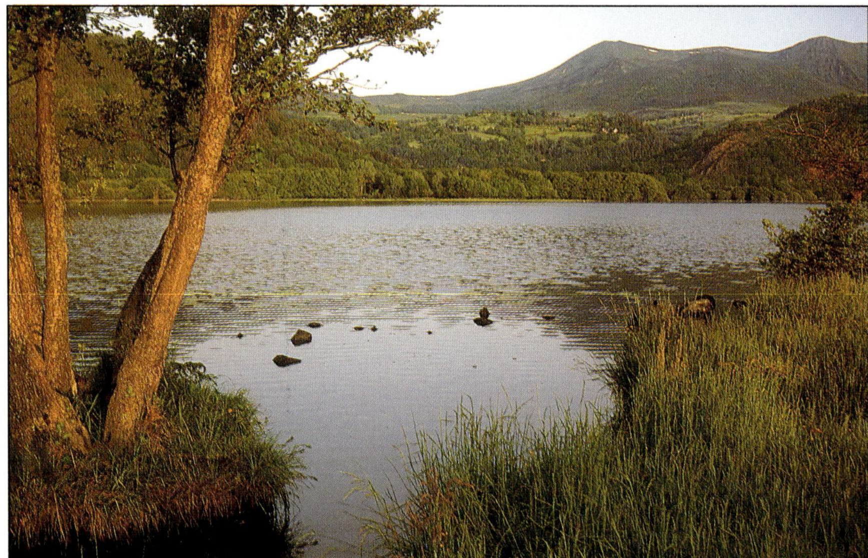

6 ◀ MORNING GLOW

Although Mike got a number of shots he liked, he was still after one more before we left. However, the light was beginning to disappear. We packed up for the evening, but returned bright and early next morning to make one more attempt before moving on. This shot contained everything we were after – interesting shapes in the background, bright foreground detail and the strong line of the tree framing the shot on the left hand side. The post-dawn light gives a warm glow that is accentuated by the warm up filter. The polarizer is also in use here.

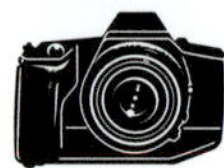 ## SLR tips

❏ On an overcast day such as this one, when you are using a narrow aperture to achieve a wide depth of field and a slow film speed for a high quality result, you will inevitably have to set a slow shutter speed to obtain the correct exposure.

This means that you have to use a tripod. However, even if you are shooting on a bright day and using a wide aperture, you should still make use of a tripod.

Getting the horizon absolutely straight is difficult when hand holding the camera. Even if you line it up perfectly level, you may still knock the camera on to a slight angle when you press the shutter release.

Slightly tilting horizons may not be noticeable when you are looking through the lens, but they are when you view your results.

❏ To use a number of filters at the same time, you need a 'system' filter holder. Mike's enables him to use three filters – for example, a neutral density grad, a polarizer and a warm up filter (Mike favours either an 81C or an 81EF).

Remember that each filter you use will reduce the amount of light entering the lens, each time necessitating a slower shutter speed. This is another reason why tripods are essential.

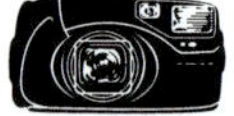 ## Compact tip

❏ Most basic compacts are equipped with fixed focal length lenses – normally around 33-35mm. This makes them quite suitable for the majority of landscape shots.

If you have a zoom compact, however, don't automatically select the wide angle setting. Survey the scene very carefully and pick out the most interesting part of the landscape before you shoot. If this is some distance away, you may obtain a better picture if you zoom in to the telephoto setting.

Be careful of foreground subjects if you are using a telephoto lens, however. The narrow depth of field is likely to throw them out of focus.

Weather conditions

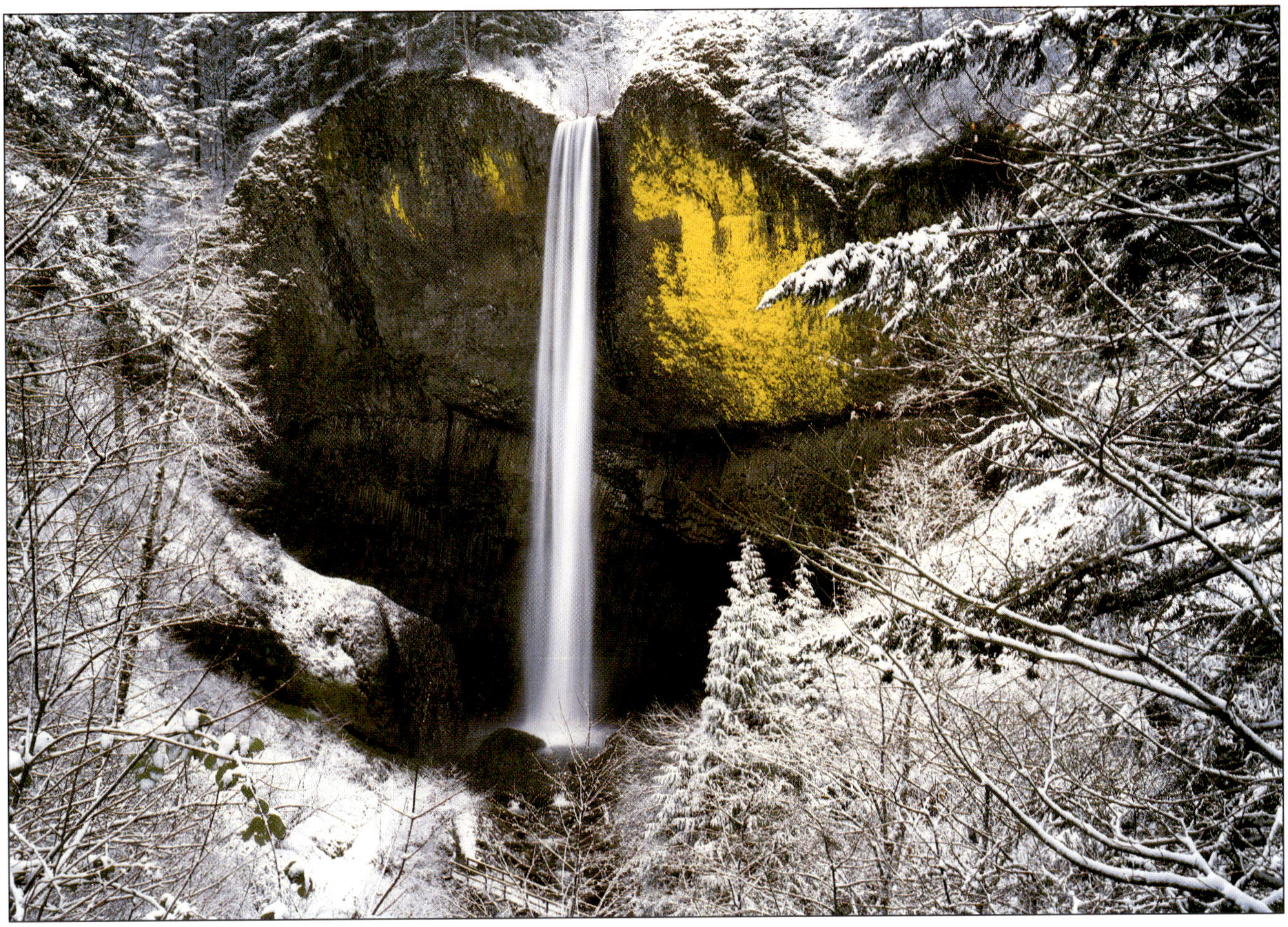

Poor weather shouldn't be an excuse to put your camera away. If you know what you are doing, you can get great pictures in rain, fog, haze and snow.

Photographers are often put off by bad weather, only venturing out with a camera when it's a bright, sunny day. But there are some interesting, and often unusual, shots to be had when the weather takes a turn for the worse.

On the next few pages, we look at various ways of photographing snow and ice. Dramatic, snow-heavy clouds, frosty mornings and falling snowflakes can all be readily captured if you are prepared to dress both yourself, and your camera, up warmly.

Moving on to rain and storms, we show you how to keep the water out of your camera and into your pictures. The scope for dramatic pictures is huge – from lightning and rainbows to spider webs covered in raindrops.

Finally, we look at how to capture moody, monochromatic pictures in the mist and fog; and discover the ways in which haze adds atmosphere to a photo, such as shimmering heat on a road or the blurring of distant mountains.

▲ **WINTER WONDERLAND**
A fall of snow has transformed this landscape into a fairytale scene. The scattering of light by the snow and clouds means that every detail of the scene is clearly visible. A slow shutter speed recorded the waterfall as a blur.

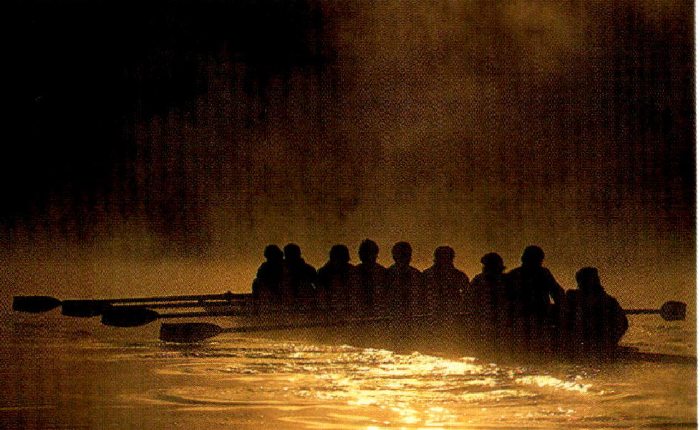

◀ **MORNING GLORY**
Early morning mist has added an eerie atmosphere to this river scene. The mist also helps the silhouettes of the oarsmen to stand out clearly against the dark hills beyond.

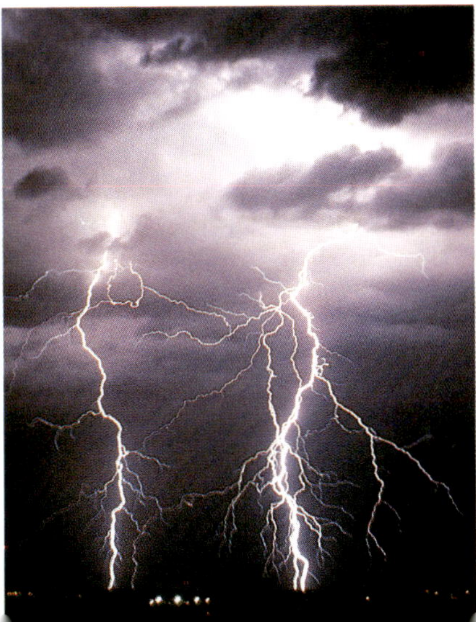

▶ **STORMY WEATHER**
Lightning is one of the most dramatic products of a storm. A tripod and a long exposure were all that were needed to capture this impressive shot.

Photographing snow

From the bleakness of a landscape blanketed in white to traditional 'Christmas card' scenes, snow creates some wonderful opportunities for photographers. Fresh fallen snow is the most appealing because it looks clean, crisp and white.

But snow alone doesn't make a great picture – you need to include some other detail in the frame to break up the scene. A tree, person or river works well and provides that all important focal point.

Exposure The most important thing to remember when shooting snow is that it is a highly reflective surface. This means that you will get a falsely high meter reading from it, resulting in pictures that are underexposed. The snow will appear grey rather than white.

Therefore, you need to compensate for this. If the snow fills the frame, overexpose by 1 1/2-2 stops; but if half the frame is blue sky, less compensation is needed (1/2-1 stop). To be on the safe side, bracket a few shots to get the exact result you want.

Portraits Whether snowballing,

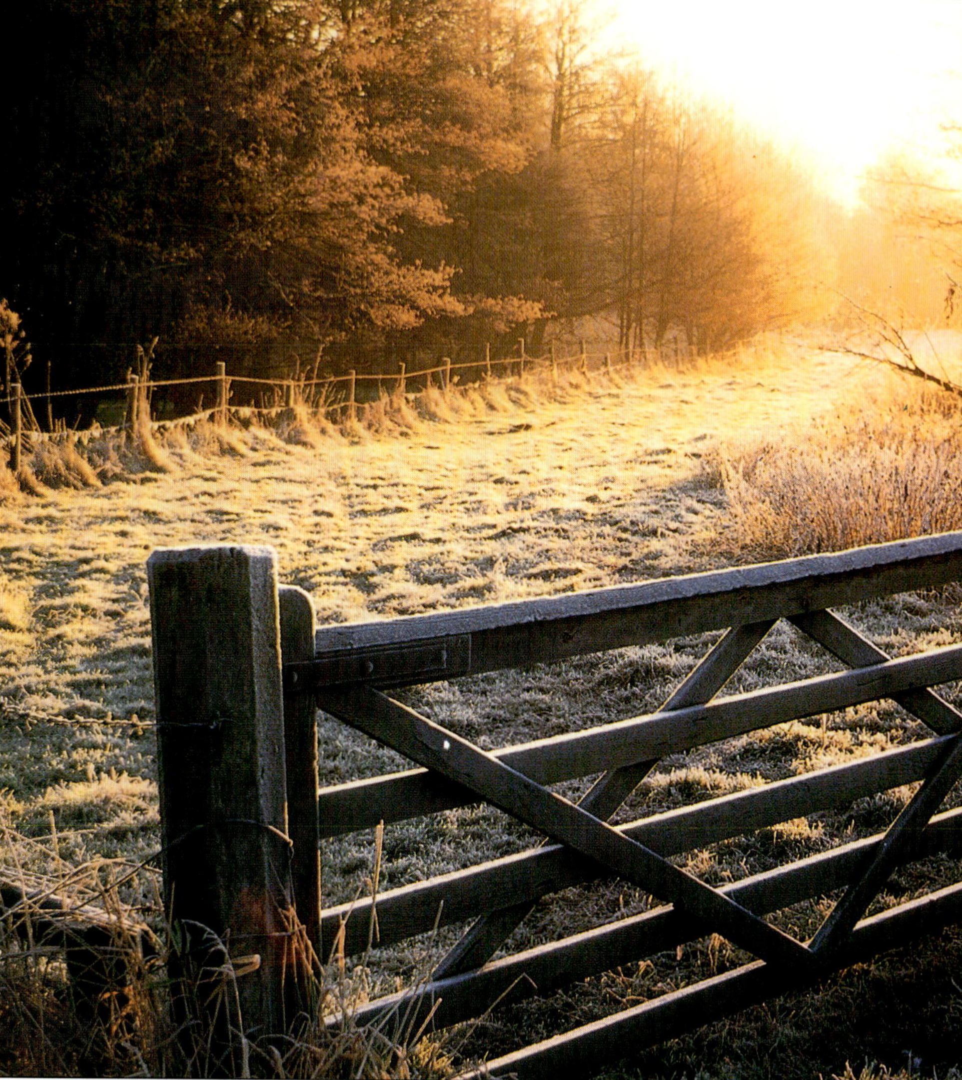

▶ **TINGED WITH PINK**
The low winter sun has transformed this landscape by bathing it in a warm, pink glow. Without it, this scene would have lacked the colours and the shadows which pick out the various textures of the land.

putting the finishing touches to a snowman or sledging down a hillside, kids look great playing in the snow, wrapped up in their colourful winter woollies.

Snow acts as a useful shadow fill-in for outdoor portraits, but you need to take a reading from your subject's face, or from your own hand, to get the right exposure for their skin. Alternatively, you can take an incident light reading.

Altered hues Snow reflects the colour of its surroundings and this can greatly affect the mood of your

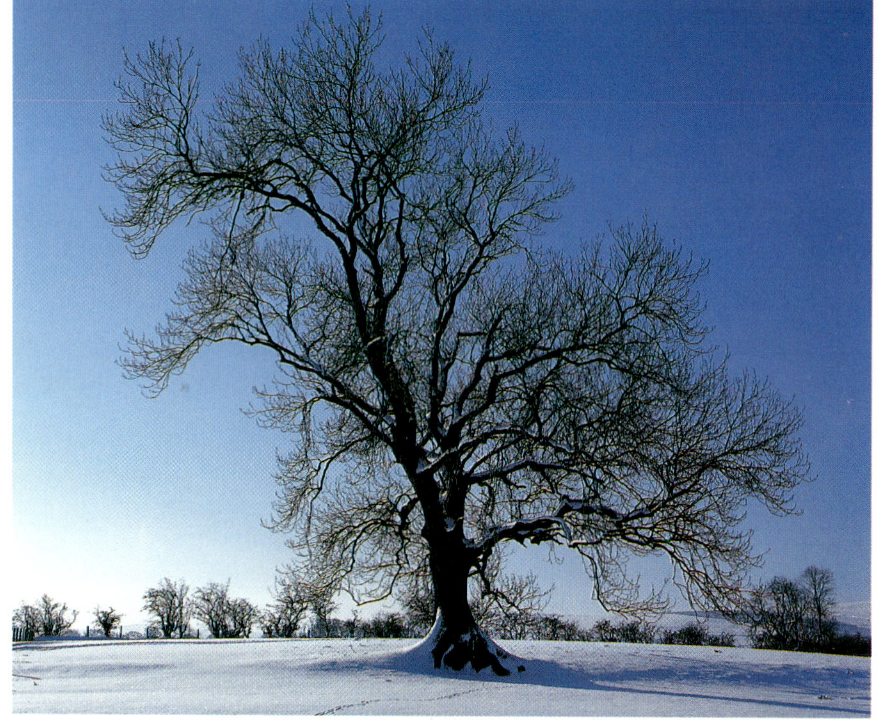

◀ **WINTER BRANCHES**
Snow-covered landscapes lend themselves to simple, bold compositions. In this picture, the combination of a clear blue sky and snow-covered ground bring out the stark silhouette of a leafless tree.

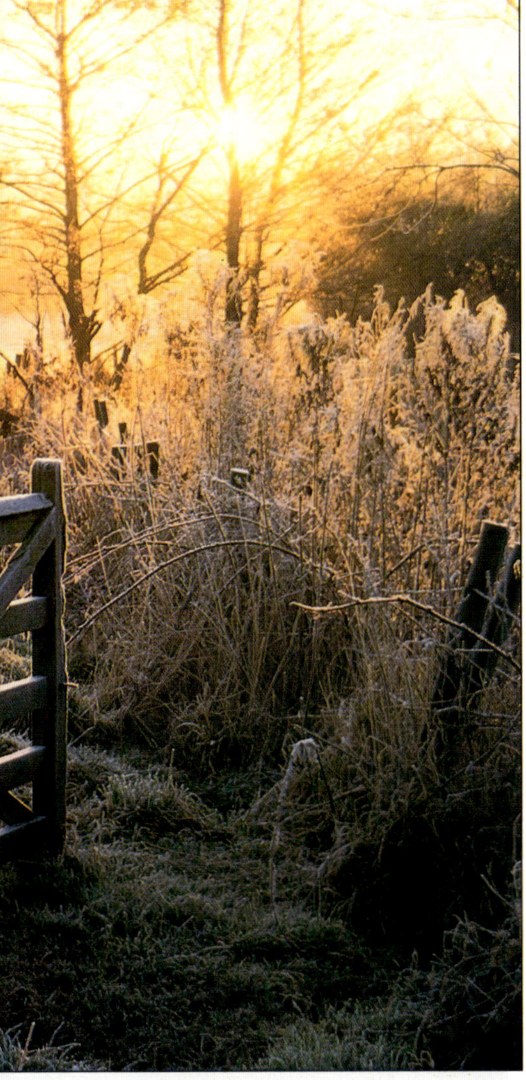

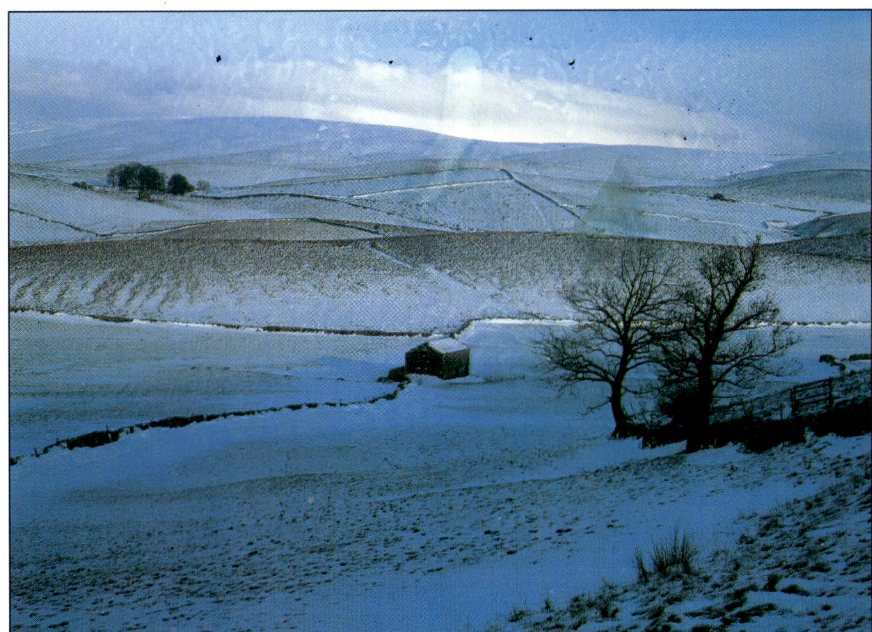

▲ FEELING BLUE
This landscape is awash with blue because the snow, most noticeably in the shadows, has reflected the blue sky.

This cold cast emphasizes the isolation of the farmhouse and the chilliness of the wintry morning.

shots. When the sun is low in the sky, snow has a warm orange/pink glow to it. The angle of the sun also helps to reveal the texture and contours of the land.

Or you may prefer to take advantage of the chilly effect when snow reflects a clear, blue sky. You can use a pale blue filter or tungsten balanced film to exaggerate this cold look. (If you want the snow to look white, fit a skylight or warm up filter.)

Capturing falling snowflakes on film can look very atmospheric and wintry too. A shutter speed of 1/125th sec should be fast enough to freeze them, while a speed of 1/30th sec will produce an attractive blurred effect.

Tip — Protection

If you're using your camera outside a great deal, it will need protecting. For maximum cover, put it in a plastic bag with an opening for the lens. Then fit a UV filter over the lens and attach a lens hood.

Batteries can seize up in wintry weather, too, so tuck your camera into your coat between shots, and if you are out for a long while, take spare sets of batteries with you for both camera and flash so you can alternate them while keeping one set warm in your pocket.

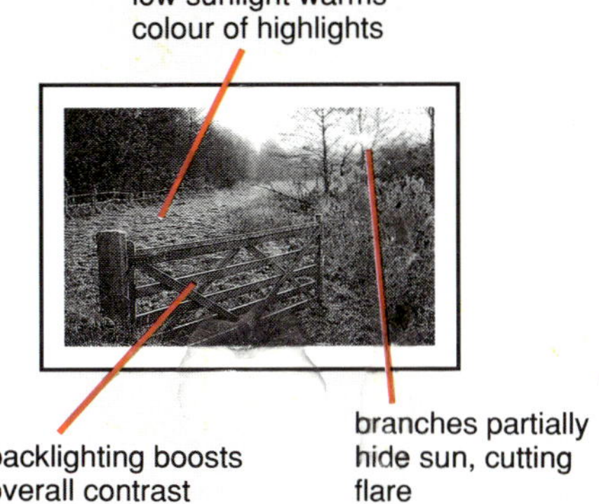

► SNOW-BOUND SYMMETRY
A thick covering of snow hides colour, detail and form, creating a stark, monochromatic landscape. Here, the absence of distracting elements helps focus attention on the symmetrical pattern formed by the trees.

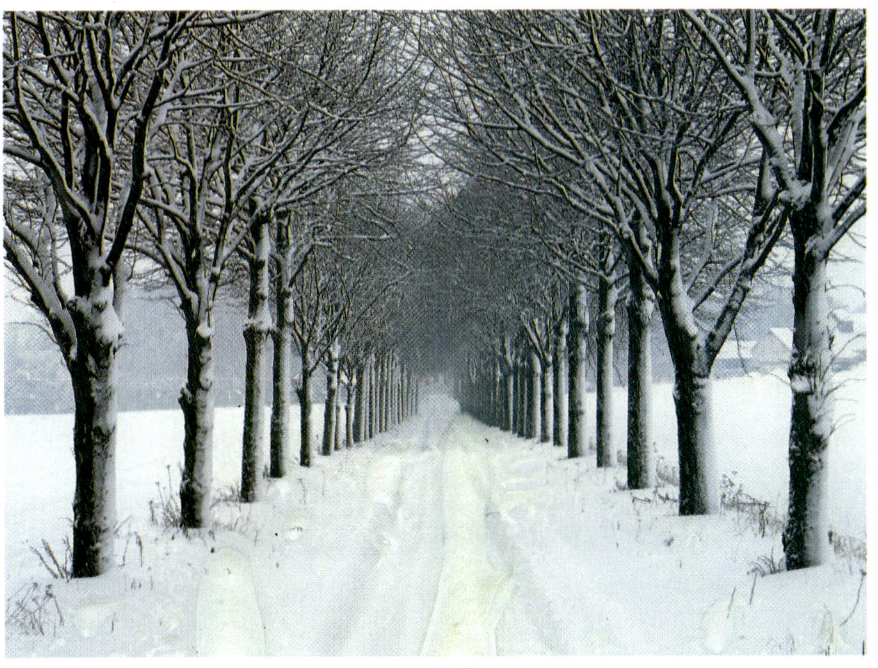

Frosty mornings

In very cold weather, water droplets freeze overnight, coating everything in sight with a thick layer of ice crystals. Although you have to get up very early to capture frost before it melts, the results are well worth the effort.

Take a low viewpoint to contrast white, encrusted branches against the clear, blue sky that often accompanies a frosty morning. Use a polarizing filter to deepen the blue of the sky, and heighten the contrast further.

Frost-encrusted cobwebs look spectacular, especially when the frost starts to melt. Position your camera so that the sun adds sparkle to the crystals, and shoot against an out of focus background.

Ice works

Ice, too, can produce some attractive, chilly pictures. Keep an eye out for icicles hanging from drainpipes and car bumpers. Or capture delicate ice patterns on windows by moving in close and using a telephoto or macro lens to fill the frame.

When photographing icicles you can create an impressive starburst effect of the sun by positioning it behind the tip of an icicle and using a narrow aperture.

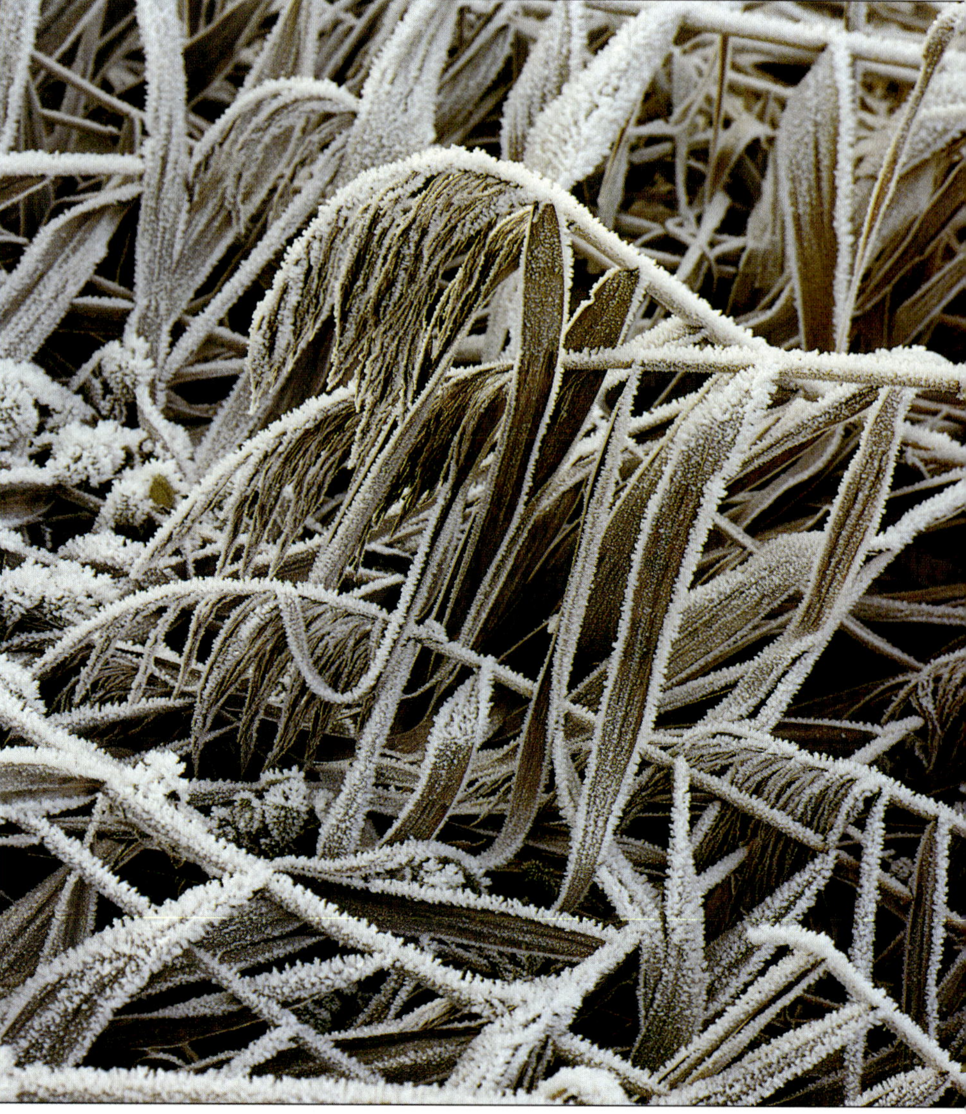

▲ **FROSTY LOOKS**
To catch superb hoar frost pictures such as this one you need to be an early bird. The photographer used an 80mm telephoto lens to fill the frame and capture as much detail as possible. An overcast sky kept the image monochromatic and gave a slightly blue tinge to the scene.

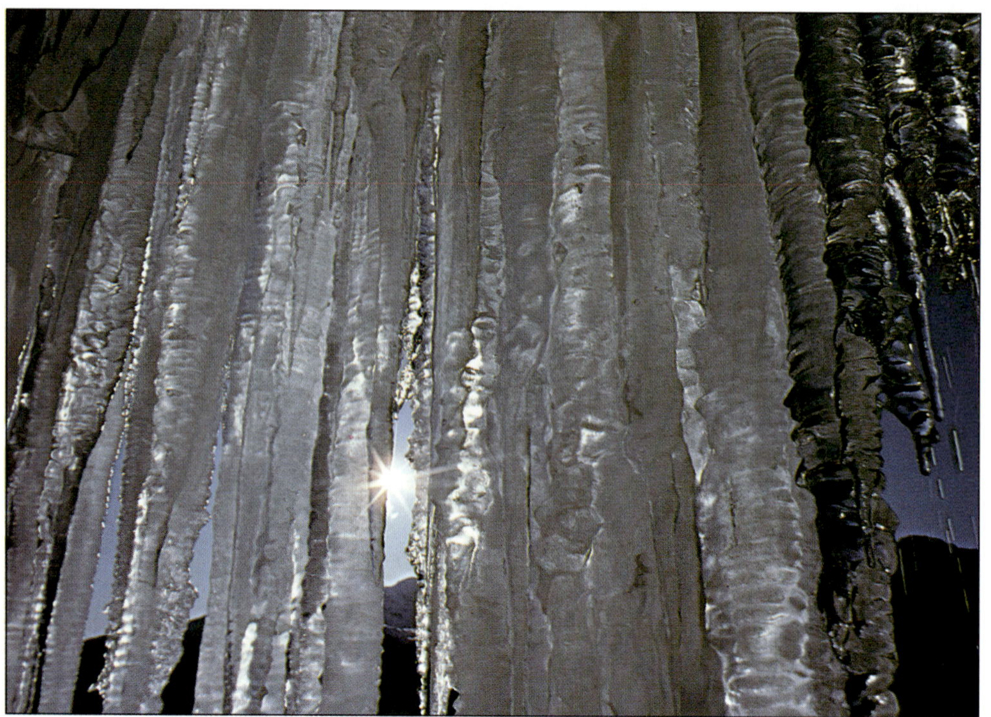

◀ **FROZEN FINGERS**
Icicles are not a common occurrence so it is well worth taking plenty of shots when you come across some. Here, the photographer made sure that the icicles were backlit to reveal their texture and translucency.

Rain and storms

Low light levels and grey skies needn't mean dull pictures. The changing light and colours which accompany rainy days offer tremendous creative scope to the photographer who's prepared to get a little wet.

In many parts of the world the weather rarely stays the same for long. Sooner or later the wind changes direction bringing the rain clouds along with it, if only briefly. The dark, looming clouds that gather just before a storm breaks can produce some particularly dramatic scenes.

Look out for shafts of light which appear when the sun is partly hidden behind a cloud, picking out a church spire or clump of trees, say, like a spotlight on a stage. Or capture the menacing shadows thrown on to the land by oncoming clouds.

When storm clouds mask the sun, it can be tricky to expose correctly to deal with the contrast. It's a good idea to bracket your shots since underexposed pictures of clouds often have more impact.

Use a graduated filter to exaggerate the darkness of an overcast sky, while leaving the landscape unaffected. Or use a red filter with black and white film to darken a blue sky, creating the impression of an impending summer storm.

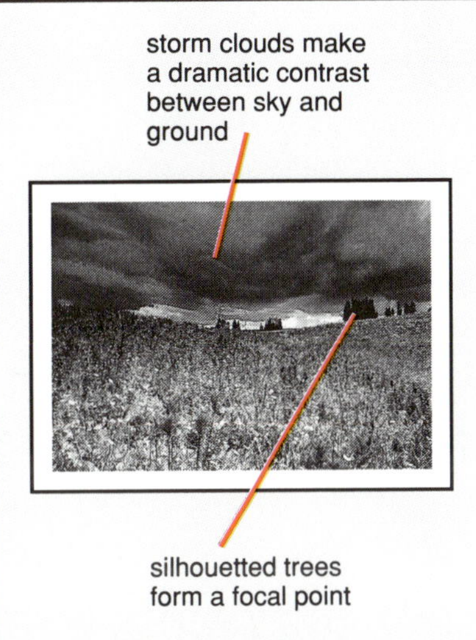

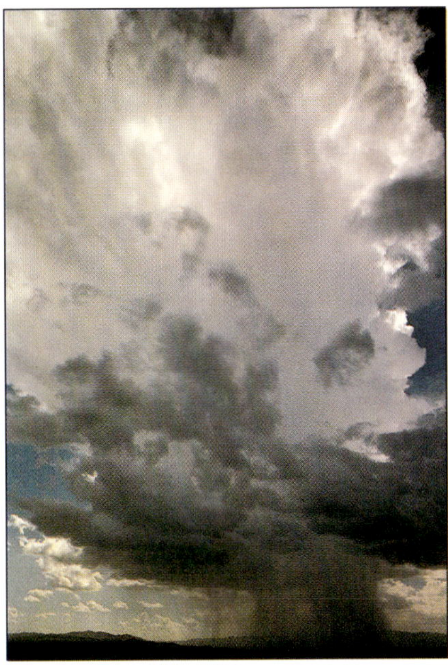

▲ IN A WHIRL
Using the portrait format helps to fill the frame with the sky and also draws the eye down to the tornado columns on the horizon.

▼ GATHERING STORM
By dividing the frame equally between the foreground and gathering clouds above, the photographer has captured the tension before the storm breaks.

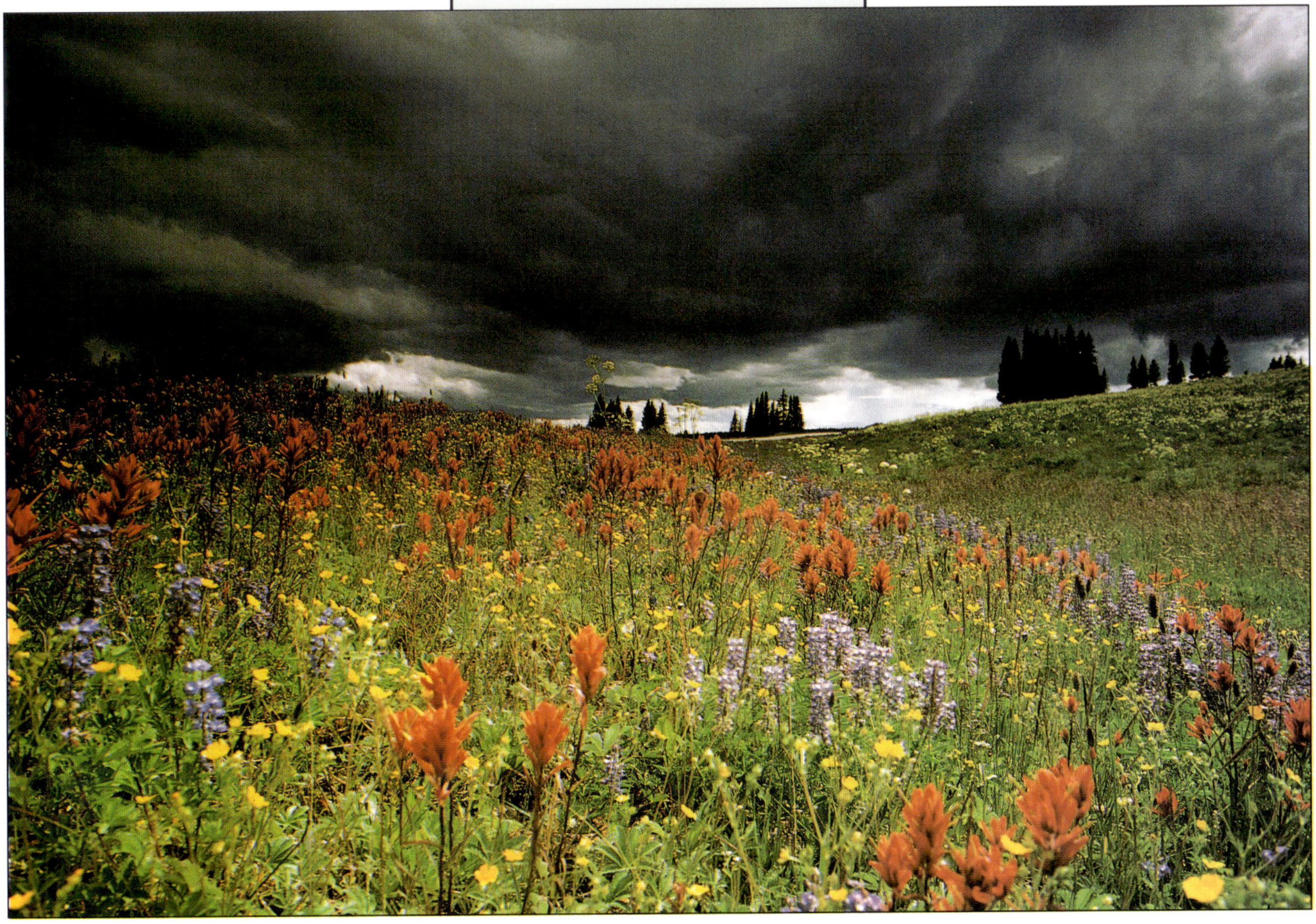

Shooting in the rain

There are plenty of subjects to photograph once the heavens finally open and the rain comes down. Close-ups of rain splattering into puddles, interesting patterns formed by a sea of umbrellas and raindrops on windows are all evocative. It is often a time for recording unusual wildlife too – some creatures only come out when it's wet.

When it's raining, lighting conditions are similar to those of a stormy sky. The light is bluer than it appears to the eye, and often very dim. It is tempting to load up with high speed film so that you can use fast shutter speeds. However, you really need to use slow film to make the most of the weak colours and poor light.

Because it's transparent, rain is more difficult to capture in motion than snow. To shoot individual raindrops you need a fast shutter speed and backlighting against a dark background. This is quite a tall order, so do grab the chance for some stunning shots if you come across these conditions.

However, the best sense of raininess often comes from your choice of subject. People with umbrellas, children in wellington boots, puddles on pavements, wet, shiny roads and animals sheltering under trees all give photos a strong feeling of rainy weather.

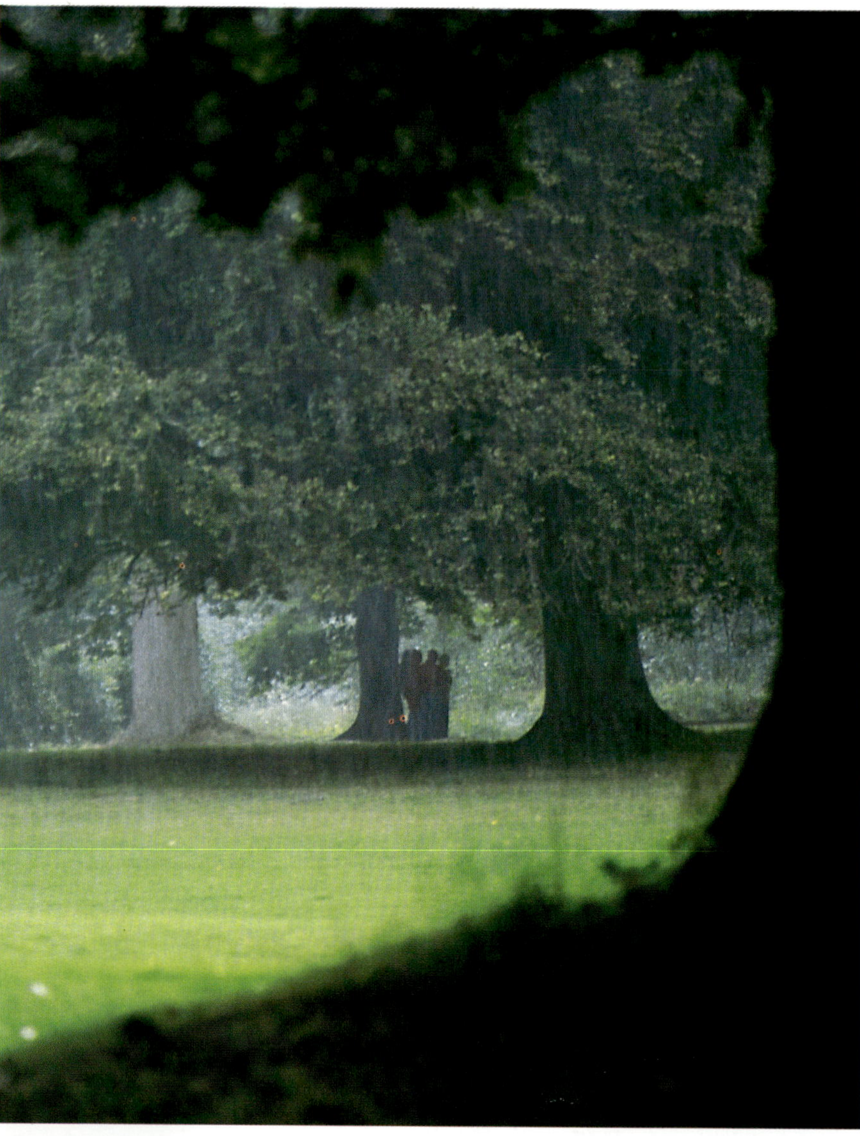

▲ SUMMER SHOWERS
The inclusion of people sheltering under a distant tree reflects the melancholy atmosphere surrounding this shot of a rain-soaked landscape. By using the tree in the foreground as a natural frame, the photographer cleverly suggests that he too is sheltering from the downpour.

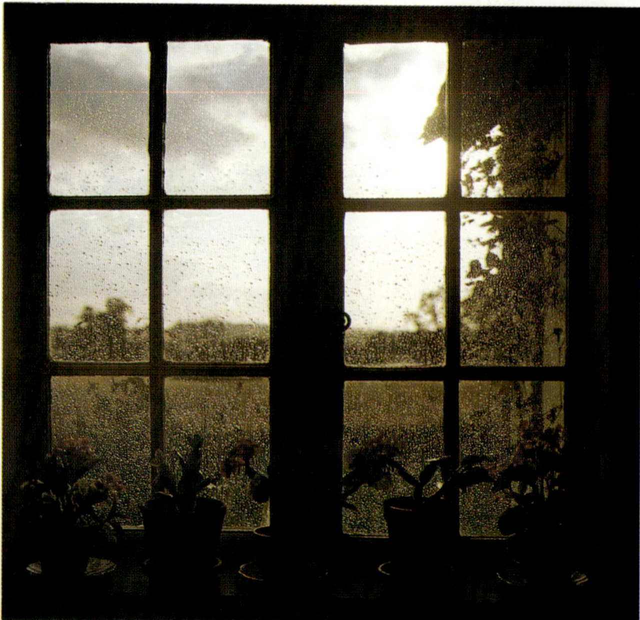

◀ RED AND DRIPPING
You needn't venture outside to capture a rainy scene. Backlighting places the window frame in silhouette and also helps to reveal the translucency of the drops of water. The red flowers add just the right amount of colour to this otherwise moody, monochromatic scene.

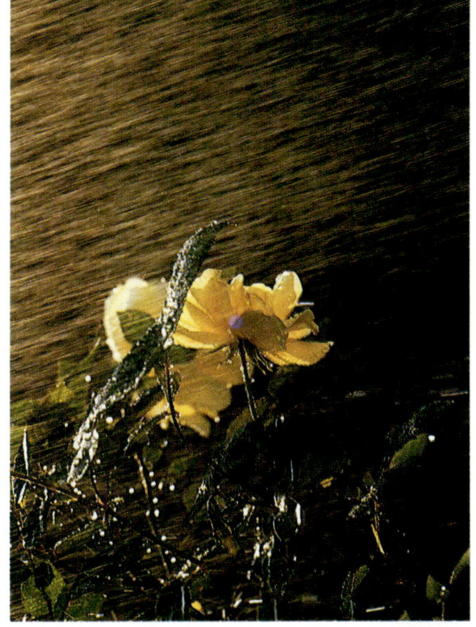

▲ BACKLIT RAIN
When you do come across backlit rain against a dark background you can capture some impressive shots of falling rain, because the droplets show up clearly. A carefully chosen shutter speed has blurred the falling sheets of rain.

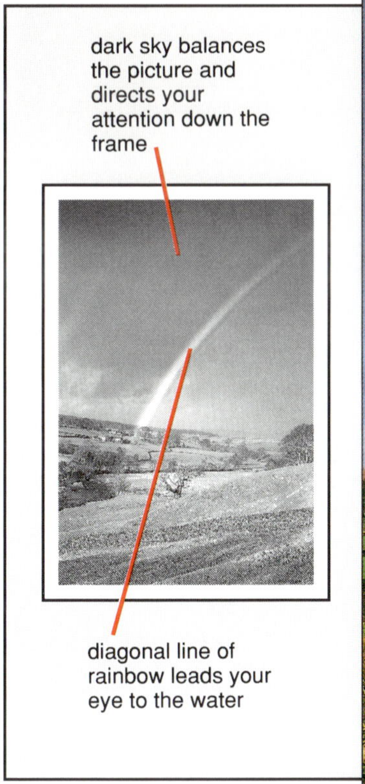

Rainbows are a rare bonus in any skyscape – but you have to act fast, because they disappear just as quickly as they show. Rainbows occur when the sun comes out while it is still raining. Each raindrop works like a tiny prism, splitting the light up into all its constituent colours.

Use a telephoto lens to bring the rainbow closer, and intensify the colours by underexposing by one or two stops. If you can see most, or all, of the rainbow use a wide angle lens to include as much of it in the frame as you can.

Calm after the storm The moments after the rain stops are magical too, but you need to be out in the rain in the first place to catch them. The air is very clear and objects look shiny, as if painted with a coat of nail varnish. Colours are more saturated after rain – think of rain-washed cars, shiny leaves and bright paintwork.

dark sky balances the picture and directs your attention down the frame

diagonal line of rainbow leads your eye to the water

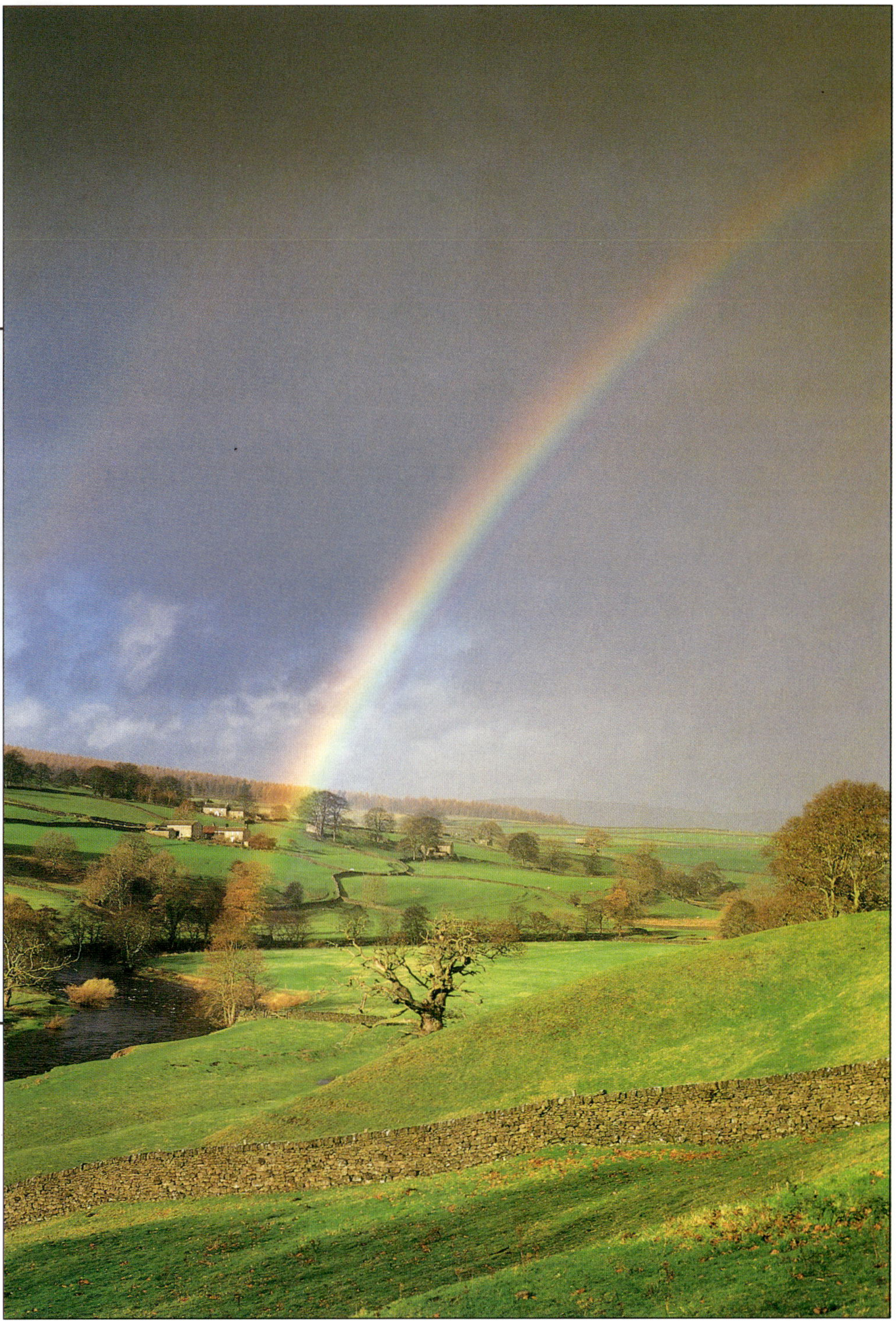

▶ RAINBOW DAYS
In order to see, and so photograph, a rainbow you need to have the sun behind you. Here, the photographer slightly underexposed the shot to intensify the colours of the rainbow, and to heighten the contrast between the storm clouds and the sunlit land.

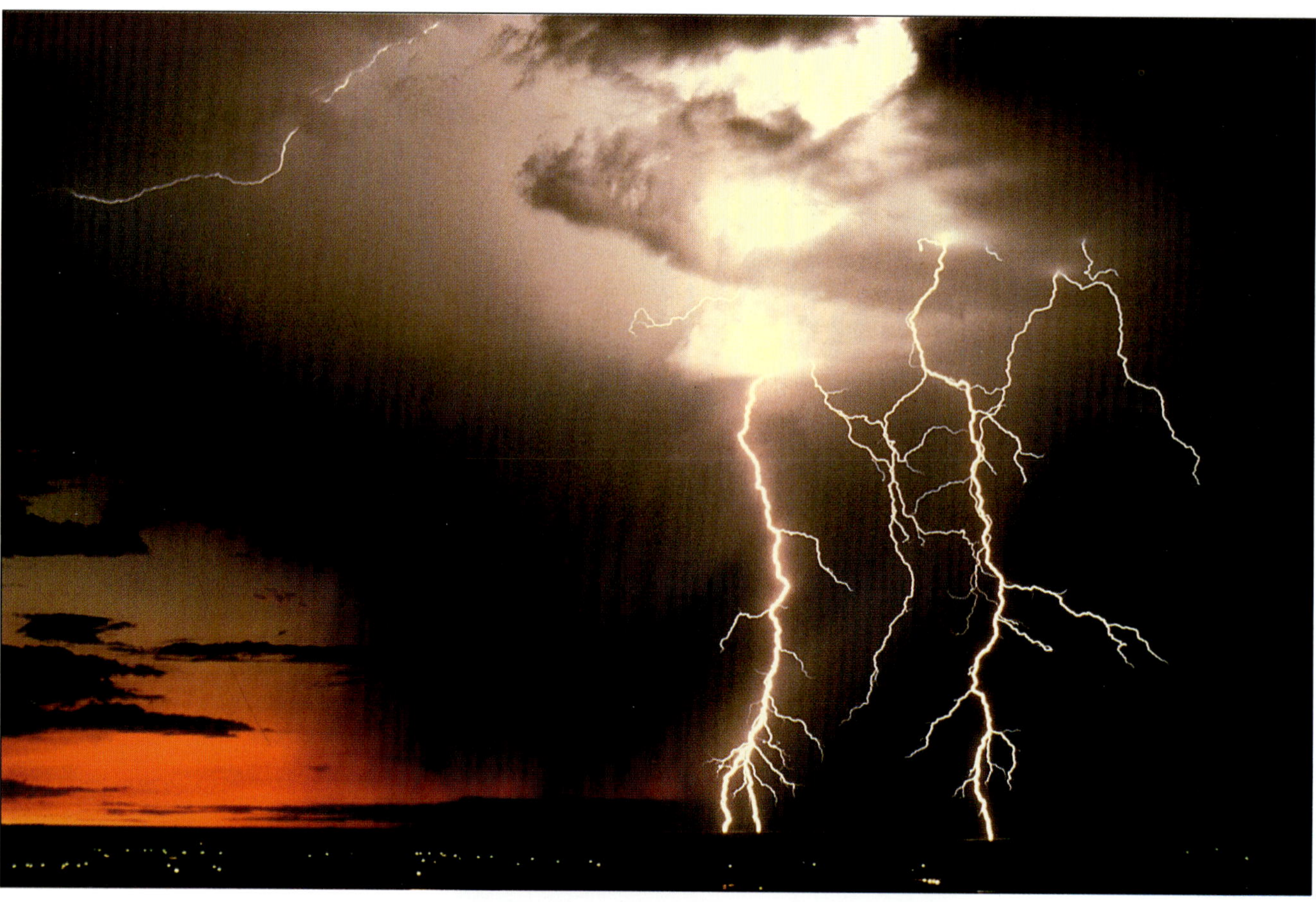

Lightning

One of the most spectacular visual effects the sky has to offer, is lightning. Since it is impossible to predict the exact moment the lightning is going to appear, it is best to photograph it at night so that you can leave the shutter open without overexposing the shot. If there is any light in the sky you can help prevent overexposure by fitting a neutral density filter.

First identify the direction of the storm and set up your camera on a tripod so that you can leave the shutter open for several minutes. At the height of a storm you shouldn't have to wait longer than ten seconds between flashes. You should even be able to capture three or four bursts on one frame before the lightning moves out of the camera's field of view.

▶ FAKE IT
Alternatively, for the 'perfect composition', do as this photographer has and capture your spectacular lightning on film first, shoot a cityscape at night, then copy the images one by one on to a duplicating film.

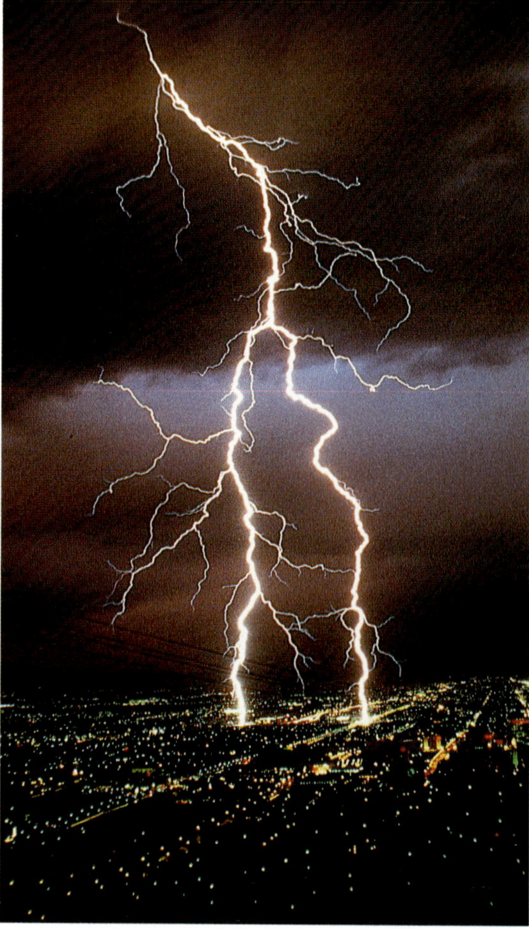

▲ IN A FLASH
The only reliable way to capture lightning on film is to set the camera on a tripod, facing the storm, and hold the shutter open with a lockable cable release for several minutes. Only do this if the lightning is in the distance, for safety.

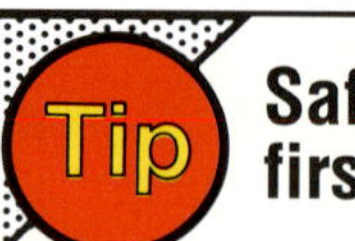

Safety first

Whatever you do, don't risk your life for a photograph in a thunderstorm. Don't set up your tripod in a bare, open space as it makes an efficient lightning conductor and so could attract a lethal bolt.

Try not to stand in open spaces, and don't shelter under trees. The safest vantage point to shoot storms is from a window in your own home.

Mist, haze, dust and fog

With a little bit of imagination mist, haze, dust and fog can be used to create interesting and dramatic photographs. Mist and fog produce a moody, muted atmosphere, while haze and dust help to provide aerial perspective.

Although usually invisible to the naked eye, air contains dust, pollutants and tiny water particles which scatter the light rays travelling through them. If the particles are dry, like smoke or dust, haze is produced. If the particles are made up of water, then mist, and sometimes fog, result. You can use these effects in your compositions to lift them out of the ordinary.

Misty conditions provide wonderful opportunities for creating atmospheric images, if you are prepared to set the alarm clock early. Mist dissolves background details, muting colours and flattening contrast, producing moody, almost monochromatic, scenes.

Distinctive shapes of trees, buildings, farm machinery and animals all stand out well against a blanket of mist. Mist is usually most obvious above water in the early morning – think of anglers silhouetted against a white haze, or swans, shrouded in white, on a lake. This is also the perfect time of day for capturing pale mist floating in the hollows of a landscape or cloaking open grassland.

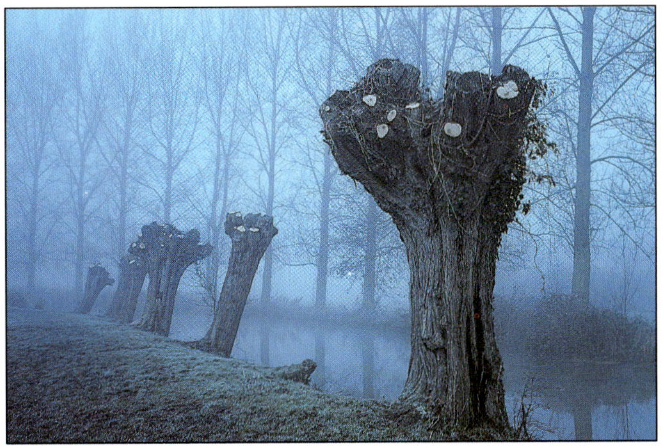

◀ MORNING BLUES
Early morning mist subdues colours to create a strange, muted atmosphere. Subjects in the background fade away and the use of a pale blue filter emphasizes the natural blueness of mist.

early morning mist creates a blue cast on landscape

contrast flattened and all shadows filled

▼ SCOTCH MIST
Clouds of mist filling the valleys of this landscape in the Scottish Highlands obscure detail and create an unearthly effect.

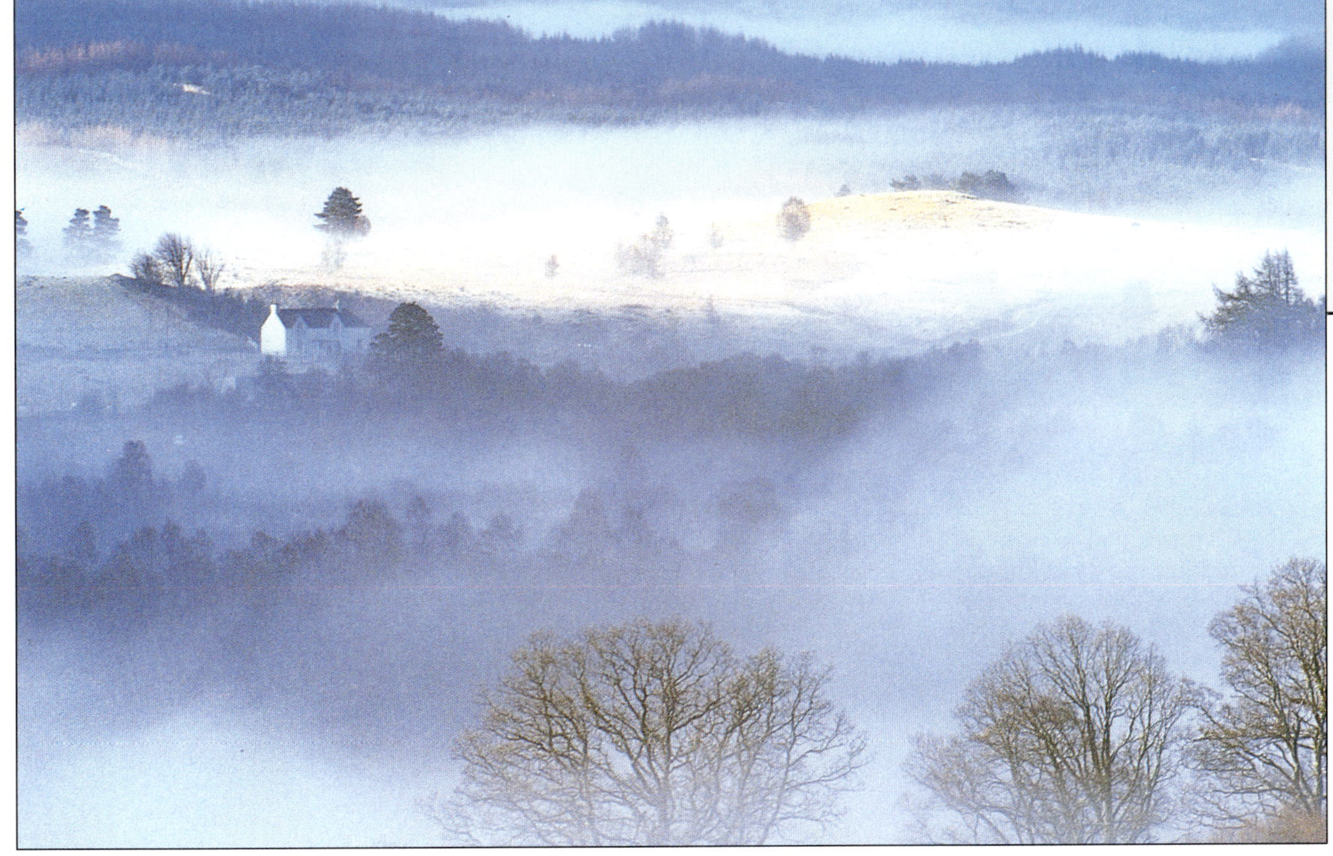

Ways with haze

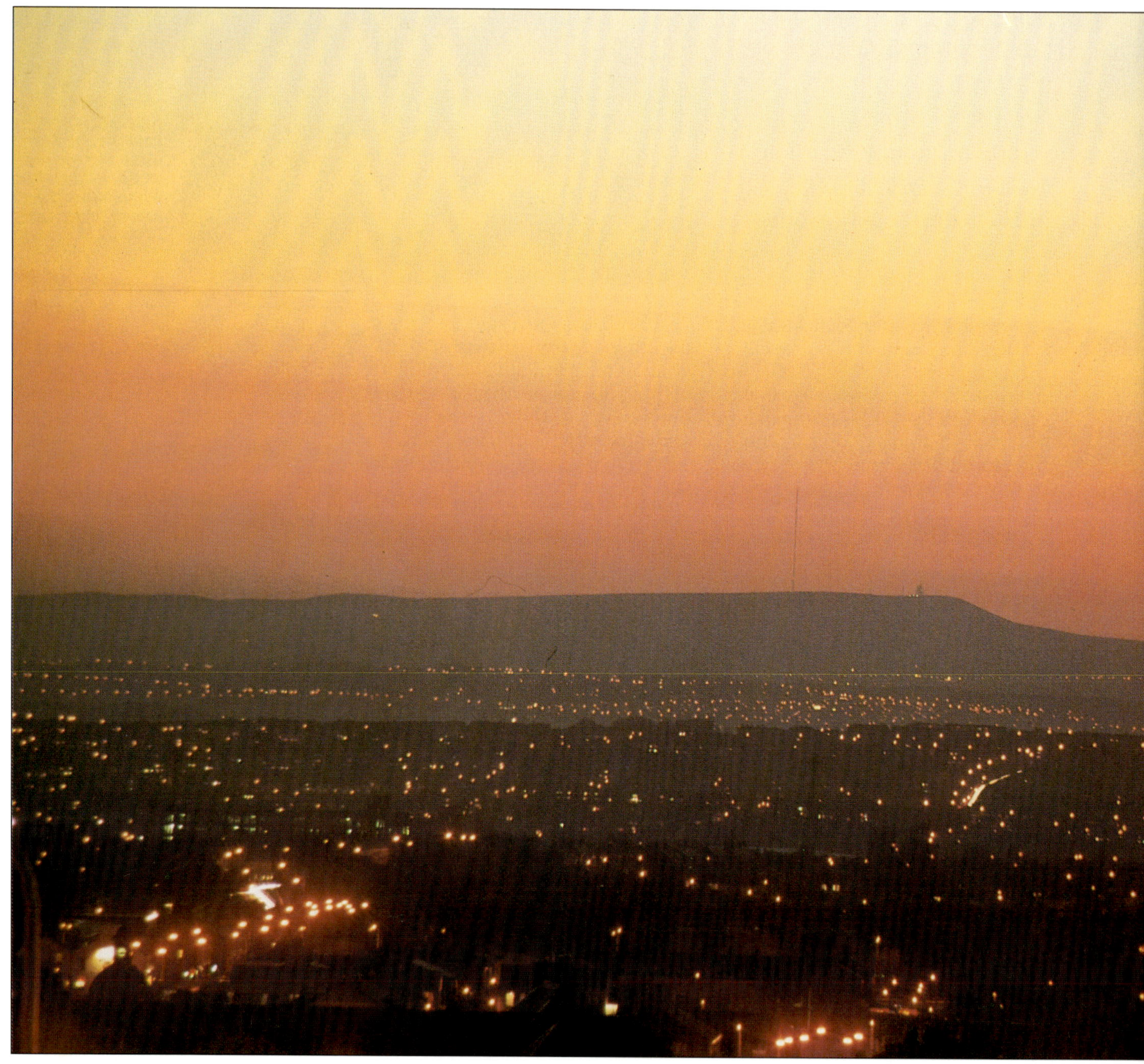

Haze is caused by the scattering of light by fine dust and pollution in the atmosphere. Fine dust makes the distant horizon appear paler and bluer than the foreground.

This effect, called aerial perspective, helps to increase the sense of depth in a scene.

This natural phenomenon is exaggerated in a photograph because film is sensitive to ultraviolet (UV) radiation, which is invisible to our eyes. Dust and pollution scatter UV even when visible light is unaffected. So even on a seemingly clear day, the effects of haze will show up on film.

Haze affects a photograph in two ways. It lightens and narrows the tonal range, so that the colours appear paler. It also softens sunlight, reduces contrast and fills in shadows.

Dust and pollution can create enormous amounts of haze in cities and industrial landscapes. Try to shoot such scenes at sunset when haze is at its most noticeable.

▲ HAZY EVENINGS
Industrial haze created by dust and pollution is a feature of most cities. Sunset is the best time to take advantage of its effects – when it spreads the light to give a pink glow.

Backlighting, too, exaggerates the smoky effect.

On very hot days, road surfaces sometimes become so hot that you can see the air shimmering above them. Use as low a viewpoint as possible if you want to enhance this effect.

Dealing with dust and smoke

Since dust particles are coloured, they produce views with a yellow or brownish tinge. Dust is a very active condition, needing wind or other movement to remain in the air, and so adds atmosphere to your photographs.

Think of swirling clouds of dust churned up by a truck or a herd of galloping wild horses. Backlighting shows dust off to the best advantage.

Dust can be very damaging to your camera, so before venturing out do make sure that all but the lens is enclosed in a plastic bag, and that a skylight or UV filter covers the lens.

Smoke can also be used creatively. Against a dark background smoke appears pale, while against a pale background it appears dark.

Shutter speed also affects the appearance of smoke. With a short exposure time you'll record billowy, cloud-like shapes. A long exposure time creates the impression of long fluffy streaks.

▼ UP IN SMOKE
When smoke is backlit it appears blue, when frontlit it appears brown. In this picture the photographer has used backlighting to create a strong silhouette of the man.

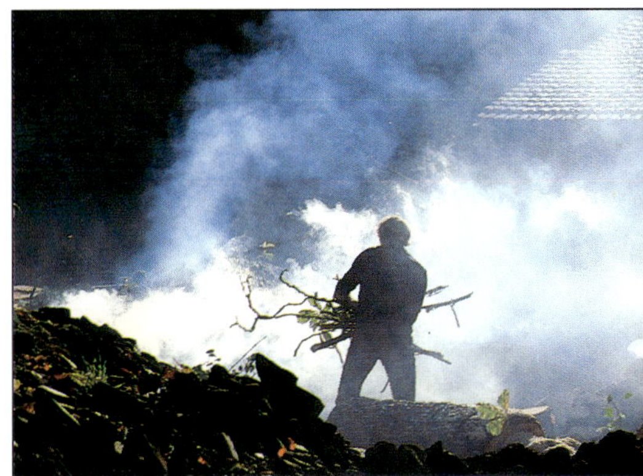

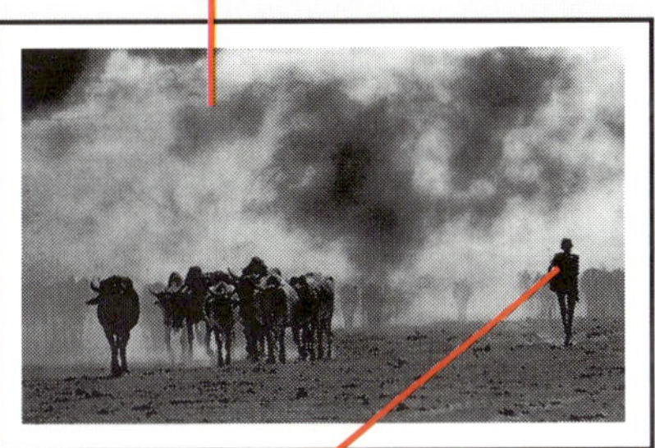

▼ DUSTY DESERT
The swirling, rising dust kicked up by the herd of cattle creates a dramatic picture. Dust gives a yellowish brown tinge and, when backlit, produces dark silhouettes.

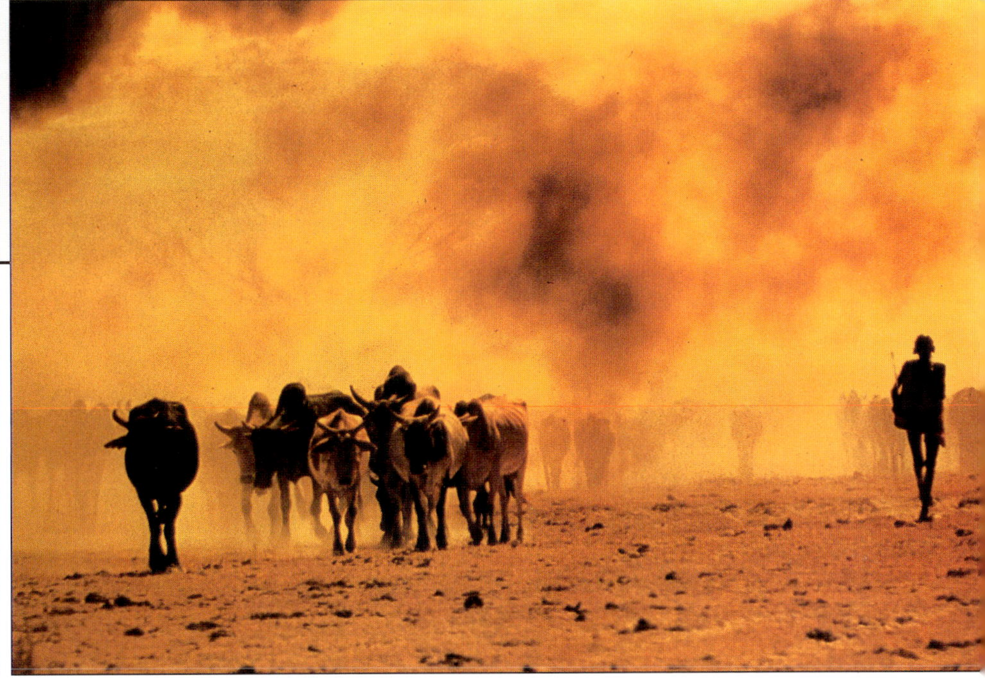

The effects of fog

Although fog can be so dense as to make even nearby objects difficult to see, it still offers opportunities for a number of interesting images. For example, shooting against the light in fog creates an eerie silhouette of your subject. Alternatively you could wait until the fog starts to lift, to capture an unworldly white halo over a brightly coloured landscape.

Getting an accurate exposure can be a problem in foggy conditions. Lightmeters tend to be confused by the abundance of scattered white light leading to a false reading. So don't forget to overexpose the shot slightly.

Fake it

A fog filter reduces colour saturation and contrast in much the same way as fog and mist do. Use a graduated fog filter so that just the upper half of the frame is affected. This gives a more natural view of the fog, which appears to increase with distance.

◀ **FOG AND LIGHT**
Thick fog can reduce a complex subject like this road and woodland scene to an image of stark, almost monochromatic simplicity. The scene is enhanced by the diffused light from the car headlamps caused by the dense fog.

▲ **GHOSTLY IMAGE**
The dark, solid mass of the streetlamps and wall contrasts starkly with the pale shapes of London's Houses of Parliament in the background. If you're not lucky enough to come across a scene like this, you can cheat by using a graduated fog filter.

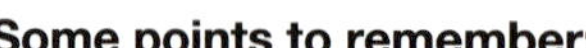

Some points to remember:

❑ Haze creates an increased sense of depth
❑ Mist produces flat, moody scenes

❑ When the effects of haze are unwanted, use a skylight, UV or polarizing filter
❑ In foggy conditions, overexpose slightly

Misty mornings

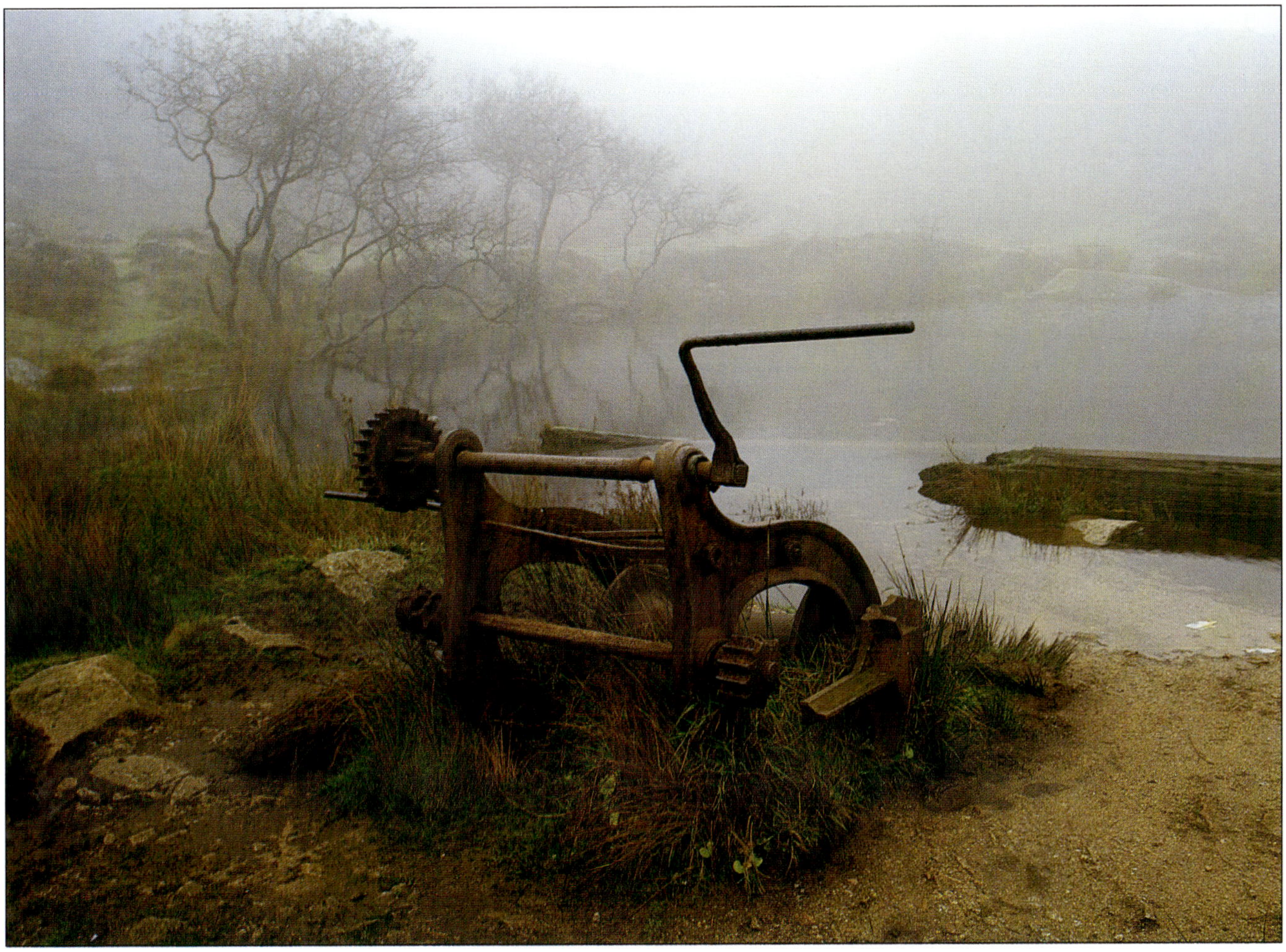

At certain times of the year, morning mist can be a virtual certainty. Check the weather forecast and be willing to get up at dawn, if you want to take advantage of a wonderful range of picture opportunities.

Unexpected surprises lurk around every corner. Clinging cloud softens the hard edges of the city, and turns familiar, colourful landscapes into strange, unreal worlds of white. Heavy mist is often fairly slow to clear, so you may have an hour or more to find the best composition.

Low lying mist, on the other hand, is a rarer bonus for the photographer who gets up early. Blanketing the ground or hovering over water, it can rise suddenly and disappear just as quickly while your back is turned.

▲ SIMPLE BACKGROUND
Interesting outdoor subjects, like this winch, can be disappointing on film if they are too similar to the background in colour or tone. But visit the same spot on a misty morning, and you may find that nature has provided a perfect backdrop. Here the mist picks out the winch handle, separating it from the muddy shallows of the lake.

▼ VITAL DETAIL
By its very nature, mist often creates photographs with large areas of grey tone in subtle shades. Such images appeal precisely because of their simplicity, but you may find the lack of detail a little bland. The answer is to spice up the picture with a few small but significant details. Here the swans and horse were included for more interest.

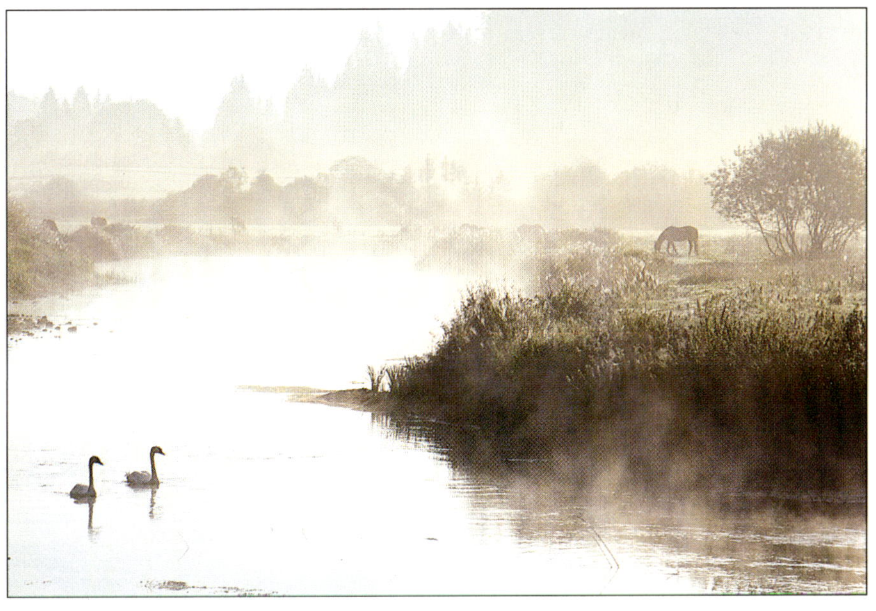

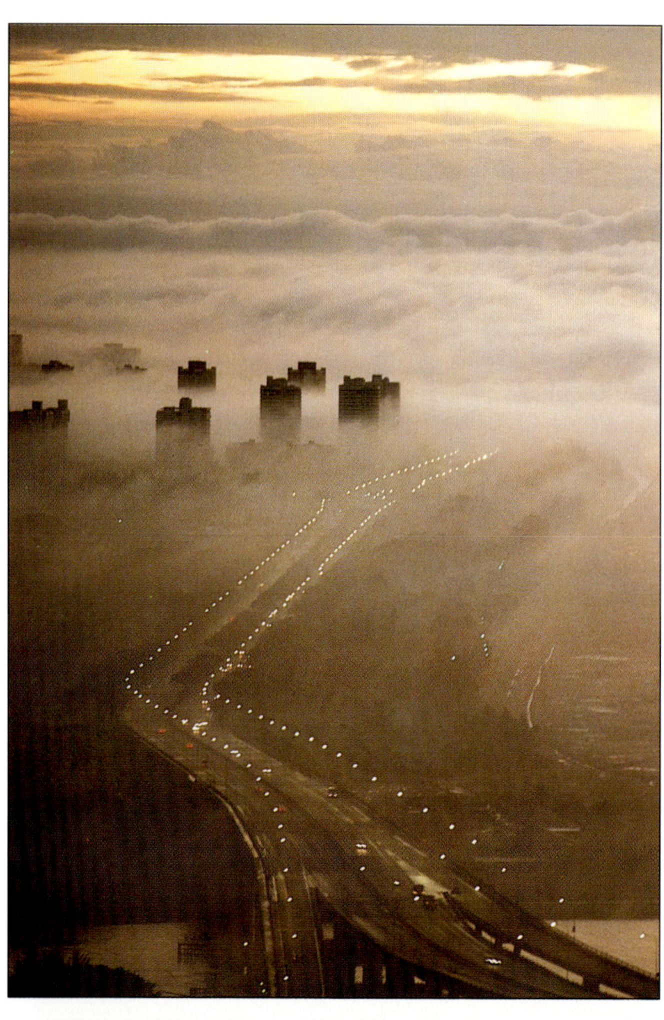

◄ CITY MASK
Some regions are vulnerable to low lying mist. Visit an area regularly to learn what sort of weather conditions create these spectacular effects, and plan your early morning visit accordingly.

In this photo of Singapore, the weather isn't entirely responsible – traffic fumes help hide the city's streets beneath a soft white carpet.

▼ QUICK SHOOTER
The warmth of the rising sun can burn off early morning mist very quickly. This often limits the time available for shooting, so if the atmospheric effects look right, fire off some frames immediately. In this example, just a few minutes of sun would be enough to lift the mist from the distant hills, and destroy a great photo opportunity at the same time.

► USE A FILTER
A veil of white doesn't make for colourful pictures! If you are lucky enough to arrive with the sunrise, the sun's warm tones can help by tinting the mist with gold. But when nature won't oblige, you can always resort to filters. For the most natural looking result, use only bluish and yellowish filters – green and purple filters look unrealistic.

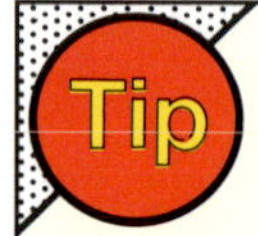

Wrap it up

On a cold day, potentially damaging condensation can form on your camera when you bring it back indoors. So put it in a plastic bag while you're outside, and let the equipment warm to room temperature before removing it.

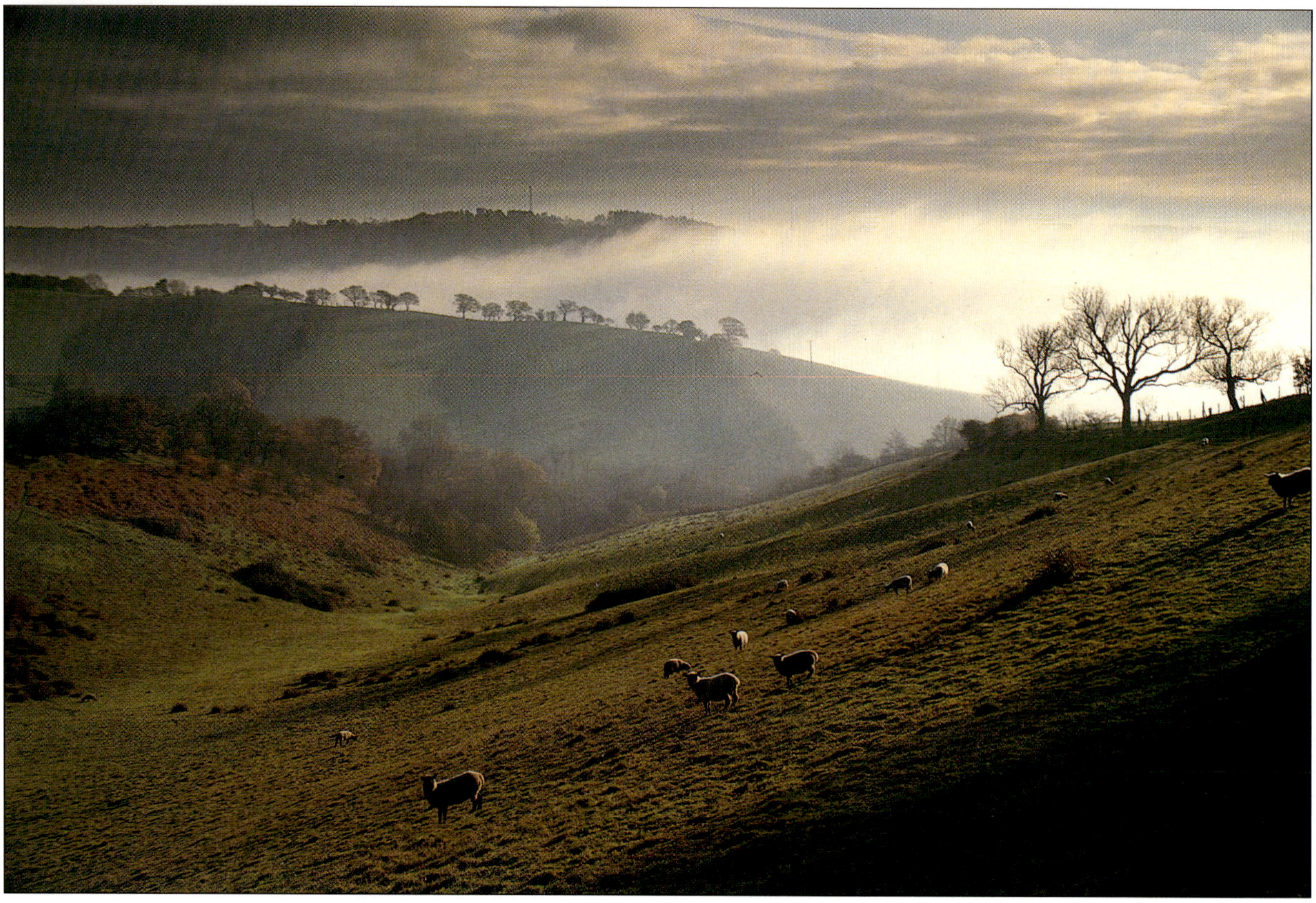

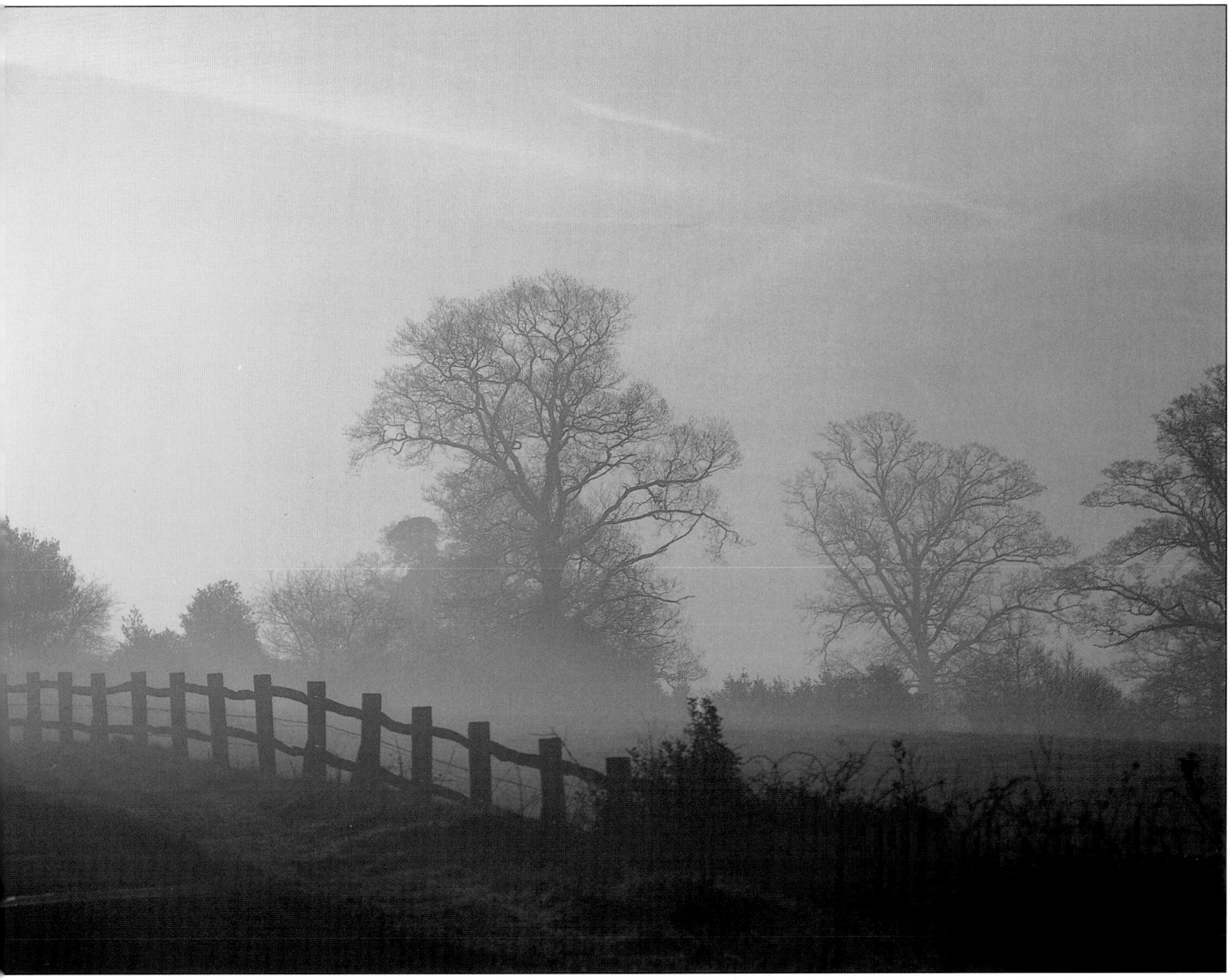

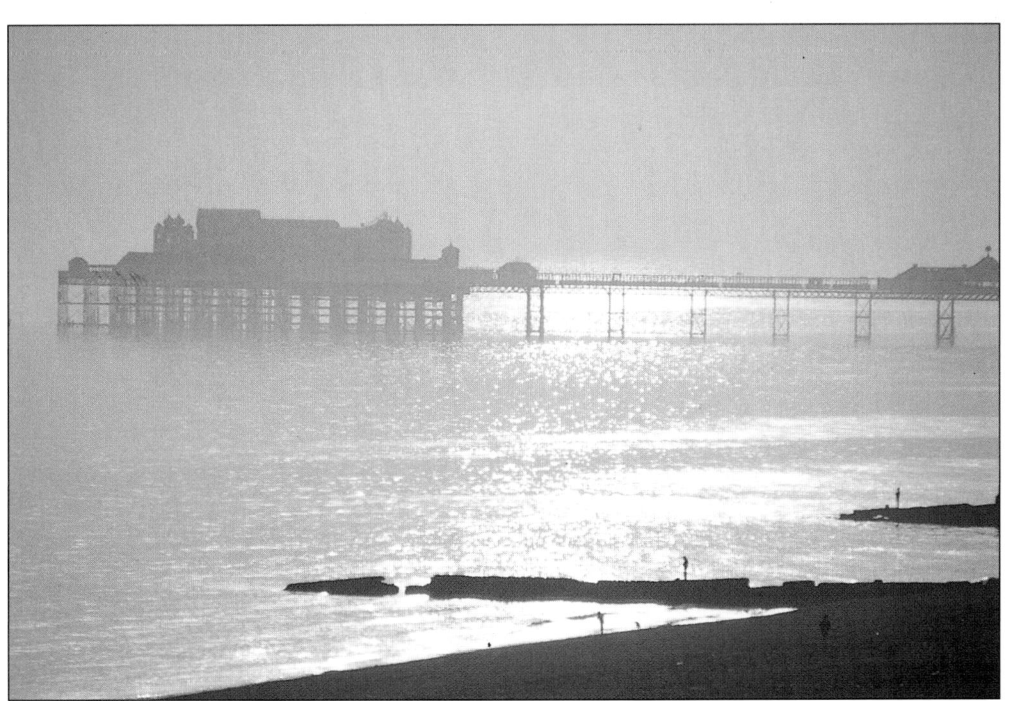

◀ **GENTLE TONES**
Turning the camera towards the rising sun usually creates marked contrasts, which split the picture into extremes of dark and light. Mist, though, shortens the tonal range without sacrificing the brilliant sparkle of the sun. To keep tones light, follow the example of the photographer who framed Brighton pier, and use a long exposure.

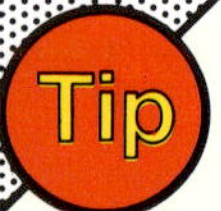

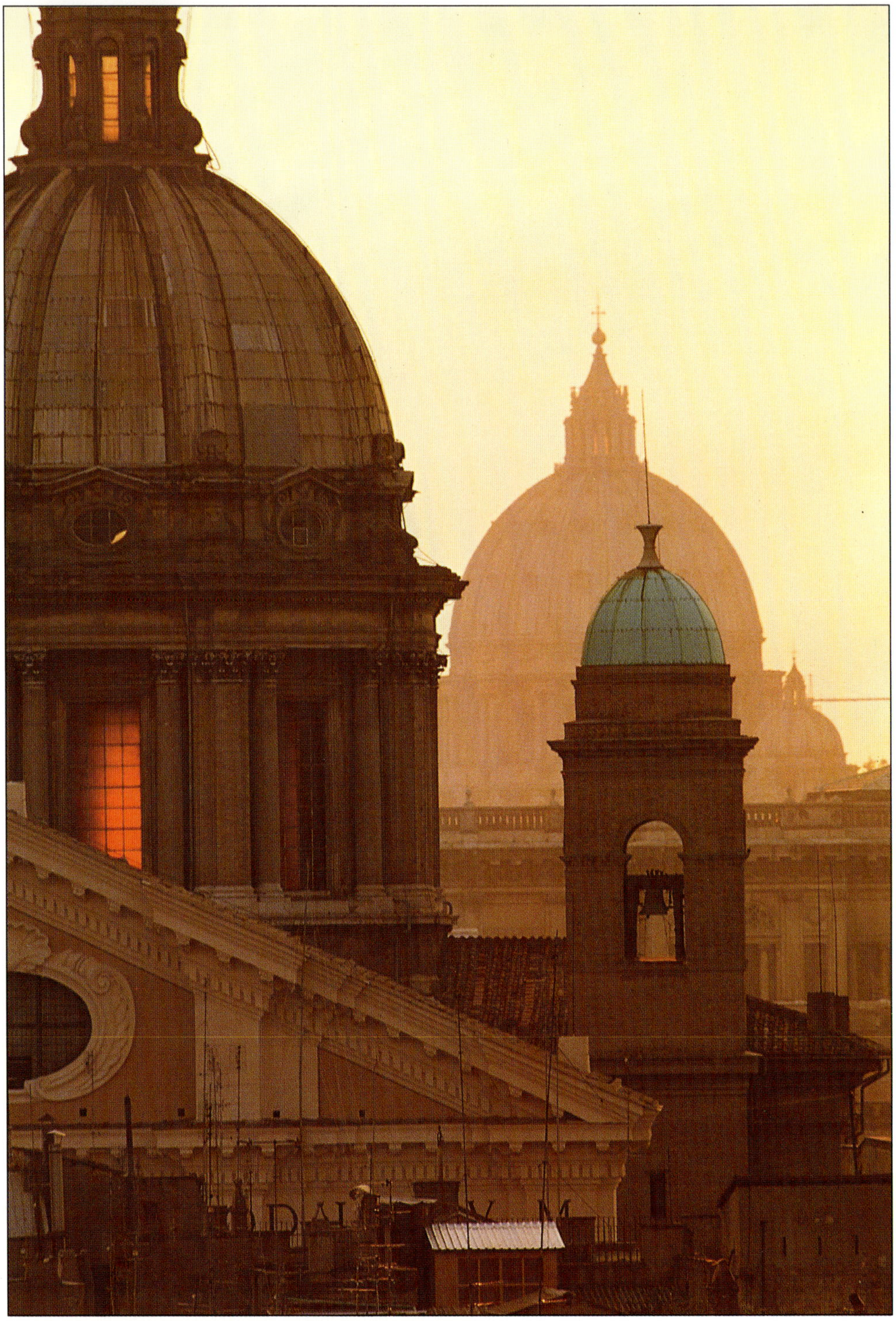

Tip

Weather report

To avoid disappointment, remember to check the weather report the night before you intend to set out on a photo expedition. If mist is forecast, pack up your gear in advance, so you can make an early start in the morning and not waste time.

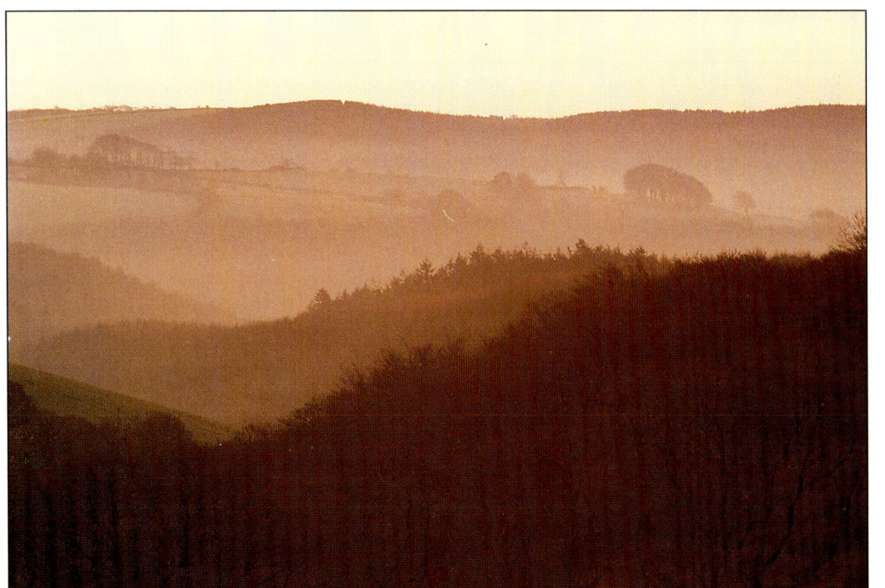

◄ **DISTANT HILLS**
The classic use of mist and haze is to give a sense of distance. Notice how each 'layer' of hills is paler than the one in front of it. Look for scenes with overlapping layers, like the interlocking V shapes here, to convey a landscape stretching to infinity.

Mountain landscapes

Mountain scenery gives the landscape photographer a great deal of scope, but for a really strong image you need to find a focal point. Mike Busselle took to the craggy hills of Spain to show David Jones how to bring upland scenes to life.

The mountains of Andalucia in southern Spain are full of dramatic and distinctive views. The foothills are rolling, comparatively grassy and covered with groves of olive trees, but higher up the landscape becomes rocky, forbidding and far more spectacular. Mike was keen to try photographing both types of view.

We set out early on a clear and sunny spring morning, and within half an hour were driving through the rolling green foothills. The groves of hillside olive trees looked very picturesque in the early morning light, but I was looking for a more dramatic, rocky scene so I didn't bother taking any pictures.

Mike did though, and produced a nice shot with olive trees in the foreground and green hills and white farmhouses behind. This scene had only limited potential, though, and Mike soon packed away his equipment and we set off again.

Higher ground

As we drove up into the mountains the scenery became harsher and rockier, and by the time we'd reached a height of around 3000 metres it was really dramatic and bleak. This was exactly the sort of landscape I'd been hoping for, so once I'd spotted a promising view I asked Mike to pull over and started shooting.

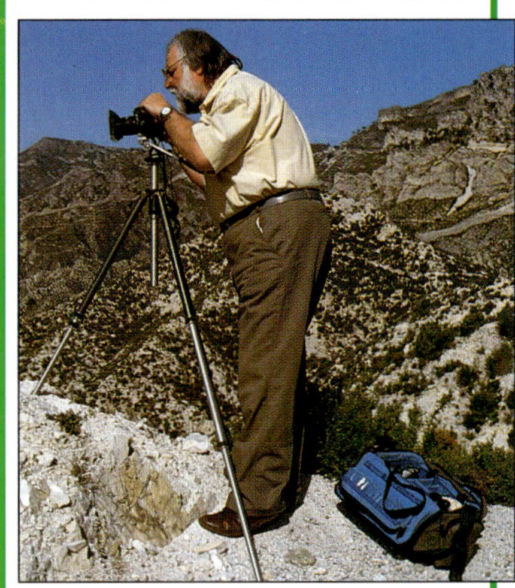

The set up

Mike and David were shooting in the mountains and hills due east of Malaga in Andalucia, southern Spain. The weather was excellent, with constant sunshine and a clear, cloudless sky, but the slight morning haze hung around all day and significantly reduced visibility. David used a Nikon F801. Mike mounted his Nikon FE2 on a tripod so he could use the long exposures he needed.

▼ David had high hopes for this shot, because he liked the way the distant mountains give it a sense of depth. But the heat haze has diminished this effect and left them looking indistinct.

Because he used a fast shutter speed and didn't use a polarizer the colour in the shot is very washed out. There's no real focal point either.

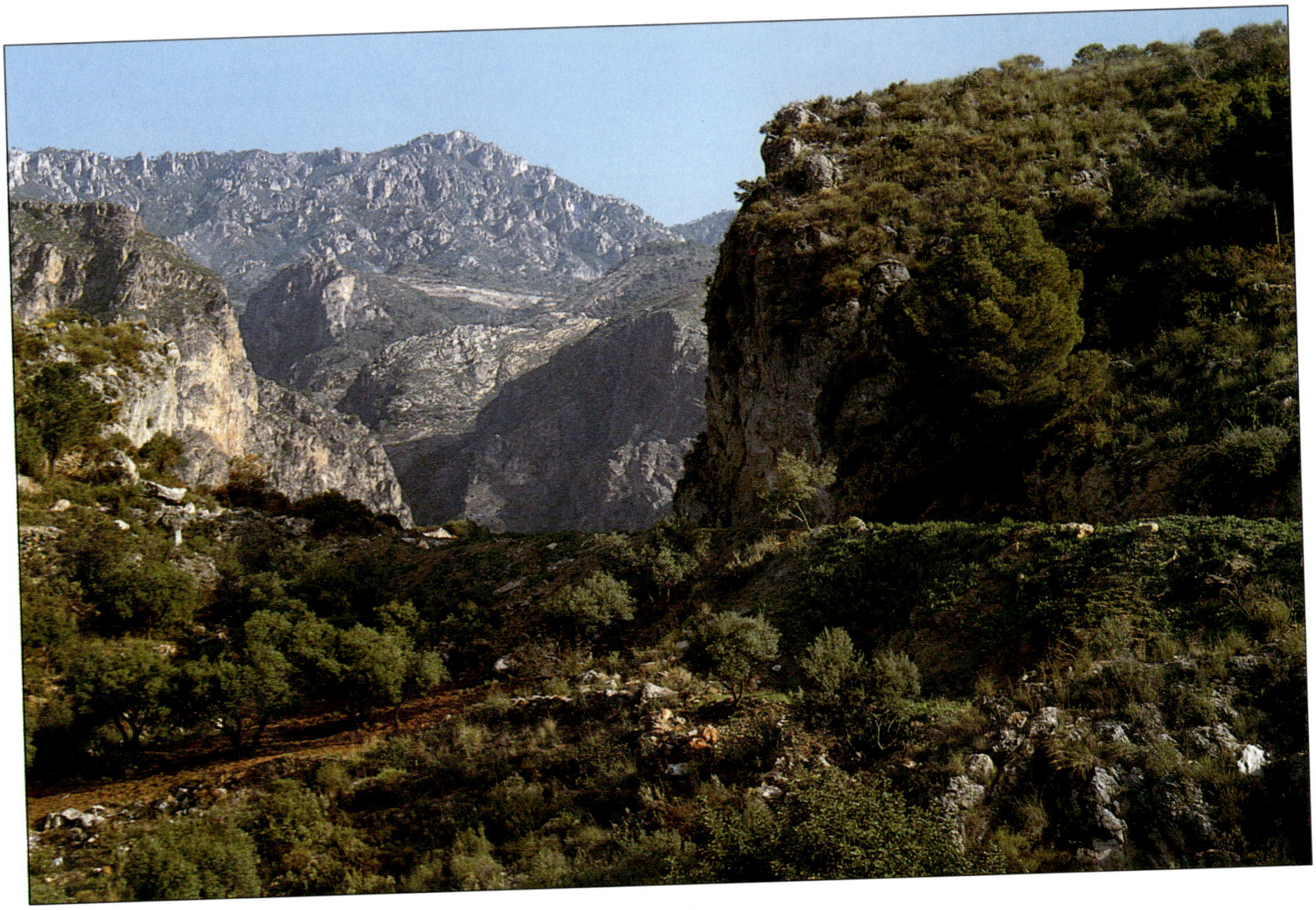

FINDING A FOCAL POINT

1 IN THE FOOTHILLS
Mike took this picture early in the day before the sun got too high. The olive trees make a very strong impact in the foreground, but the background is less convincing. Partly because of the haze, the hills behind look flat and colourless, and the untidy clump of weeds in the left hand corner doesn't help much either.

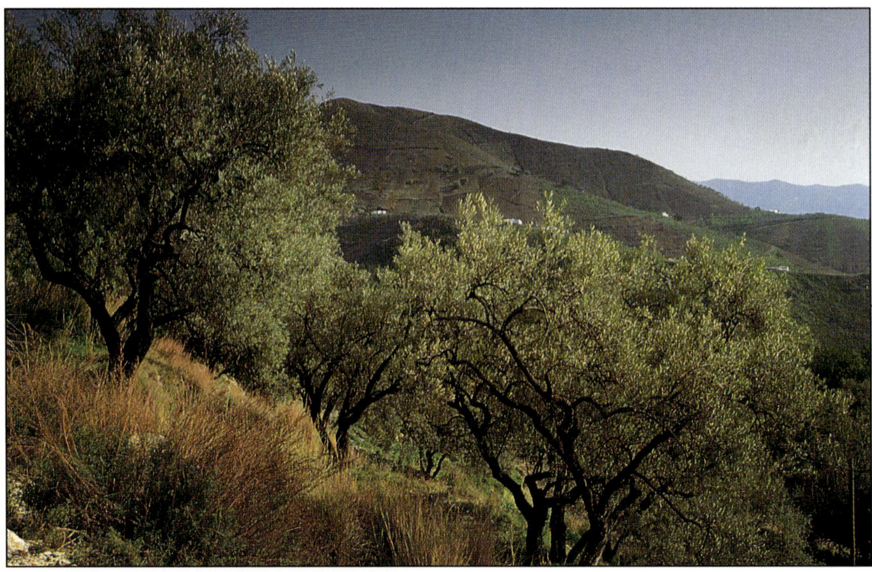

2 A ROCKY VIEW
Higher up, the landscape became far more dramatic. Mike really liked this view of the sheer cliff face, but he knew it wouldn't work on its own. It needed something in the foreground to provide perspective, and this clump of rocks and heather did the trick . But the shot lacks colour and the sky's a bit dull.

3 A TOUCH OF COLOUR
Slightly further on Mike came across another spectacular mountain view, and this time there was a vivid green pine tree in the foreground to add a dash of colour. A polarizing filter helped Mike to capitalize on what colour there was.

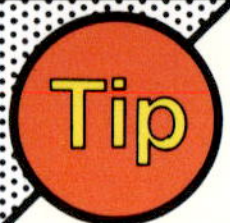

Coping with haze

Haze can be a big problem on sunny days, drastically reducing the depth of field so vital to strong landscapes. An ultraviolet filter will help you cut through it and keep your image sharp. If you're using a polarizer it should have a very similar effect. It's sometimes worth waiting a few hours to see if the sun burns the haze off.

The most reliable way to eliminate haze, though, is to take pictures in the early morning when the air is clearer.

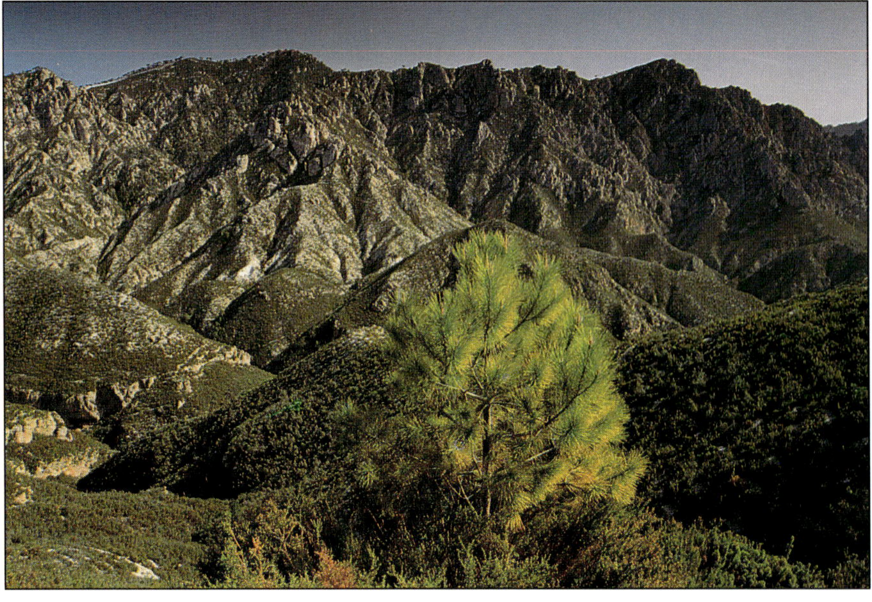

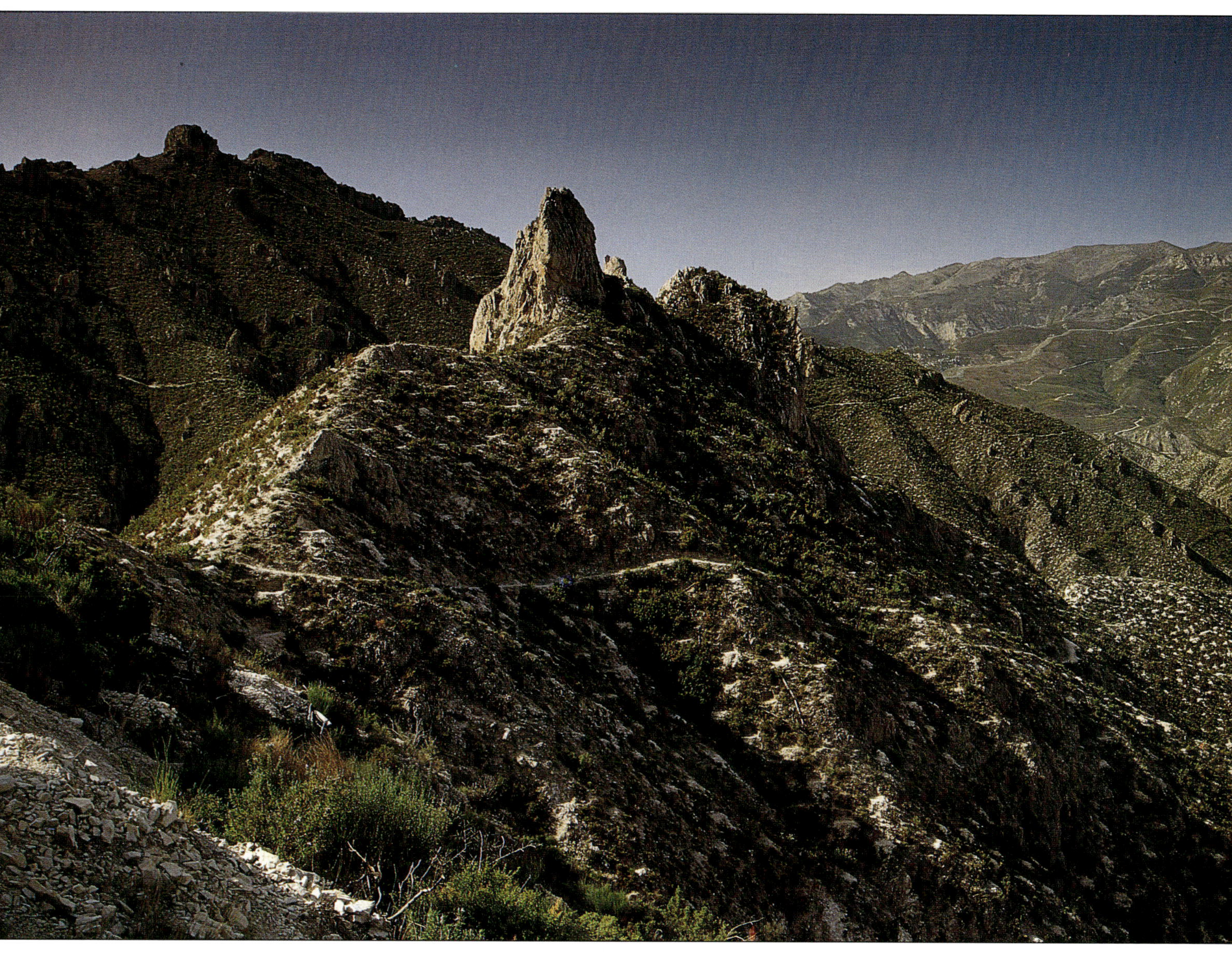

I used a Nikon F801 with a 28-70mm zoom lens and Fuji ISO 50D slide film, and chose a shot with rocks in the foreground and high, desolate mountains behind. I liked the shape of the big outcrop of rock in the foreground, and I was hoping the distant mountains would give the shot a sense of depth. I tried a few different angles before settling on the one I wanted, and shot half a roll to make sure I ended up with something good.

But the resulting shot lacked any strong focal point to draw the eye into the frame. The mountains behind look hazy and indistinct, and because the sun was directly overhead the colours look weak.

A better viewpoint

When I'd finished Mike drove on a bit further in search of a clearer view of the mountains themselves. He soon came across a sweeping and spectacular view of the peaks which he made stronger by including a big clump of rocks in the foreground. This provided a focal point at the front of the frame and gave the picture a sense of scale.

Mike used a Nikon FE2 on a tripod with a 24mm wide angle lens and shot on Fuji Velvia ISO 50 slide film. He used a long exposure to get better colour saturation, a polarizing filter to darken the sky and an ultraviolet filter to cut through the heat haze.

4 THE PERFECT PEAK
Mike thought the distinctive peak on top of this arid hill made a perfect focal point in the middle of the frame. He tried a few close-ups of the rock first, but decided that there was more interest and contrast in a long shot. A little more colour would have helped though.

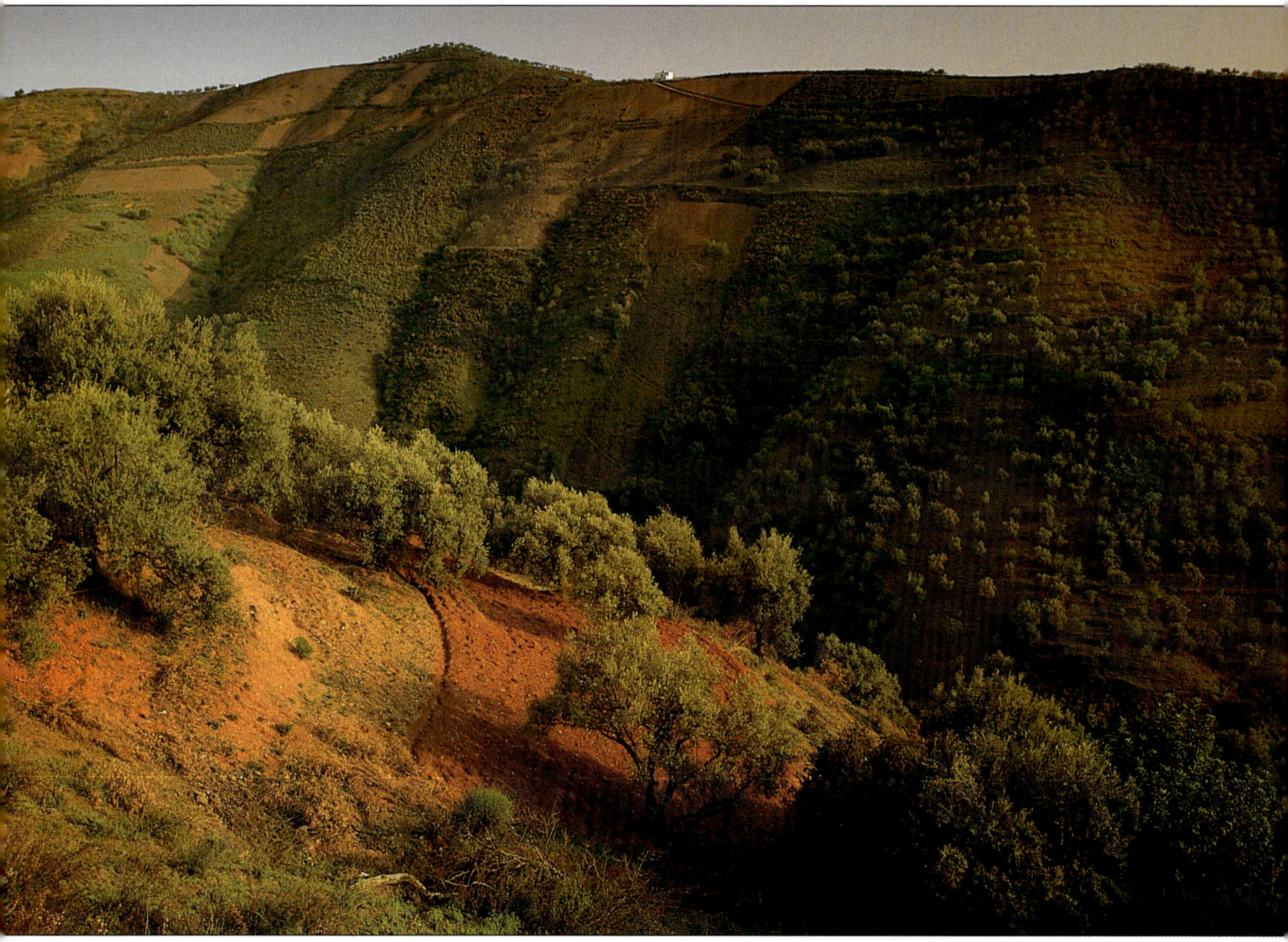

5 TWILIGHT GLOW

Mike came across this spectacular view in the foothills at the end of the day. This scene has all the colour the more dramatic mountain landscapes lacked. The red soil stands out in the foreground and there are plenty of subtle shades in the hills behind. It's the evening light that makes it really special.

Strong focal points

Further down the road he found a better view of the mountains with a splash of colour provided by a vivid green pine tree in the foreground. But the tree was almost too dominant, so we soon moved on again. By trying different locations, Mike made sure there'd be a wide variety of different shots to choose from afterwards.

The next view that caught Mike's eye was a rocky outcrop on top of a scrub-covered hill. The strange rock formation made a perfect focal point, and Mike used a zoom lens to try both long shots and close-ups. The only thing the landscape lacked was a bit of colour.

Evening light

By now it was quite late in the day, so we decided to turn back and go home. But on the way down, Mike spotted a remarkable twilight scene. The evening light had lit up the orange soil of an olive grove, which was backed by rolling green hills.

It was a chance Mike wasn't prepared to miss, so he pulled over and took a whole roll, bracketing widely to make sure he got it. 'It's amazing how often you get your best shot at the end of a day', he concluded.

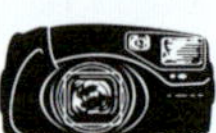

Compact tip

❏ Distant scenery on sunlit hillsides can be very bright, and if you're not careful your compact will record a very dark background and a correctly exposed but indistinct horizon. Solve the problem by finding some foreground detail and brightening it up with fill-in flash.

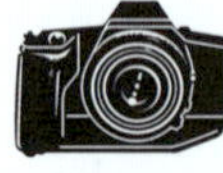

SLR tip

❏ If you're walking in the hills, don't bring too much heavy equipment with you. Use zoom lenses instead of individual ones to avoid extra weight, and pack smaller items in a waist pouch. Take bulky equipment in a back pack rather than a shoulder bag.

Snow covered scenery

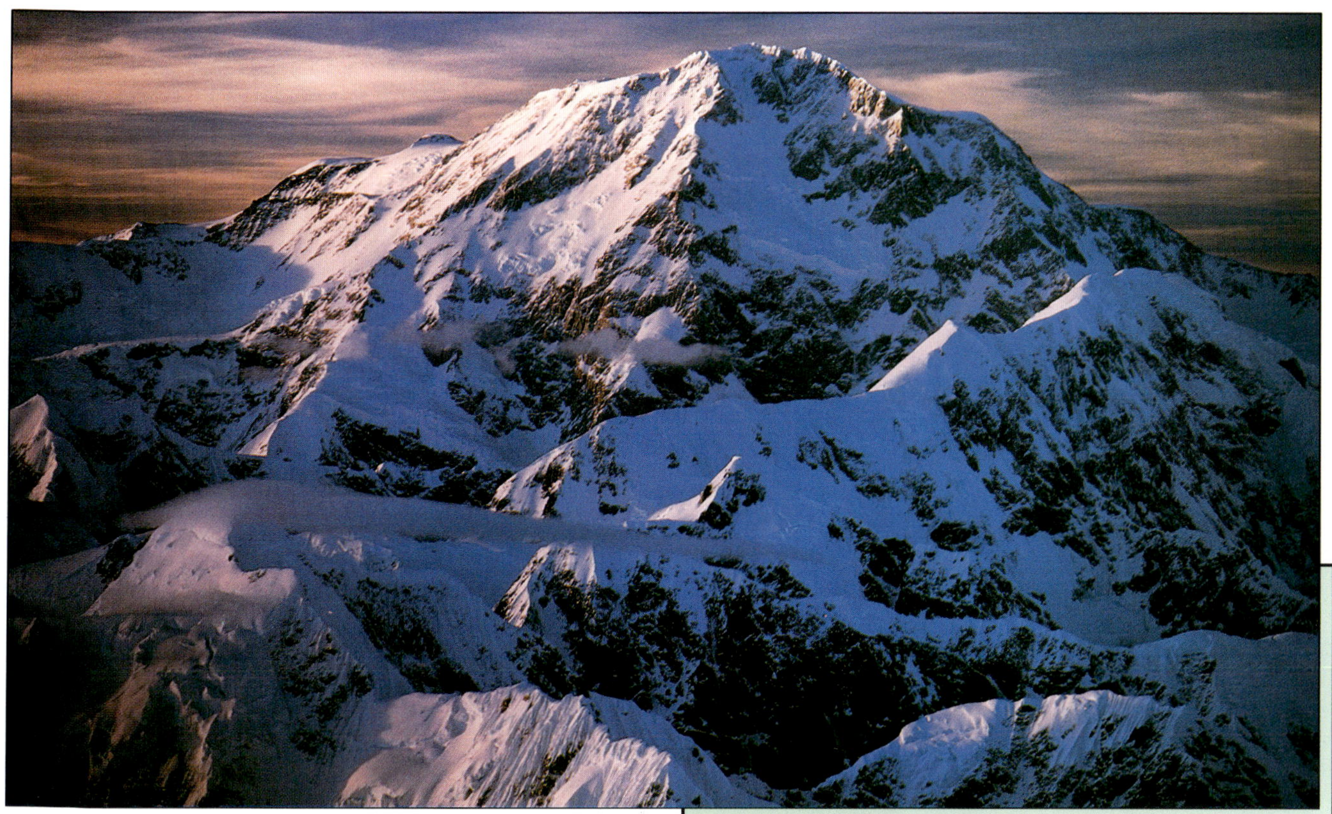

Snow scenes are one of the most attractive – and most photographed – kinds of landscape.

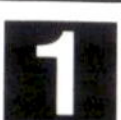

1 Exposure

Snow scenes are notorious for fooling camera meters. The predominance of bright, highly reflective white surfaces will almost certainly lead your meter to underexpose if it is left on automatic. As a result, the snow appears 'dirty' in the final shot.

With an SLR, the solution is to switch to manual and bracket your exposures by half stops. You'll find that you need to increase the exposure by $1\frac{1}{2}$ stops. For this, use the method you find easiest.

Depending on the camera, you could set exposure manually, or set a slower film speed, or use the exposure compensation control.

▲ *In this shot of a mountain in Alaska, shadow areas take on a blue tinge, conveying intense cold.*

▼ *The high lighting level allowed the photographer to use a narrow aperture for good depth of field.*

2 Weather

On a day where the sky is a uniform white, the ground and sky tend to merge into one, so it's best to avoid shooting then. Brilliant blue skies show off the white snow best – a polarizer is a must here, because it darkens the sky and also reduces glare.

Alternatively, you could shoot when there are murky grey clouds or during a snow fall. This can result in a really atmospheric image.

3 Protection

You can brush snowflakes off a cold camera, but don't take your camera from a warm room into a snowstorm – snowflakes will melt, then later freeze on. Cold impairs battery performance, so tuck the camera under your coat between shots, or keep spare cells in a warm pocket.

Before you come indoors, wrap equipment in plastic bags until it has warmed up, or condensation will form.

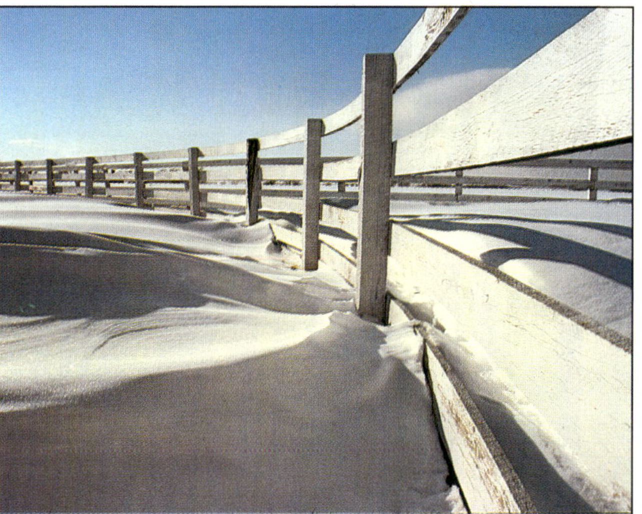

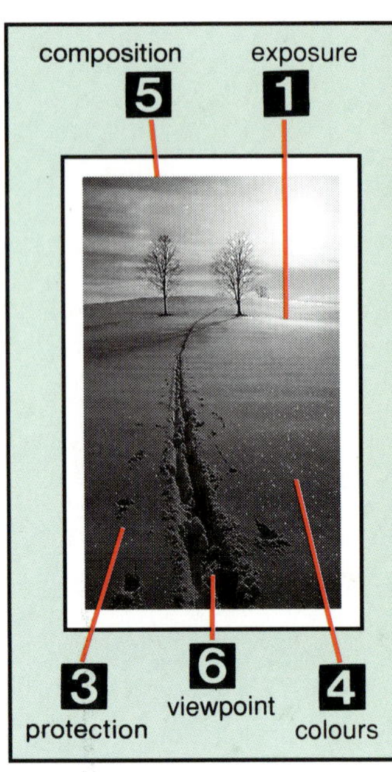

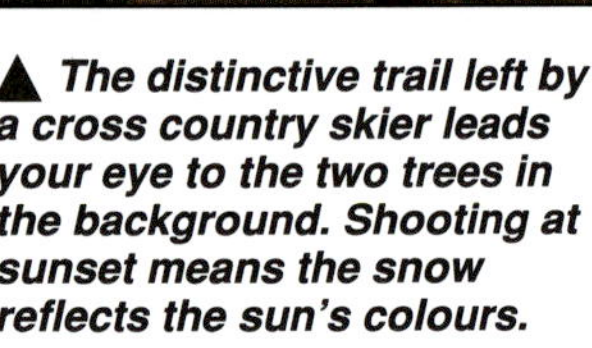
▲ *The distinctive trail left by a cross country skier leads your eye to the two trees in the background. Shooting at sunset means the snow reflects the sun's colours.*

4 Colours

Snow tends to reflect the colour of its surroundings. Your eyes can compensate at the time, but the image on film may turn out to be disappointing.

Often, highlight areas are white but the shadows have a blue tinge. That's fine if you want to convey a cold, bleak landscape – you don't have to use any extra filters. You probably also won't need any if the highlight and shadow areas are present in roughly equal amounts.

However, if shadows dominate the scene, use an 81EF filter to remove the blue cast. To introduce warmth, shoot at sunset, when the snow takes on an attractive golden hue.

5 Composition

With everything covered by a blanket of snow, the landscape takes on a completely different feel. Ground which was once separated into paths, grass and rock, for example, becomes one uniform layer of white.

You can turn this to your advantage. For instance, one

▼ *Trees that would look boring in summer take on a fascinating appearance when snow covered.*

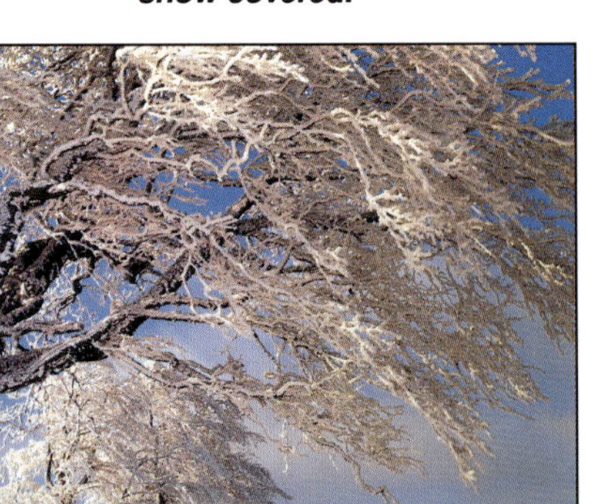

feature which is taller than the rest or an unusual shape – whether it's a bird table or a building – can stand out and become the focus of the picture. Anything which looks interesting is a possible subject.

Alternatively, base the shot on a landmark that's conspicuous precisely because it isn't hidden by snow, and so displays a different colour and texture. This could be a river, a well trodden path or the cleared roof of a house.

6 Viewpoint

Where you walk is very important. Unless you're after specially created footprints, you don't want pristine snow – or eyecatching footmarks that are already there – ruined by your own tracks.

If you're taking a series of shots from different positions, start with the furthest away view. Only when you're satisfied with your pictures from that position should you move further in. A zoom telephoto lets you get closer without marking the snow.